From Personal to Political

HOW WOMEN AND FEMINISM
CREATED SOCIAL CHANGE

Bassim Hamadeh, CEO and Publisher
Carrie Montoya, Manager, Revisions and Author Care
Kaela Martin, Project Editor
Christian Berk, Associate Production Editor
Miguel Macias, Senior Graphic Designer
Alexa Lucido, Licensing Associate
Don Kesner, Interior Designer
Natalie Piccotti, Senior Marketing Manager
Kassie Graves, Vice President of Editorial
Jamie Giganti, Director of Academic Publishing

Cover image Copyright © 2017 iStockphoto LP/izusek.

Printed in the United States of America.

ISBN: 978-1-5165-3654-2 (pbk) / 978-1-5165-3655-9 (br)

From Personal to Political

HOW WOMEN AND FEMINISM CREATED SOCIAL CHANGE

Second Edition

JoAnna Wall

To Q & A—Thank you for being young feminists. Stay gold, be kind, and speak up.

CONTENTS

ACKNOWLEDGMENTS

The inspiration of the second edition of this book belongs to every woman who marched, who shared #MeToo, and who continues to work for equality. I am indebted to my amazing team at Cognella, especially Carrie Montoya and Kaela Martin, who always provide excellent support. I am forever thankful to Lisa Funnell, who joins me at every march, analyzes every new movement with me, and keeps me updated on trending social media posts. Nikki Jones Edwards, I can't even begin to thank you for how amazing you are. Lastly, I'd like to thank my mother and my sister, Ann Woolridge and Shea Woolridge Johnson. You all make my world a better place.

FOREWORD

Lisa Funnell

When we think about social justice and the struggle to create a more equitable society, it is important to recognize the role that women have historically played, particularly in the United States over the past 100 years. From the fight for universal suffrage, bodily autonomy, and equal pay to the advocating for and introducing of laws ensuring safe relationships, homes, neighborhoods, schools, and workplaces, women have long served as leaders and change-makers even if their work—much like the gendering and devaluing of most "women's work"—has gone largely unacknowledged. History is, after all, written by "the victor" and reflective of social privilege. It matters whose stories are told (and why) and who has largely been overlooked.

In our current social and political climate replete with fake news and ideological echo-chambers, the United States seems more divided and divisive than ever. In the process, civil rights and liberties are being challenged and contested leading many to question if the American dream is still possible when various groups (women, LGBTQA+ individuals, racial minorities, immigrants, the disabled, the lower and working class, and so forth) are not being given an even playing field. It becomes more important than ever to explore the ideas, actions, and accomplishments of empowered targeted group members who have developed a liberatory consciousness and have laid the foundation for, if not provided us with, blueprints for achieving social change.

While the cultural, legal, political, and ideological contributions of women are often overlooked, this book focuses squarely on women's activism in various facets and forms. From the creation of art in community spaces to the organizing of marches in public spaces to the writing and advocacy of laws in political spaces, women have challenged social and institutional norms and practices that have historically defined and delimited privilege. This book not only reflects on this history but also serves as a warning that freedom, a bedrock American principle, is essentially reliant on its citizens to strive for and ensure. *From Personal to Political* provides both an informative and inspirational account of activism that encourages women to keep striving for social equality in order to further transform "America"—as both a place and idea—into a more inclusive, equitable, and aspirationally perfect union.

Feminist Organizing and Creating Social Change Movements

The following section is a brief introduction to what feminist organizing looked like in the second wave. Many movements were created and sustained, while others faltered after serving their initial purpose. Some feminist movements found difficulty in organizing due to internal politics and some divided and became completely separate movements. Working together for the common good was not always first on the agenda, yet these movements eventually earned their place in second-wave history and assisted in activism for equality.

CHAPTER 1

Doing the Work of the Movement
FEMINIST ORGANIZATIONS

By Myra Marx Ferree and Patricia Yancey Martin

Among the most fundamental developments in American society in the past thirty years is the reemergence of feminism as a significant, though controversial, force. The political visibility of feminist ideas ranges from A(nita Hill) to Z(oe Baird). Indeed, Jo Freeman argues that the primary political parties in the United States are engaged in nothing less than a polarized culture war over the place of feminism in American society: "The two political parties have now completely polarized around feminism and the reaction to it…. On feminist issues and concerns the parties are not following the traditional pattern of presenting different versions of the same thing…. They are presenting two different and conflicting visions of how Americans should engage in everyday life" (1993, 21). In families and workplaces around the country, feminism is invoked to explain conflict and justify change as well as to attack proponents and decry efforts to challenge the status quo. The very centrality of feminism to American social and political debates, however, suggests that the women's movement has successfully called into question many taken-for-granted ideas about male dominance and institutionalized privilege based on gender.

Feminism's impact is evident on many fronts. When a judge in New York scolds attorneys for their attempt to depict a rape victim as a "loose woman," this reflects a change in consciousness, one outcome of twenty years of work by rape crisis centers. When the Association of American Colleges makes inclusion of scholarship on women a criterion for acceptable liberal arts curricula, credit must be given to the decades of work by women's studies programs, women's research centers, and women's caucuses in the academic disciplines. When citizens by the hundreds of thousands take to the streets of Washington to press for a Congressional guarantee of women's reproductive rights, their mobilization represents the grassroots organizing done by hundreds of local chapters of national feminist organizations and community-based programs.

As these examples attest, the movement's impact can be attributed in large part to the activities of feminist organizations that have worked for change—in the law, the courts, universities, corporations, local communities and individual women's lives. Few people have remained untouched, directly or indirectly, by these organizing efforts. The cultural changes they have triggered are one important indicator of their success. A second measure of the effectiveness of feminist organizations is the vehemence of the countermovements they have generated, evident in the mobilization of anti-feminist organizations such as Eagle Forum, the National Association of Scholars, and Operation Rescue.

A third measure is the sheer number of feminist groups. Literally thousands of organizations—including rape crisis centers, battered women's shelters, women's studies programs, women's health clinics, and women's bookstores, restaurants, theater groups, credit unions, and other profit and nonprofit organizations—were founded during the past three decades. Many have survived, some have prospered, and most have had a profound impact on the lives of women they touched. The women's movement exists because feminists founded and staffed these organizations to do the movement's work. Some are as tentative as volunteer-run hotlines, others as intense as illegal abortion collectives, still others as massive as the nationwide National Organization for Women. All these organizations sustain women and are sustained by them. They are tangible evidence of the movement in many feminists' lives and in the social and political life of the nation. But few of them have been studied in the depth and detail they deserve.

Despite dramatic growth in the number of feminist organizations in this generation, feminism itself is not new. Its roots go back well over a hundred years (Flexner 1959; Buechler 1990b), even though the term "feminist" came into common use only at the turn of the century (Cott 1987). To be sure, when scholars spoke of feminism before the late 1960s, they were referring to the remnant of early twentieth-century feminism that persisted on a small and declining scale through the 1950s (Rupp and Taylor 1987). But in the 1960s a new type of women's movement emerged as a clarion call to millions of women to rethink their priorities and question the social arrangements that defined them as second-class citizens. Many long-institutionalized organizations of the earlier feminists, such as the National Women's Party, the League of Women Voters, and the American Association of University Women, provided organizational resources and a sense of history to the nascent movement and were themselves revitalized by the new mobilization. The women's liberation groups that grew out of the student left and new women's rights organizations such as the National Organization for Women gradually defined themselves as part of a single larger movement

that they came to call feminism. The term feminism thus was expanded and rejuvenated, to cover a multitude of movements: among them, efforts for reproductive rights, employment and pay equity, and the political representation of women at all levels; against battering, rape, and other forms of violence against women, to name a few.

Some of the activists involved claimed to have invented a unique type of organization, a *feminist* organization, which they defined as embracing collectivist decision-making, member empowerment, and a political agenda of ending women's oppression. Working with women, for women, they encountered tensions and problems in their inevitable collisions and collaborations with what they called "the male-stream." For some, the tension between separatist culture and mainstream political change proved unmanageable, but a large number of rape crisis centers, feminist women's health centers, shelters for battered women, women's studies programs and research institutes, bookstores, art galleries, and theater collectives did survive. As chapters in this volume demonstrate, the organizations that did not collapse changed, though not necessarily in the direction of stultifying bureaucracy and displaced goals predicted by Robert Michel's "Iron Law of Oligarchy."[1] Although often classified as a social movement "of the 1960s," the second wave of the women's movement has organizationally outlived many of its contemporaries. This book addresses the fundamental questions of how and why so many feminist organizations managed to endure. What price did they pay? What effects have they had? What promise do they hold?

A Story of Survival and Effectiveness

Feminism is not dead, we believe, largely because of the number and variety of organizations it generated, nurtured, and influenced. Indeed, feminism can no longer be easily classified into bureaucratic or collectivist forms, if it ever could (Ferree and Hess 1985, 1994). Contemporary feminist organizations mix both elements in their structures, practices, and goals as they work to survive and to transform society. We see four aspects to the picture of survival and effectiveness drawn by the essays in this collection.

First is the issue of *institutionalization*. By institutionalization we mean the development of regular and routinized relationships with other organizations. Many feminist organizations founded in the decade 1965 to 1975 are celebrating their twentieth or twenty-fifth anniversaries. Their survival provides evidence that they became institutionalized in at least some respects. While organizations that would not or could not institutionalize folded, they served an important purpose nevertheless, as chapters in this volume by Strobel, Whittier, and Staggenborg attest. The important, and largely unasked, question about feminist organizations that survived is what their institutionalization means for feminism. Such organizations were surely co-opted in some ways, but did they abandon their feminist goals, practices, and agendas? To invoke a standard of feminist purity, as some have done (Ahrens 1980), obscures awareness of the ways in which organizations continue to seek and sometimes achieve significant change. The articles in this volume illustrate how feminist organizations question authority, produce new elites, call into question dominant societal values, claim resources on behalf of women, and provide space and resources for feminists to live out altered visions of their lives.

A rape crisis counselor, no matter how institutionalized her relationships with the police may become, is unlikely to feel indifferent about rape. Caring deeply about it, in her own life and in the lives of other women, she may work hard and long to combat it. It may be a central issue for her long after she stops working in a center. The personal passage through a feminist organization by feminist activists has been and remains transforming for many (Remington 1990, 1991). Organizational experiences can shape world views, politics, and a sense of self in relation to society, as many women can testify. It is important not merely to see individuals as resources used by organizations (as much social movement theory does) but to consider how individuals use the organizations they found or join, and how they employ the lessons learned in one group when they move to another. The empirical evidence gathered by Spalter-Roth and Schreiber, Reinelt, Eisenstein, Matthews, and Katzenstein challenges the claim that institutionalization necessarily leads to deradicalization. Chapters by Strobel, Barnett, Whittier, and Christiansen-Ruffman raise further questions about the political learning that goes on within movement organizations. In evaluating any feminist organization, we think it appropriate to ask: Were any of the activists or women on whose behalf they worked transformed? Did society change at all as a result of their efforts? Do the organizations continue to make a difference?

Second is the issue of *the relationship of feminist organizations to the movement*. We argue that the women's movement exists in a dynamic and reciprocal relation with its organizations, giving them their broad purpose, specific agenda, and supply of activists, while drawing from them a set of practices, political and material resources, and a supportive context within which activists can carry on their lives while struggling for change. This is a relationship that Mansbridge's chapter calls "accountability," and it exists as both an individual and a collective tension in the movement (see also Leidner 1993). Although social movements cannot be reduced to their formal organizations, such institutions are vital. The resource mobilization perspective on social movements has often severed the study of social movement organizations from the study of the movement as a fundamental challenge to the status quo, as if survival and institutionalization were the *goals* rather than the *means* of movements. Scholars are only now recognizing what activists have long known: the transformative intent and impact of feminist organizations (see Leidner 1991; Blanchard 1992; Martin et al. 1992). We think it appropriate to ask, as Staggenborg does in this volume: How does organizational survival help or hinder the accomplishment of the movement's broader agenda? What are the short- and long-term effects on policy, mobilization potential, and the surrounding culture?

Third is the issue of the *tensions arising from the multidimensionality of feminist politics.* The feminist movement is not coherent, singular, or unified. It does not and cannot pursue a single strategic course. It is a multifaceted mobilization that has taken different forms at different times, in different areas of the country, in different socioeconomic and political contexts, and among women of diverse racial, ethnic, class, and age groups, as chapters by Christiansen-Ruffman, Whittier, and Arnold particularly demonstrate. It is possible to appreciate this variety most when we look at movement organizations, for they vary in scale, scope, intent, form, and practice in amazingly rich and multiple ways. This diverse movement is constantly engaged in internal political relations: that is, in negotiations among participants that allow decisions to be made and work to be done (see Melucci 1989). This process is evident in women's movement organizations and their practices. The vitality and tensions of these organizations must be seen in the context of the social movement they represent.

Feminist organizations are an amalgam, a blend of institutionalized and social movement practices. They have changed over time in response to their own needs, the needs of the women they serve, and the demands of their environment (see Schmitt 19941). In the position of *outsider,* they pursue a feminist agenda that has barely begun to alter the social arrangements that disempower and victimize women. Yet as *insiders,* many have achieved a measure of respect and acceptance from the mainstream, becoming so familiar as to be no longer newsworthy, becoming so successful as to arouse resentments, angry reactions, and sometimes violent attacks. A movement organization is not a contradiction in terms, but it is, by definition, in tension. It is always a compromise between the ideals by which it judges itself and the realities of its daily practices, as the essays by Farrell, Morgen, Matthews, Pardo, Tom, Arnold, Spalter-Roth

and Schreiber, Mueller, and Acker bear witness. To understand the tensions intrinsic to feminist politics, we need to ask: What compromises are made, and at whose expense? Which groups of women set the agenda for the practical politics done in and by the organization, and on whose behalf? How are the day-to-day negotiations for survival carried out and with what effect?

Fourth, feminist organizations are the outcome of *situationally and historically specific processes.* In each time and place, feminism reflects its history and prior developments as well as present opportunities and constraints, as shown particularly in chapters by Gelb, Barnett, Pardo, Eisenstein, Simonds, and Christiansen-Ruffman (see also Katzenstein and Mueller 1987; Gelb 1989). The global women's movement consists of many diverse movements that coexist and often are quite dissimilar. The specific shape and nature of the women's movements in the United States in the 1990s reflects distinctive features of American history: for example, the relative weakness of a socialist tradition, the continuing significance of race, a decade of an antifeminist national administration. In addition, American feminism has been shaped by distinctive political practices and opportunities such as the prominence of lobbying groups, grassroots voluntary organizations, and a tradition of nonprofit community services to supplement a weak welfare state, as well as by the exceptionally active mobilization from the right, which has both attacked and borrowed from feminism, as we see in the chapters by Marshall, Hyde, and Simonds. These factors contribute to the plenitude of women's movement organizations of all sizes, shapes, and orientations. As Gelb's chapter points out, no other nation-state has as large and diverse a set of feminist organizations as the United States. American feminists work through these organizations to influence organizations of many other types—political, educational, religious, and commercial. Appreciation of the variety of their forms, practices, goals, ideologies, and effects will increase understanding of second-wave feminism's survival and its varying, albeit partial, successes. In evaluating a feminist organization we should ask: How are its options expanded or limited by the features of the legal, political, or economic situations with which it has to deal? by the specific generational, economic, or racial/ethnic experiences and identities of its members? by its history?

Activists' experiences within feminist organizations provide a rich and largely unmined source of data for the development of social theory. The editors come from two areas of sociology—namely, political sociology (Ferree) and the sociology of organizations (Martin)—that have not taken much theoretical account of these developments. In considering why this is so, we hope to encourage this pattern to change.

Why Have Feminist Organizations Been Ignored?

Despite a quarter-century of successful organization, feminist groups have largely been ignored by organizational scholars. Most sociologists of organizations, and their favored theories, have focused on large corporations, state bureaucracies, and labor unions that presume men to be their primary members and that relegate women, and women's life circumstances and experiences, to the margins (Acker 1990). Concern with big-budget, politically powerful organizations is consistent with the sociopolitical standpoint of men who have many qualities in common with the similarly (or more) privileged men who run large business and state organizations. These sociologists are unlikely to perceive small, grassroots, social movement organizations founded by feminists as interesting or important. If the dominant models and norms that guide organizational theory, research, and publication view such low-budget, high-commitment, women-run organizations as uninteresting, women scholars (who have low status within the discipline, the academy, and the subspeciality of organizational research) may be reluctant or unable to challenge them. Biases toward managerial needs and rational-technical control in large public and private organizations strongly encourage women organizational scholars to attend to similar issues.

To change this situation, a critical mass of feminist scholars in many disciplines must cooperatively develop new theory and discourse about feminist organizations. Such theory should have practical value for feminist activists who work in organizations to produce social transformations that benefit women. The felt need for such study can be seen in efforts of activists themselves to take stock of where they are and where they are going (see esp. Remington 1990, 1991). We have assembled this book as the first scholarly step in that direction.

We intend this volume also to challenge the preconceptions in feminist theory. Until recently, much of the women's studies perspective and research on feminist organizations reflected ideological judgments more than systematic observation of their forms, practices, and effects (as Ryan [1992] argues; see Ferguson 1984). In "Rethinking Feminist Organizations," Martin (1990b) sets an agenda within sociology for research on feminist organizations that focuses on their concrete forms and practices and on the dilemmas and effects their participants experience. Several popular claims are questioned, including the assumption that bureaucracy is inherently antithetical to feminism, and its corollary, that institutionalized feminist organizations cannot be agents of change. Martin calls for a more open-ended approach to the study of feminist organizations and a focus on what they do, how they work, and their transformative impact on members, other women, and all of society. Ferree and Hess (1985, 1994) have also argued against prejudging one type of feminist organizational strategy as more central or effective than another; rather, different organizational forms (such as grassroots and participatory service-delivery, mass-membership mobilization for lobbying or demonstrations, expertise-centered educational efforts, and identity-oriented, culture-building work) all play important and distinctive roles in the movement of which they are a part. Staggenborg (in this volume) proposes that outcomes that count as successes can be found in policy, organizational, and cultural arenas, and that all three are important. This book will, we hope, move the scholarly agenda toward a more balanced accounting of the successes and failures of feminist organizations and of feminist protest, organizing, and activity from within other organizations.

Biases in theories of gender and social change have also led scholars away from the study of feminist organizations. Theoretical models such as the old sex role paradigm led to countless studies of attitude change about women's roles but neglected feminist efforts for structural and political change. For example, although many studies of attitudes about rape were conducted, few asked whether or not changes in rape-processing laws or procedures affected women's experience of sexual assault and, either way, how and why so? On the one hand, within social movement theory, those who define themselves as working on new social movements (e.g., Melucci 1989; Rucht 1988) have singled out some types of feminist activism for attention (especially the identity-centered small groups) but discounted those organizations that cooperate with the mainstream as co-opted or inconsequential. On the other hand, many political scientists and sociologists who work within the resource mobilization paradigm have focused almost exclusively on mass-membership organizations such as the National Organization for Women, taking institutionalization for granted, and ignoring grassroots organizations where membership is difficult to define and where formal structures and survival dilemmas are difficult to see. The chapters by Barnett, Christiansen-Ruffman, Taylor, and Staggenborg further develop this critique.

In sum, a number of theoretical biases and limitations have contributed to pervasive inattention to feminist organizations. As submerged networks of actual and potential mobilizers, the women's movement is sustained by the organizations it has produced, and these *less than totally institutionalized* organizations may be more challenging and disturbing to the status quo than some critics seem to think (Martin 1994). The police may, for example, think rape crisis staffers are *raving feminists* who demand immediate, profound change; and college administrators may view their *radical* women's studies programs with alarm, with little regard for how conforming and mainstream such organizations try to appear and, indeed, in many ways are (see Martin 1994). What if the police and college administrators are correct, and movement scholars who focus on the failures of rape crisis centers and women's studies programs to be "truly" radical are wrong? Social movement researchers who deplore the ideological and procedural imperfections of feminist organizations may be underappreciating these groups' practical situations and their role in producing fundamental political and social change (as critiques by Marshall, Reinelt, Katzenstein, and Eisenstein in this volume suggest).

Feminist organizations are, we argue, a form of movement mobilization in the present and a resource for feminist mobilization in the future. Indeed, the most important outcome of any wave of social movement mobilization may be the institutionalized resources it provides for future mobilizations (Tarrow 1983; Mueller 1992). Organizations reach across individual life spans, connect generations, and transmit their members' memories, hard-earned wisdom, and unrealized hopes. Organizations define boundaries between insiders and outsiders, establish hierarchies, garner resources, provide a home base for activists, and institutionalize mistakes as well as successes. Thus the women's movement of the future will, for better or worse, reflect today's feminist organizations, just as these organizations reflect a movement with an extensive, complex, and contradictory past.

In recent years, research on feminist organizations has increased (e.g., Morgen 1986; Sealander and Smith 1986; Tudiver 1986; Gelb 1989; Staggenborg 1989, 1991; Leidner 1991,

1993; Solomon 1991) and an outpouring of case study material on women's protest activities has appeared (e.g., Mansbridge 1986; Bookman and Morgen 1988; Echols 1989; Blumberg and West 1990; Mathews and DeHart 1990). These scholars have begun to ask about what a range of feminist organizations are doing, why they are making the choices they make, and what effects they are having on their members and society. When we learned of the number of individual scholars struggling with these questions, we thought the time was ripe to bring them together into a broader discussion of feminist organizations.

The tie that binds us in this book, and many of the pioneers who studied feminist organizations before us, is feminism, not our disciplines or specialities within disciplines. The scholars confronting these questions are diverse in discipline, and many do not define their specialities as either social movements or formal organizations. Some are interested in women's politics, some in women's history, some in feminist practice, some in social change, and only a few in feminist organizations per se. With this book we collectively attempt to legitimate a new field of interdisciplinary study and to share the insights and questions that we have discovered we hold in common.

■ ■ ■

Discussion Questions

1. What are some examples of feminist impacts given in the reading?

2. What are the four aspects of survival and effectiveness of feminist organizations?

3. Why have organizational scholars largely ignored feminist organizations?

4. Second-wave feminist organizations provided institutionalized resources for future generations. What are some current examples you can think of?

What You Can Do

- Familiarize yourself with local and regional feminist organizations and lend them support
- Volunteer at a feminist organization to learn more about it and how you can help
- Promote and patronize feminist organizations' special events
- Become an advocate for feminist causes

CHAPTER 2

Organizational Learning in the Chicago Women's Liberation Union

By Margaret Strobel

The Chicago Women's Liberation Union (CWLU) was a major force in the women's movement in Chicago in the first half of the 1970s.[1] Moreover, it influenced developments in other women's unions nationwide. Its eight-year existence, from its founding in 1969 to its dissolution in 1977, was longer than that of most of the dozen or so other women's unions sharing similar politics: a radical vision that came to be identified as socialist feminism (K. Hansen 1986; Strobel 1990).[2]

I utilize the example of the CWLU to examine how individuals learn about organizational process and structure, how they use that learning in organizations, and what structures organizations put in place to promote members' learning. When I refer to organizational learning—that is, learning about organization—I am referring to one of these three questions. The CWLU experience transformed the lives of women members; in addition to learning about organization, they learned significantly about themselves and the world. Here, however, I narrow my focus to learning that is related to issues of organization. From studies of the origins of second-wave feminism, we know that many of the women's liberationists of the late 1960s came from the civil rights movement, the New Left, Students for a Democratic Society (SDS) and other parts of the student movement, and the antiwar movement. These studies emphasize how women's liberarionists took away ("learned") from these experiences the understanding that the male domination within society at large was also found in oppressive hierarchical organizations dedicated to achieving justice, equality, and freedom from oppression. I argue that those who formed the CWLU learned other, more positive, lessons about organization as well (K. Evans 1980).

My interest in working on the CWLU developed when I moved to Chicago in 1979 to become director of the Women's Studies Program at the University of Illinois, Chicago Circle (as it was then named), and discovered over time that many of the women I worked with and liked had been members of the CWLU. During the period of its existence I was a member of the New American Movement in Los Angeles, a socialist feminist group that shared the CWLU's politics in many ways. Hence I am both an insider (in terms of shared beliefs, friendships, and the historical moment) and an outsider (not a participant in CWLU events). The CWLU began placing its documents in the Chicago Historical Society as early as 1973, which shows an unusual self-consciousness of their role as agents of history compared with other women's and radical organizations. I have used and added to this archive. In addition, I have interviewed forty-six members and leaders of the CWLU, many of them several times, as well as thirty-two members of other women's unions, and two other individuals.[3] The forty-six CWLU women are broadly representative of the organization's membership, numbering perhaps one-quarter to one-third of its most active members over its lifetime.[4] They were involved in all the major and most of the minor work groups, projects, and chapters. They represent all the major political persuasions. They were both leaders and followers, central and more peripheral actors. They include heterosexuals, lesbians, and bisexuals. All are European American except for one Asian American.

An Organizational Overview

The CWLU was founded in 1969 as an umbrella organization that brought together individuals and groups of women who had been active in a variety of activities: for example, consciousness raising, community organizing, or underground abortions. The founders saw themselves as supporters of women's liberation, as radical women who argued for tying women's issues to other issues (such as the war in Indochina, Black liberation) and for establishing a broad base among Black and White working-class women. The CWLU's "Principles of Unity" stated a feminist, anticapitalist, anti-racist position; a "gay principle" was added in 1972.

From its founding, the CWLU was structured to demand a great deal of participation on the part of its members. Not uncommonly, a woman who was involved in a CWLU project (called "work groups") was also in another affinity grouping (called "chapters") for purposes of discussing CWLU business and personal development. The organization early on rejected the impulse to form consciousness-raising groups, instead choosing to establish action projects. This preference for action, a New Left legacy, characterized the Chicago union throughout its existence and differentiated it from others more theoretically oriented, such as the Berkeley-Oakland Women's Union (interviews: Lawhon, Ehrensaft). Indeed, the widely circulated paper for which the CWLU is best known, *Socialist Feminism: A Strategy for the Women's Movement,* was written as a strategy

for and evaluation of direct action (Booth et al. 1972; CHS/1/7).

Members could select from a wide variety of work groups, which were classified as involving education, service, or direct action (these categories are further discussed below). Educational initiatives included public speaking engagements handled through the Speakers Bureau, courses offered through the Liberation School, and various newspapers. Organized earlier than most women's studies programs, the Liberation School offered a series of courses that enrolled about two hundred students per session. The Union produced several newspapers designed to interest women in women's liberation and in the CWLU itself. *Womankind* introduced women to various aspects of women's liberation, often linked to CWLU projects in health, employment, and so on. *Secret Storm,* named after the soap opera, had two incarnations, the first with a group organizing in a factory, and the second for those women who organized teams and challenged Chicago Park District discrimination against women. Later, *Blazing Star* was produced by and for the lesbian community.

Music, art, and film formed an early focus within the Union, crossing the categories of education and service. The Chicago Women's Liberation Rock Band, which made a record, played for fund-raising and other events. They "saw their role as both outreach [to diverse constituencies] … and internal unification and stabilization, scheduling dance concerts when they perceived conflict and low morale in the Union" (personal communication: Weisstein, August 26, 1993). Band members wrote a "Culture Paper" in which they assessed the sexism and insurgent potential of rock music and posited the role of such groups as theirs in advancing a visionary, socialist feminist movement (*CWLU Newsletter,* January 5, 1973, CHS/19/6; "Developing a Revolutionary Women's Culture" 1972). In addition, the Graphics Collective produced a wide range of posters and other materials, and CWLU members helped produce *The Chicago Maternity Center,* a film about the medical establishment's closing of a home-delivery center (interviews: Cooper, Davenport, Rohrer).

The CWLU provided various services for women, including pregnancy testing (in the days before kits were available at the local pharmacy), the Legal Clinic, and the Prison Project. The Legal Clinic offered legal advice, primarily about simple divorces, plus some work on landlord-tenant problems (interviews: Pascal, Geraghty). Prison Project members did support and advocacy work for female prisoners at Dwight Correctional Institution and taught classes there.

Perhaps the most dramatic of the service projects under the Union's umbrella was the Abortion Counseling Service, an underground abortion collective some of whose members had helped found the CWLU. "The Service," as they called themselves, later came to be popularly known as "Jane." From 1969 to 1973, members performed an estimated 10,000 abortions and achieved a safety record better than or comparable to that of licensed medical facilities in New York or California (Bart 1987; Schlesinger and Bart 1983; interview: Arcana).[5]

Jane was concerned with more than merely providing an immediate service, and the umbrella structure of the CWLU facilitated linking different types of projects and forging connections across issues. For example, service members also taught courses on women's bodies and women's health in the Liberation School (interview: Arcana). Then, after abortion was legalized, the Abortion Counseling Service disbanded, and the Abortion Task Force worked to ensure that Chicago area hospitals actually provided safe abortions.[6]

Other CWLU direct action groups engaged in struggle to bring concrete changes, not only service, as a strategy. Direct Action for Rights of Employment (DARE) had various incarnations. DARE women supported strikes and organized in local factories. They lent support to African American "janitresses" at City Hall and successfully joined with NOW to sue the city for sex discrimination. Also as part of a direct action strategy, CWLU members organized ACDC, the Action Coalition for Decent Childcare, a multiracial coalition that succeeded in bringing about changes in city codes regarding licensing of day care centers and gaining $1 million in state funding for child care (interview: Booth).[7]

CWLU members often worked on one or more of these projects. If a member was also in a chapter (the affinity-based group) or in a leadership position or volunteering in the office, she could easily attend four or five meetings a week. Although such a high level of participation made the experience very intense for those who could maintain it, many women—those with children and/or full-time jobs—found it hard to embrace so heavy a commitment.

Thus, for all its theoretical understanding of the importance of reaching working-class women and women of color, the CWLU was in fact relatively homogeneous (see Rothschild-Whitt and Whitt 1986) in terms of age, race, and socioeconomic status (for comparison with Bread and Roses, see Popkin 1978). Over its lifetime, its membership hovered between 200 and 250 dues-paying individuals, of whom the members I interviewed are broadly representative. All forty-six were born between the years 1915 and 1954, with the median year being 1945. Except for one Asian American, all were European American, including a substantial Jewish contingent (43 percent). Although they tended to be single and childless, a large minority (35 percent) were married or were parents. A substantial portion were lesbian (39 percent) or bisexual (26 percent). Most grew up in suburban areas (54 percent, compared with 50 percent urban, 28 percent small town or rural), although a substantial minority reported their family as below middle class (17 percent working class, 28 percent lower middle class, 48 percent middle class, 24 percent upper middle class). The vast majority were getting or had received college degrees while in the CWLU (15 percent had only a high school diploma; 39 percent had a B.A. or B.S., 24 percent an M.A. or M.S., 15 percent a Ph.D. or equivalent). Their parents were relatively liberal but not radical (52 percent Democratic, 20 percent liberal; 24 percent Republican, 7 percent conservative; 7 percent socialist; 7 percent communist).[8] Despite periodic efforts to recruit beyond a homogeneous base, CWLU members remained concentrated in the Lake View and Hyde Park neighborhoods that were home to many progressives. This overall homogeneity hindered recruitment among women who did not fit the profile. For example, one older woman whose daughter had recommended that she "belong to the women's lib" did attend one meeting, she wrote to the CWLU, but decided that she wanted a group of women her own age.[9]

Although the Union had few women of color as members, it successfully worked in coalitions with Black and Latino organizations. The Abortion Task Force early on linked legal abortion with the need to stop sterilization abuse, a link that led the CWLU, the Puerto Rican Socialist Party, and Mujeres Latinas en Acción to form, in Chicago, the Coalition to End Sterilization Abuse. This coalition work resulted in other cooperation: in 1975 the Puerto Rican Socialist Party asked the CWLU to provide a speaker for its May Day celebration.[10] And in 1974 the CWLU organized a large and diverse coalition to celebrate International Women's Day, attracting nearly 4,000 people.[11]

The CWLU had little interest in employing mainstream structures or playing mainstream politics. Apart from the janitresses' case, which it undertook with the Chicago chapter of the National Organization for Women, the Union preferred to agitate rather than sue. The late Mayor Richard J. Daley's grip on the Chicago machine made work with reform politicians seem futile, even had the CWLU been ideologically predisposed to electoral politics, which it was not.[12]

What held all these disparate projects and affinity-based chapters together? Where did the vision come from for creating the CWLU as an umbrella with a unifying center? How did the CWLU develop new structures, approaches, and strategies? The answers to these questions lie in an exploration of organizational learning.

Structure, Change, and Organizational Learning

Organizational learning was evidenced in the CWLU in two ways. First, individuals used legacies from previous movement experience to shape the Union. Key founders brought from their prior SDS experience ideas about organization, structure, and accountable leadership. Second, the CWLU structured organizational learning into its processes through formal courses and elaborate evaluations of individual performance, actions, and programs. I examine several critical moments in the CWLU's development that illuminate both the lessons its members drew and the process by which the group approached making decisions, and I analyze the various mechanisms the CWLU used to foster organizational learning. In the latter analysis I look at mechanisms for skills transfer in, for example, the Speakers Bureau, the extensive practice of evaluation and criticism/self-criticism, and, finally, the CWLU's reflexive examination of its activity using a grid of education, service, and direct action.

NEW LEFT LEGACIES

The founders of the CWLU came out of the New Left and brought what they had learned from that experience. According to Wini Breines, "participatory democracy, small group consciousness raising, and the slogan 'the personal is political'" constitute the New Left legacy to the women's movement in general (1982, xiv). Specifically, several key founders of the CWLU came from SDS, a central New Left organization with national headquarters in Chicago after 1965 (Miller 1987, 235). Jo Freeman claims that "Chicago, more than any other city, had a movement almost entirely rooted in the New Left" (interview: Freeman).[13] The SDS and former SDS women who founded the CWLU came from the "Old Guard" period of SDS, rather than its disintegrating, Weather Underground period; their experience in community organizing and other organizing gave them an appreciation of the need for organization, strategy, and program.

SDS moved into community organizing in summer 1964 with Economic and Research Action Projects (ERAP) in northern cities. ERAP sought to address urban poverty and powerlessness under the rubric of organizing "an interracial movement of the poor" (Gitlin 1987, 165–66; Miller 1987, 184–217).[14] SDS women had more organizing success than did the men. They had the one-on-one communication skills, and the women they talked to were rooted in the communities. In contrast, the men's constituency was largely guys on street corners—unemployed men, teenaged gang members or potential gang members—and the men's skills, such as speech-making, were less significant in community organizing (S. Evans 1979, 145–55; Gitlin 1987, 366; Miller 1987, 203, 257).

Several women central to the CWLU's founding had been active in SDS and community organizing. Vivian Rothstein had worked earlier in JOIN—"Jobs or Income Now," Chicago's ERAP project.[15] Heather Tobis (now Heather Booth) worked in the Coordinating Council of Community Organizations and Student Nonviolent Coordinating Committee (SNCC) in Chicago.[16] Amy Kesselman worked as an organizer with Citizens for Independent Political Action, one of whose activities was to organize a community-based women's group. All were part of the Westside group, an informal gathering that met in Jo Freeman's apartment from approximately September 1967 to April 1968 (interview: Freeman).

The Westside group's legacy to the CWLU lay in the organizational structure that embodied principles of the women's liberation movement and New Left. Schooled in community organizing and other kinds of organizing, and in contrast to most other women's liberation organizers,[17] the CWLU founders sought to establish leadership positions that were accountable to the membership and also to develop democratically the capacity of many women to become leaders. CWLU members adopted a clear (if awkward and not completely effective) umbrella structure intended to assure democratic participation at a time when many women's liberation groups, chary of authoritarian structures, fell victim to the "tyranny of structurelessness" (Freeman 1973). And, in a critical early period, CWLU leaders, mindful of the collapse of SDS and seeking to preserve the integrity of their organization, affirmed its right to remain a multi-issue autonomous women's group and successfully avoided takeover by the Socialist Workers Party/ Young Socialist Alliance.

The CWLU's unique and most valuable contribution to women's liberation was its notion of accountable leadership and structured democratic participation (see Sirianni 1993). Its leadership initially created a decentralized structure and modified the structure as their experiences warranted.

Those who attended the CWLU's founding conference established a structure involving a Steering Committee of representatives from each work project group and chapter, plus periodic citywide membership meetings at which policy decisions would be made. Thus, Steering Committee members represented only a minimal level of leadership; individuals voted directly on policy. But this structure proved unwieldy, because the Steering Committee was the only authorized group that could respond quickly to requests for endorsement of activities. Since it was not clear where the ultimate political authority lay, the Steering Committee devoted part of its July 1970 retreat to that issue. The chapters and work projects, committee members argued, were the "basic functioning units." The Steering Committee was largely an administrative and supervisory body whose task was to "guide the general policy and politics of CWLU activity." The citywide meeting was "a membership, action, and policy forum."[18] Whereas the Steering Committee was representative of the chapters, the citywide meetings provided at-large members who were not in chapters with a forum. In reality, both these types of members were part of the CWLU, but the tension between them continued throughout the life of the Union.

In addition to citywide meetings, at periodic conferences CWLU members evaluated the effectiveness of these structures and modified them over time, empowering leaders to speak and act for the benefit and in the name of the CWLU. Moreover, they strengthened representative, rather than direct, democracy by authorizing the Steering Committee—not only the general membership—to make policy decisions. By 1973 the organization had decided to elect co-chairs to provide accountable leadership beyond that of the Steering Committee. A year later a Planning Committee was established to do long-range planning for financial security and outreach, which often got lost amid everyday activity. At each of these levels of political responsibility, leaders were elected, given concrete tasks, and asked to report back to those who had elected them.

The question of defining membership emerged in the first year, and the debates surrounding this issue illustrate several points. First, the founding leaders with SDS and community organizing experience brought that experience to bear. Second, their definition of membership showed CWLU leaders' profound commitment to organizational learning, to the evaluation of past activity and redirection of effort based upon that evaluation. At issue was who might attend the first annual membership conference in a decision-making capacity.

The 1971 conference was the first major conference since the CWLU's founding. The founders had negative past experiences with the Socialist Workers Party/Young Socialist Alliance, a Trotskyist organization: "The [SWP/YSA] would recruit people off the street to vote their way" (interview: anonymous). Hence the founders took decisive action to protect CWLU from what they saw as infiltration and takeover by the SWP/YSA.[19] As one member recalls, "A fundamental difference [between us and the

SWP/YSA] involved our sense of sisterhood and sectarianism, so a small grouping decided to, in effect, go to war on this question. Not to move for exclusion on the basis they were SWP[/YSA] and fall into red-baiting,[20] but to try and figure out … a self-definition of what we stood for."

Laying out the philosophy that decisions and change should develop out of an organization's evaluation of its past activity, Vivian Rothstein argued that those attending should "be in similar places politically in order for discussions to get anywhere." People should come who had worked together and could therefore evaluate that work. Having done some work with the Union should be seen as a requirement for membership, and only those people should attend the spring 1971 conference.[21] Essentially labeling this notion as elitist, SWP/YSA supporters argued for very open criteria, based simply on agreement with the CWLU's political principles. Their statement appealed to notions of sisterhood and democracy: "Each woman's experience because she is a woman is valid and valuable for our movement. It is on the basis of our common experience *as women* that we must come together and not on the basis of some esoteric knowledge of the inner workings of a select group of active women" ("Position Paper #2," *CWLU Newsletter,* November 11, 1970, CHS/19/3). Ultimately, the membership voted in support of Rothstein's notion of a conference of members who shared and could evaluate activity instead of the broader SWP/YSA proposal (written communication: Wessel).

If the membership debate was a critical moment in which CWLU members learned about establishing organizational boundaries and debated issues of structure and democracy, it also contributed significantly to their understanding of how to organize. Because of their notions of sisterhood and commitment to inclusiveness, it was difficult to persuade union members to exclude other women, even on principled grounds. "People felt it was a terrible thing to ask them to do," explained one member. "As the vote came close, we felt an enormous pressure to move for that victory and didn't build enough of a core that in fact felt participatory enough and owning enough of the core decision…. We alienated people who were close to us, though we won the vote overwhelmingly…. I still feel, for the survival of the Women's Union, it was the right outcome." Reflecting on the episode, Heather Booth noted that "the questions of when [one is] organizing, creating a core of support, ensuring that friendship patterns reinforce political objectives, and keeping the human relationships primary—that lesson will stay with me for the rest of my life. It reinforced my antagonism to 'pure line' sectarianism."

In addition to establishing organizational boundaries by defining membership in terms of participation, the 1971 conference affirmed representative democracy (decision-making by the Steering Committee) over direct democracy (citywide votes on organizational matters). And, reflecting women's experiences in such large groups as SDS, they decided that "important decisions will be talked over in the small groups with women we work with and know, rather than made in large meetings in which many of us do not speak, or understand the procedure."[22]

Thus, CWLU members consciously learned from the experiences of those with prior organizational and movement experience, in terms of maintaining organizational integrity (preventing takeover by the SWP/YSA) and promoting internal democracy (ensuring representative democracy and small group structures).

In addition to voting changes in structure in 1971, CWLU members changed their attitude toward paid staff. From the beginning, the Union had a (barely) paid staff of one to three women, who coordinated activities of the various work groups and, with volunteer labor, produced a fairly regular monthly newsletter. "Initially," wrote Day Creamer (now Piercy) and Carole Whiteside, "we argued that since capitalism is so concerned with money, we should not be." Most workers were volunteers, since "paying someone to do it would be a new form of oppression."[23] Over time, however, members came to believe that paying staff made it possible for

low-income women or single mothers to take these jobs and experience the benefits in terms of personal growth. They accepted a division of labor between paid staff and members, while clearly articulating expectations that chapters (but not work project groups) held some responsibility vis-à-vis routine maintenance of the organization. The Union staff echoed sentiments similar to those of Old Guard members of SDS regarding the importance of effective organization (Breines 1982, 76). In the words of staffer Betsy V., "If we don't deliver better than the institutions we are attempting to supplant, how are we going to make a revolution?" ("Please Note," *CWLU Newsletter*, May 1972, CHS/19/5).

The particular influence of the Chicago SDS/ JOIN experience on the CWLU can be seen in differences between the Union and Bread and Roses, the more anarchistic Boston area group of similar politics, which was formed three months earlier in 1969 and collapsed much sooner (Popkin 1978, 1979). The two groups drew members from the same segment of the population in terms of age and ideology. But Bread and Roses members were suspicious of formal structure. Their structure, based upon primary affiliation with a small group, work groups, and mass meetings, did not include a formal center that held the organization together; formal leaders were not selected. In comparison with the CWLU's vast array of minutes of meetings (in some cases summarizing the statements of each person on each issue), Bread and Roses kept no minutes of meetings and had no organizational newsletter. Two part-time staffers were chosen by lottery from among members. Meredith Tax, who later joined the CWLU, summarized her Bread and Roses experience this way: "Inevitably, most of the real decision-making got done informally, … leading to a feeling of exclusion and resentment on the part of the majority and a feeling of overwhelming responsibility on the part of the informal leadership. I learned all about anarchism in practice in Bread and Roses; the experience turned me into a Leninist for a while. Fearing an SDS model of leadership, we fled from representatives and elections and ended up with de facto leadership of people who had the most experience and confidence: rule by friendship clique, a popular form of oligarchy in the feminist movement."[24]

The early membership of the CWLU drew upon the same kinds of women as Bread and Roses and other women's liberation groups around the country; indeed, two JOIN organizers became leaders in Bread and Roses. Yet Bread and Roses members did not draw the same conclusions as did the CWLU membership: to create accountable leadership, representative democratic committees, and membership based on shared political work.[25]

INTERNAL LEARNING PROCESSES

Organizational learning in the CWLU did not consist merely of heeding the political advice of more seasoned activists. As the organization evolved, its leaders and members adopted a number of procedures that institutionalized organizational learning. They established a Liberation School course on the political history of the CWLU in order to transmit to new members the lessons learned from their past CWLU work and struggle, as well as the policies of the Union. Both individuals and work projects as a whole were evaluated periodically in an effort to learn from experience and correct emerging problems. They drew upon Chairman Mao Tse-tung's notion of criticism/self-criticism, incorporating into each meeting an evaluation of self and of the group. As member Sarah Bornstein reported, "I've been through formal and informal constant appraisals of what I did, through criticism and self-criticism. I felt [that I was] held very accountable for my work in the Women's Union, more so than I've been on paid jobs" (interview: Bornstein; communication: Davenport; see also Rothschild 1986, 84–91). In addition, each work project published an elaborate evaluation in the newsletter for public discussion at the annual conference.

In its first year the CWLU developed an important schema for evaluating and analyzing its activity. In this analysis, the overall work of the Union was to be balanced in terms of education, service, and direct action. (As another example of organizational learning, this schema was adopted by other women's unions.) These three aspects were intended to be mutually supportive and to define success in relation to the CWLU's call for fundamental changes in U.S. society. Without taking direct action to challenge power, education and service activity could not bring about real change.[26] Without education, discrete actions could be viewed in isolation rather than seen as part of a broad strategy; in addition, education was necessary to change and deepen women's understanding of themselves and their world. The service component of the Union's work was intended to meet the real needs of women, but merely building counter-institutions nurtured the illusion that "problems can be solved in the spaces between existing institutions"; moreover, service-providing activities could not "alter the power relations if they [made] no demands on those in power" and hence needed to be combined with direct action (Booth et al. 1972, 14). Although the Union continued to experience the centrifugal force wherein women's intense identification with a particular project competed with their identification with the organization as a whole, the leadership attempted systematically to unify the organization by having members utilize the education/service/direct action schema to discuss the relationship of projects and chapters to one another and to the CWLU's overall program.

Members and leaders also built on their experiences to develop strategies for democratic participation. Initially, Steering Committee representatives rotated frequently, reflecting an implicit assumption that the role of the Steering Committee was to be a conduit for information rather than a leadership and decision-making body; for the former purpose it was useful to rotate representatives, thus encouraging participation and familiarity with the larger group. In mid-1971, as the role of the Steering Committee became more important, the membership conference voted for staggered three-month terms (extended to six to nine months at the November 1972 annual conference), and the Steering Committee discussed the political implications of regular representation. Some women believed that requiring regular attendance by representatives was "anti-working class, because many women can't leave home regularly on every second Thursday." Yet irregular attendance made it hard for a woman to follow and contribute; therefore, others responded that her chapter or work group should bear the responsibility to "make it possible for her to come, doing child care, etc."[27] Ultimately, the CWLU was not able to address the kinds of problems that made it hard for some women to participate or to serve in leadership roles, but the Union did structure opportunities for members to learn concrete skills related to effective organizational work.

One such skill was public speaking. The CWLU established the Speakers Bureau in response to the barrage of requests for information about women's liberation. Within its first six months the bureau scheduled fifty speaking engagements and averaged twenty-three per month for some time after that.[28] Although the CWLU did not share the women's movement's suspicion of structure, it did reject the notion of media stars, and this attitude is reflected in its Speakers Bureau policy: everyone in the Union was expected to give speeches. Speaking engagements were rotated among chapters or work projects. The Speakers Bureau actively taught the public speaking skills necessary for spreading a message and building a movement (Strobel 1995). Women were sent in pairs to speaking engagements, and training sessions helped them learn and improve. They shared sample presentations for particular audiences and critiqued one another's efforts.

While training individuals, Union members learned from their experience and modified the speakers' policy over time. Replacing voluntarism with an expectation that everyone would learn to speak publicly helped members develop skills and self-confidence and ensured a basic level of

political knowledge. Supporters saw this Speakers Bureau policy as "structur[ing] out elitism" and as evidence that not all structure was bad. Critics, however, labeled it as coercive and claimed that the rigid policy was blind to differences in people's abilities and placed "the need of developing our members before the need of making an impact on the audience" (Rothstein and Weisstein 1972).[29] By 1973 the policy was modified to make the elected co-chairs responsible for important media contacts and speaking engagements; and work project groups were responsible for speaking on their particular subject area.[30]

Training occurred in both the Liberation School and the various work projects. Liberation School courses included such practical skills as auto mechanics, which contributed significantly to women's sense of accomplishment even if they had little relation to building an organization. Classes in silk screening encouraged neophytes to learn how to produce inexpensive political art. Those who worked on the various newspapers learned writing and layout skills, typically by being paired with more experienced women and by rotating responsibilities. Other training included such technical skills running pregnancy tests. In all these ways, CWLU members learned the skills needed to organize effectively around whatever goals the group established (written comments: Wessel, July 1992; interview: Davenport).

In both the definition of membership and the empowering of a representative Steering Committee over the general membership meeting, CWLU members rejected the notion of a barely involved but dues-paying membership and a leadership whose influence derived in part from the marginal involvement of the membership. In various decisions that empowered elected leaders (for example, creating co-chairs and a Planning Committee), union members sought to ensure accountable leaders. In their structures of evaluation, criticism, and mentoring, they sought both accountability and growth from themselves (Strobel 1995).

Lessons Learned and Not Learned

Staggenborg (Chapter 22) identifies various ways in which the CWLU was successful in terms of "mobilization outcomes and broader cultural outcomes," even if it "exerted little direct influence on public policy and accomplished none of its radical goals." Indeed, part of its success lies in the lessons about organization learned by members who went on to utilize the skills and ideas developed in the CWLU in other organizations, from women's studies programs to women's health groups.

There is not space to analyze in detail the lessons *not* learned by CWLU members, although these remain critical to the development of effective feminist organizations. Tensions existed between more feminist and more left-oriented members—for example over the Equal Rights Amendment (written communication: Weisstein, August 26, 1993). Like that of many other women's unions, the CWLU's demise was linked to an inability to deal with ideological heterogeneity within a left-feminist framework.[31]

Its other shortcomings are manifested in many other organizations. It tried to be, in Paul Starr's categories (1979), both an exemplary organization, "exemplify[ing] in its own structure and conduct an alternative set of ideals," and an adversary organization, "primarily concerned with altering the prevailing social order." This contradiction led the CWLU to try simultaneously to be an organization of organizers (of cadre) and an organization of the masses. For all its discussion of structure, it did not find a structure that was democratic and inclusive and also served the needs of people with minimal available time. The problem of how to integrate at-large members, who for lack of time or commitment never joined a particular work group, was never solved.

For all its energy, the CWLU never succeeded in broadening its base beyond a fairly narrow range of the population in terms of ethnicity, class, education level, and lifestyle. The enormous outlay of time that was expected of members built intense friendships but effectively limited the possibility of membership for many people. The intensity of relationships built solidarity but also created the sense of an in-group (Popkin 1978). Although the structures for evaluation contributed to members' learning from their own and other members' experiences, the requirement of active participation limited the extent to which CWLU members could learn from experiences of people outside the Union.

Further, largely because of the youth and countercultural orientation of its membership, the CWLU had unworkable notions about work and money. After a few months on the job, staffers, who claimed to have learned enormous amounts, would decide that it was time to move on to another position. People moved in and out of communities, barely there long enough to meet neighbors, much less develop roots upon which to build an organization based in neighborhoods. The idea of paying people to do political work was abhorrent initially and the Union included several voluntarily downwardly mobile individuals. The homogeneity of the group, which reinforced this countercultural ethos, contributed to its ineffectiveness in developing a movement in Chicago that could include working-class women who identified with neighborhoods and aspired to raise their standard of living.

Like other socialist organizations, the CWLU did not successfully communicate to the anticommunist/antisocialist society around it a compelling vision of democratic and feminist socialism.[32] The problem of developing a strategy that linked concrete reforms and victories to a larger goal of socialist transformation was not solved by the Union; neither was it solved by those who criticized the Union in its dying days for its lack of such a strategy for revolutionary change.

For all these shortcomings, the CWLU did bring some changes to the Chicago area. It helped keep a left-wing presence alive in the 1970s in the years following the end of the Vietnam War. It brought a socialist feminist perspective to the gay and lesbian rights movement. It strengthened reproductive rights activity in Chicago (see Staggenborg, Chapter 22). It helped win the janitresses' suit against the city.

Many women learned organizing skills they brought to later political work in Third World liberation, antiracism, disability rights, labor, community, peace, reproductive rights, lesbian, or other feminist activities. Thus the CWLU contributed leadership to various other progressive organizations. Many people I have interviewed comment upon the skills they learned in the Union, and, although I do not have a random sample, a remarkable number report that their present jobs embody the politics they held while in the CWLU (McAdam 1989). Membership in the CWLU affected some women's eventual career decisions. Some Jane workers went on to work in health care fields, for example (Schlesinger and Bart 1983). One woman found relevant to her later degree in marketing the collective decision-making that she had learned in the CWLU (interview: Kloiber). Others have gone into community organizing, labor organizing jobs, youth work, or nontraditional careers (interviews: Blacksin, Norris, Schmid, Hurst).

The impact on personal lives too is striking. One Jewish woman attributes her marriage to a Mexican American to the exposure she got in the CWLU to a broader range of people and cultures (interview: Morales). The radical questioning of heterosexuality generated by the women's liberation movement in the early 1970s occurred in the CWLU as well.[33] One woman who came out as a lesbian during her years in the Union says, "It gave me ... the ability to be able to look a little deeper into myself and explore my own sexuality, which took a long time, a lot of years. But I felt that there was always a lot of support from the people in that group to figure out who you were" (interview: Maloney). Another lesbian agreed that as a married housewife with children, living in the suburbs at the time, she would not have come out as a lesbian without the CWLU. Although it was sometimes criticized by the lesbian separatist community as basically heterosexual (a claim the CWLU rejected), the Union provided her with space and acceptance that she did not find in the separatist community (*Secret Storm* group interview). The CWLU provided a deep sense of sisterhood. As one woman put it: "I grew very fond of all the women in the group…. They gave me a feeling of self-worth in being a woman…. I had never had [the camaraderie] from a group of women before, in high school, whatever. Women were just somebody you knew. This was the first time I could ever be close to women and not be afraid to tell them how I feel."

In retrospect, many view the Union as having been an appropriate vehicle for its time and its ending as closure on an intensely meaningful period, organizationally and personally.[34] In the words of former co-chair Jennifer Rohrer, "It had been for most of us, certainly for me, the most important organization for developing leadership, for transition from the left into the mainstream…. I have never felt more confident than I did then. Politics has never been more fun, and my social life has never been better than it was in the Women's Union." For most, the perspective on society learned in the CWLU— the importance of linking women's issues to those of people of color and the working class or poor people—remains, in Suzanne Davenport's words, "burned into your consciousness." That consciousness, along with the individual and organizational lessons learned, may turn out to be the CWLU's most important contribution to today's feminist movement.

NOTES

Acknowledgments: Interviews and written communications are from Judith Arcana, Sarah Bornstein, Heather Booth, Victoria Cooper [Musselman], Suzanne Davenport, Diane Ehrensaft, Jo Freeman, Miriam Geraghty, Cady Hurst, Judith Kloiber, Jane Lawhon, Jean Maloney, Esther Moscow Morales, Coral Norris, Erica Pascal, Jennifer Rohrer, Margaret Schmid, Meredith Tax, Naomi Weisstein, and Elaine Wessel.

Many former CWLU members have commented on drafts of my research. I thank them and, for their comments on this article in particular, Judith Arcana, Bill Barclay, Heather Booth, Victoria Cooper, Suzanne Davenport, Myra Marx Ferree, Jo Freeman, Patricia Yancey Martin, Vivian Rothstein, and Elaine Wessel.

The interpretation and any errors are my own. Carol Mueller suggested the phrase "organizational learning." Research was conducted with the assistance of University of Illinois at Chicago Campus Research Board grants and a National Endowment for the Humanities fellowship.

1. Because being identified as a socialist in the United States can be hazardous to one's livelihood, if not health, I have taken precautions in identifying individuals. Those who, when I interviewed them, gave me permission to use their names are cited by name. Others whose names appear in CWLU documents are referred to by first name and last initial only. As a historian, I am uncomfortable with social scientists' notion of not naming individuals at all. The women I interviewed are not merely representatives of points of view; they are particular individuals who have gone on to do other things in their lives. I wish to preserve their identities both so that the reader can follow the thread of a particular person's contribution and ideas within the article and so that this part of their lives is not lost to the historical record. Unless otherwise noted, archival references are to files in the Chicago Historical Society (CHS), identified by box and folder number. These materials were indexed *after* I read them. With the assistance of Vickie Kukulski, I have tried to cite the present location of all the documents I use.

2. Briefly, socialist feminists shared with Marxists a critique of capitalism and the vision of a society in which resources would be broadly shared; however, they agreed with feminist critiques of the male bias in Marxist theory and socialist practice.

3. Quotations not cited from documents come from these interviews, conducted between 1986 and 1993. Transcripts are in the CWLU archive at the CHS.

4. In preparation for a reunion in 1984, former members compiled a list of 436 names, which represented everyone in the extant records and in the memory of people who had been in the Union; many were names of transitory members, however. One-third to one-quarter is my estimate.

5. As was the case with various CWLU projects, members often developed a more intense commitment to the project than to CWLU itself. Thus, the Service had a tenuous connection with the CWLU: often it did not send a representative to the Steering Committee; rather, the Steering Committee sent a representative to Jane's meetings (interview: Arcana). The CWLU staff took calls for Jane, which constituted, according to one log for a six-month period, one-third of calls to the CWLU office (CHS/6/8).

6. Reports for May 1973 program meeting, CHS/19/6; *CWLU Newsletter,* May 10, 1973. CWLU's health work evolved over time into the Health Evaluation and Referral Service (HERS), which continued into the late 1980s. Some members formed the Emma Goldman Women's Health Center.

7. CHS/22/1. Heather Booth indicated that it was the most multiracial group in which she has ever worked: about half the members were White, the other half were Black and Latina.

8. The percentages do not add up to 100 because not all respondents answered all questions, and often they reported occupying more than one category in the course of their membership in the CWLU.

9. Correspondence, S.B.M., October 21, 1970, CHS/5/7. One chapter consisted of older, white, working-class women, but it was atypical demographically (interview: Starr).

10. "CWLU Planning Committee Report—1975," CHS/4/7.

11. Report and evaluation, my files; interviews: Tax, Cooper.

12. Several CWLU members, however, were involved in Citizens for Independent Political Action (CIPA), which engaged in electoral campaigns as an organizing tool rather than with the expectation of winning power (personal communication: Kesselman and Weisstein, December 30, 1989).

13. Indeed, some contemporaries joked, "If you ever wondered what a female SDS would look like, check out the CWLU" ("Evaluation/History of the CWLU," p. 82, CHS/2/5–6).

14. Jennifer Frost, a graduate student in history at the University of Wisconsin, Madison, is researching these projects (Frost and Strobel forthcoming).

15. Interview: Rothstein. Vivian Rothstein was married to Richard Rothstein, whom Breines (1982, 60) credits with "one of the most extensive and damning accounts of participatory democracy in SDS." He argued that the dismantling of formal structures in an attempt to eliminate hierarchy led to, in Breines's paraphrase, "an elite not answerable to the membership."

16. Interview: Booth. Both Rothstein and Heather Booth were married to national SDS leaders who argued for more effective national structure and against excesses of participatory democracy (Miller 1987, 246–59, on Paul Booth).

17. Feminist organizations such as NOW adopted more traditional hierarchical structures. In contrast, women's liberation groups, organized by the younger branch of second-wave feminism, eschewed hierarchy and, often, formal structure itself (see Carden 1974; Freeman 1975).

18. "On the Issue of Structure," by Carole Whiteside, notes of July 10–11, 1970, Steering Committee

retreat, mailed August 21, 1970, as a *CWLU Newsletter* (CHS/4/10).

19. SDS collapsed in the late 1960s, in part because of a takeover by the Progressive Labor Party; the Old Guard had already lost influence by then, and the CWLU founders were no longer close to SDS (interview: Booth; Breines 1982; Miller 1987). After the demise of the CWLU, a group of independent Marxist-Leninists who met and evaluated the CWLU, identified the SWP struggle as decisive in a different way, setting the tone for what they viewed as a pattern of anti-communism.

20. "Red-baiting" is the tactic of discrediting a person or group by linking them or their ideas with socialism or communism.

21. Vivian Rothstein position paper, endorsed by the Steering Committee for citywide discussion, *CWLU Newsletter*, November 11, 1970, CHS/19/3.

22. Karen W., "Report from the CWLU Conference"; and "Structural Decision Made at CWLU Conference April, 1971," *CWLU Newsletter*, April 1971, CHS/19/4.

23. "An Evolutionary Perspective," n.d, [1973], CHS/1/2.

24. Personal communication: Meredith Tax; a portion of this material appears in Tax 1988, 457–62.

25. Rothstein communication, July 17, 1993. According to Jennifer Frost (personal communication), ERAP women organizers left the other communities where ERAP projects were begun; hence there is no way of studying, with a control group, whether SDS women with community organizing experience established groups similar to the CWLU in their notions of structure and organization. I have dropped my initial hypothesis, that community organizing experience was the definitive cause of the difference between Bread and Roses and the CWLU; the precise explanation for the difference is more complex and requires examination beyond the scope of this essay. Naomi Weisstein argues that Vivian Rothstein deserves much of the credit for the CWLU's structure of democratic, accountable leadership (personal communication, August 26, 1993).

26. These ideas were developed in *Socialist Feminism* (1972). One of its authors, Heather Booth, built upon the ideas of author and political strategist Andre Gorz (1967) (interview: Booth). Breines (1982, 102, 104–5) discusses the influence of Gorz's thinking on SDS.

27. "CWLU Steering Committee notes April 8/71," personal copy.

28. "State of the Union" [1970], CHS/4/4; 140 engagements from September 1970 to February 1971, conference packet April 1971, CHS/7/7.

29. Critics: "Reconsidering the Speakers [*sic*] Policy," Ellen A., Pat McG., Jody P., CHS/18/3.

30. Steering Committee minutes, March 15, 1973, CHS/5/1; *CWLV Newsletter*, March 19, 1973 CHS/19/6.

31. This issue, and the particular manifestation of it in the CWLU, is very complicated. Some former members believe the organization was infiltrated and broken up by *agents provocateur* of the federal government, who deliberately provoked ideological battles. Others, including independent Marxist-Leninists and one of the alleged agents, believe the CWLU foundered because it did not—for lack of more systematic study of Marxism, Leninism, and Maoism—have the appropriate strategy for bringing about the revolution. Still others felt that although the CWLU had met a need at a particular historical moment, they wished to participate in more mainstream organizations. See K. Hansen 1986 for the demise of the women's unions; for discussion of the difficulty of maintaining an ideologically diverse and democratically structured feminist organization, see Leidner 1991, 1993.

32. Suzanne Staggenborg (1989) minimizes, I believe mistakenly, the effect of being a socialist organization in the midst of a capitalist society and instead identifies organizational features in discussing the differences between the CWLU and Chicago NOW. She is correct, however, in pointing to NOW's ability to set priorities, in contrast to the CWLU's more voluntarist, experimental approach.

33. The CWLU managed to avoid the gay/straight split that fractured much of the movement. In the early 1970s, however, tensions arose over claims inside and outside the Union that lesbianism was the authentic expression of feminism (written communication: Weisstein, August 26, 1993).

34. Others see its demise as a result of political errors that could have been corrected (interview: Davenport).

• • •

Discussion Questions

1. What made the CWLU's structure work?

2. What were some 'internal learning' processes?

3. What were some of the clear failures of CWLU?

What You Can Do

- Study the various organizing methods of feminist groups, determine best practices, and share your findings
- Utilize grant funding organization workshops to better understand operational structures
- Volunteer and help with organizational tasks

Women of Color and Social Change

This section covers women of color activism and movements during the second wave. The second-wave movement was notorious for being primarily white and middle class. Women of color were left with little option but to build their own movements addressing issues unique to them. Many women of color struggled to find their place between the feminist movement and the civil rights movement, often being pulled in completely opposite directions. Through collaboration and addressing racism head on, women of color built strong and lasting bonds that helped later generations find equality of both race and gender.

CHAPTER 3

Racism and Feminism

By bell hooks

American women of all races are socialized to think of racism solely in the context of race hatred. Specifically in the case of black and white people, the term racism is usually seen as synonymous with discrimination or prejudice against black people by white people. For most women, the first knowledge of racism as institutionalized oppression is engendered either by direct personal experience or through information gleaned from conversations, books, television, or movies. Consequently, the American woman's understanding of racism as a political tool of colonialism and imperialism is severely limited. To experience the pain of race hatred or to witness that pain is not to understand its origin, evolution, or impact on world history. The inability of American women to understand racism in the context of American politics is not due to any inherent deficiency in woman's psyche. It merely reflects the extent of our victimization.

No history books used in public schools informed us about racial imperialism. Instead we were given romantic notions of the "new world," the "American dream," America as the great melting pot where all races come together as one. We were taught that Columbus discovered America; that "Indians" were scalphunters, killers of innocent women and children; that black people were enslaved because of the biblical curse of Ham, that God "himself" had decreed they would be hewers of wood, tillers of the field, and bringers of water. No one talked of Africa as the cradle of civilization, of the African and Asian people who came to America before Columbus. No one mentioned mass murders of Native Americans

as genocide, or the rape of Native American and African women as terrorism. No one discussed slavery as a foundation for the growth of capitalism. No one described the forced breeding of white wives to increase the white population as sexist oppression.

I am a black woman. I attended all-black public schools. I grew up in the south where all around me was the fact of racial discrimination, hatred, and forced segregation. Yet my education as to the politics of race in American society was not that different from that of white female students I met in integrated high schools, in college, or in various women's groups. The majority of us understood racism as a social evil perpetuated by prejudiced white people that could be overcome through bonding between blacks and liberal whites, through militant protest, changing of laws or racial integration. Higher educational institutions did nothing to increase our limited understanding of racism as a political ideology. Instead professors systematically denied us truth, teaching us to accept racial polarity in the form of white supremacy and sexual polarity in the form of male dominance.

American women have been socialized, even brainwashed, to accept a version of American history that was created to uphold and maintain racial imperialism in the form of white supremacy and sexual imperialism in the form of patriarchy. One measure of the success of such indoctrination is that we perpetuate both consciously and unconsciously the very evils that oppress us. I am certain that the black female sixth grade teacher who taught us history, who taught us to identify with the American government, who loved those students who could best recite the pledge of allegiance to the American flag was not aware of the contradiction; that we should love this government that segregated us, that failed to send schools with all black students supplies that went to schools with only white pupils. Unknowingly she implanted in our psyches a seed of the racial imperialism that would keep us forever in bondage. For how does one overthrow, change, or even challenge a system that you have been taught to admire, to love, to believe in? Her innocence does not change the reality that she was teaching black children to embrace the very system that oppressed us, that she encouraged us to support it, to stand in awe of it, to die for it.

That American women, irrespective of their education, economic status, or racial identification, have undergone years of sexist and racist socialization that has taught us to blindly trust our knowledge of history and its effect on present reality, even though that knowledge has been formed and shaped by an oppressive system, is nowhere more evident than in the recent feminist movement. The group of college-educated white middle and upper class women who came together to organize a women's movement brought a new energy to the concept of women's rights in America. They were not merely advocating social equality with men. They demanded a transformation of society, a revolution, a change in the American social structure. Yet as they attempted to take feminism beyond the realm of radical rhetoric and into the realm of American life, they revealed that they had not changed, had not undone the sexist and racist brainwashing that had taught them to regard women unlike themselves as Others. Consequently, the Sisterhood they talked about has not become a reality, and the women's movement they envisioned would have a transformative effect on American culture his not emerged. Instead, the hierarchical pattern of race and sex relationships already established in American society merely took a different form under "feminism": the form of women being classed as an oppressed group under affirmative

action programs further perpetuating the myth that the social status of all women in America is the same; the form of women's studies programs being established with all white faculty teaching literature almost exclusively by white women about white women and frequently from racist perspectives; the form of white women writing books that purport to be about the experience of American women when in fact they concentrate solely on the experience of white women; and finally the form of endless argument and debate as to whether or not racism was a feminist issue.

If the white women who organized the contemporary movement toward feminism were at all remotely aware of racial politics in American history, they would have known that overcoming barriers that separate women from one another would entail confronting the reality of racism, and not just racism as a general evil in society but the race hatred they might harbor in their own psyches. Despite the predominance of patriarchal rule in American society, America was colonized on a racially imperialistic base and not on a sexually imperialistic base. No degree of patriarchal bonding between white male colonizers and Native American men overshadowed white racial imperialism. Racism took precedence over sexual alliances in both the white world's interaction with Native Americans and African Americans, just as racism overshadowed any bonding between black women and white women on the basis of sex. Tunisian writer Albert Memmi emphasizes in The Colonizer and the Colonized the impact of racism as a tool of imperialism:

> Racism appears ... not as an incidental detail, but as a con-substantial part of colonialism. It is the highest expression of the colonial system and one of the most significant features of the colonialist. Not only does it establish a (fundamental discrimination between colonizer and colonized, a sine qua non of colonial life, but it also lays the foundation for the immutability of this life.

While those feminists who argue that sexual imperialism is more endemic to all societies than racial imperialism are probably correct, American society is one in which racial imperialism supersedes sexual imperialism.

In America, the social status of black and white women has never been the same. In 19th and early 20th century America, few if any similarities could be found between the life experiences of the two female groups. Although they were both subject to sexist victimization, as victims of racism black women were subjected to oppressions no white woman was forced to endure. In fact, white racial imperialism granted all white women, however victimized by sexist oppression they might be, the right to assume the role of oppressor in relationship to black women and black men. From the onset of the contemporary move toward feminist revolution, white female organizers attempted to minimize their position in the racial caste hierarchy of American society. In their efforts to disassociate themselves from white men (to deny connections based on shared racial caste), white women involved in the move toward feminism have charged that racism is endemic to white male patriarchy and have argued that they cannot be held responsible for racist oppression. Commenting on the issue of white female accountability in her essay "'Disloyal to Civilization': Feminism, Racism, and Gynephobia," radical feminist Adrienne Rich contends:

> If Black and White feminists are going to speak of female accountability, I believe the word racism must be seized, grasped in our bare hands, ripped out of the sterile or defensive consciousness in which it so often grows, and transplanted so that it can yield new insights for our lives and our movement. An analysis that places the guilt for active domination, physical and institutional violence, and the justifications embedded in myth and language, on white women not only compounds

false consciousness; it allows us all to deny or neglect the charged connection among black and white women from the historical conditions of slavery on, and it impedes any real discussion of women's instrumentality in a system which oppresses all women and in which hatred of women is also embedded in myth, folklore, and language.

No reader of Rich's essay could doubt that she is concerned that women who are committed to feminism work to overcome barriers that separate black and white women. However, she fails to understand that from a black female perspective, if white women are denying the existence of black women, writing "feminist" scholarship as if black women are not a part of the collective group American women, or discriminating against black women, then it matters less that North America was colonized by white patriarchal men who institutionalized a racially imperialistic social order than that white women who purport to be feminists support and actively perpetuate anti-black racism.

To black women the issue is not whether white women are more or less racist than white men, but that they are racist. If women committed to feminist revolution, be they black or white, are to achieve any understanding of the "charged connections" between white women and black women, we must first be willing to examine woman's relationship to society, to race, and to American culture as it is and not as we would ideally have it be. That means confronting the reality of white female racism. Sexist discrimination has prevented white women from assuming the dominant role in the perpetuation of white racial imperialism, but it has not prevented white women from absorbing, supporting, and advocating racist ideology or acting individually as racist oppressors in various spheres of American life.

Every women's movement in America from its earliest origin to the present day has been built on a racist foundation—a fact which in no way invalidates feminism as a political ideology. The racial apartheid social structure that characterized 19th and early 20th century American life was mirrored in the women's rights movement. The first white women's rights advocates were never seeking social equality for all women; they were seeking social equality for white women. Because many 19th century white women's rights advocates were also active in the abolitionist movement, it is often assumed they were anti-racist. Historiographers and especially recent feminist writing have created a version of American history in which white women's rights advocates are presented as champions of oppressed black people. This fierce romanticism has informed most studies of the abolitionist movement. In contemporary times there is a general tendency to equate abolitionism with a repudiation of racism. In actuality, most white abolitionists, male and female, though vehement in their antislavery protest, were totally opposed to granting social equality to black people. Joel Kovel, in his study White Racism: A Psychohistory, emphasizes that the "actual aim of the reform movement, so nobly and bravely begun, was not the liberation of the black, but the fortification of the white, conscience and all."

It is a commonly accepted belief that white female reformist empathy with the oppressed black slave, coupled with her recognition that she was powerless to end slavery, led to the development of a feminist consciousness and feminist revolt. Contemporary historiographers and in particular white female scholars accept the theory that the white women's rights advocates' feelings of solidarity with black slaves were an indication that they were anti-racist and were supportive of social equality of blacks. It is this glorification of the role white women played that leads Adrienne Rich to assert:

> … It is important for white feminists to remember that—despite lack of constitutional citizenship, educational deprivation, economic bondage to men, laws

and customs forbidding women to speak in public or to disobey fathers, husbands, and brothers—our white foresisters have, in Lillian Smith's words, repeatedly been "disloyal to civilization" and have "smelled death in the word 'segregation,'" often defying patriarchy for the first time, not on their own behalf but for the sake of black men, women, and children. We have a strong anti-racist female tradition despite all efforts by the white patriarchy to polarize its creature-objects, creating dichotomies of privilege and caste, skin color, and age and condition of servitude.

There is little historical evidence to document Rich's assertion that white women as a collective group or white women's rights advocates are part of an anti-racist tradition. When white women reformers in the 1830s chose to work to free the slave, they were motivated by religious sentiment. They attacked slavery, not racism. The basis of their attack was moral reform. That they were not demanding social equality for black people is an indication that they remained committed to white racist supremacy despite their anti-slavery work. While they strongly advocated an end to slavery, they never advocated a change in the racial hierarchy that allowed their caste status to be higher than that of black women or men. In fact, they wanted that hierarchy to be maintained. Consequently, the white women's rights movement which had a lukewarm beginning in earlier reform activities emerged in full force in the wake of efforts to gain rights for black people precisely because white women wanted to see no change in the social status of blacks until they were assured that their demands for more rights were met.

At the beginning of the 20th century, white women suffragists were eager to advance their own cause at the expense of black people. In 1903 at the National American Woman's Suffrage Convention held in New Orleans, a southern suffragist urged the enfranchisement of white women on the grounds that it "would insure immediate and durable white supremacy." Historian Rosalyn Terborg-Penn discusses white female support of white supremacy in her essay "Discrimination Against Afro-American Women in the Woman's Movement 1830–1920":

> As early as the 1890s, Susan B. Anthony realized the potential to the woman suffrage cause in wooing southern white women. She chose expedience over loyalty and justice when she asked veteran feminist supporter Frederick Douglass not to attend the National American Woman Suffrage Association convention scheduled in Atlanta. ...
>
> During the National American Woman Suffrage Association meeting of 1903 in New Orleans, the Times Democrat assailed the association because of its negative attitude on the question of black women and the suffrage for them. In a prepared statement signed by Susan B. Anthony, Carrie C. Catt, Anna Howard Shaw, Kate N. Gordon, Alice Stone Blackwell, Harriet Taylor Upton, Laura Clay, and Mary Coggeshall, the board of officers of the NAWSA endorsed the organization's states' rights position, which was tantamount to an endorsement of white supremacy in most states, particularly in the south.

Racism within the women's rights movement did not emerge simply as a response to the issue of suffrage; it was a dominant force in all reform groups with white female members. Terborg-Penn contends:

> Discrimination against Afro-American women reformers was the rule rather than the exception within the woman's rights movement from the 1830s to 1920. Although white feminists Susan B. Anthony, Lucy Stone, and some others encouraged black women to join the struggle against sexism during the

nineteenth century, antebellum reformers who were involved with women's abolitionist groups as well as women's rights organizations actively discriminated against black women.

In their efforts to prove that solidarity existed between 19th century black and white female reformers, contemporary women activists often cite the presence of Sojourner Truth at Women's Rights conventions to support their argument that white female suffragists were anti-racist. But on every occasion Sojourner Truth spoke, groups of white women protested. In The Betrayal of the Negro, Rayford Logan writes:

> When the General Federation of Women's Clubs was faced with the question of the color line at the turn of the century, Southern clubs threatened to secede. One of the first expressions of the adamant opposition to the admission of colored clubs was disclosed by the Chicago Tribune and the Examiner during the great festival of fraternization at the Atlanta Exposition, the Encampment of the GAR in Louisville, and the dedication of the Chickamauga battlefield. ... The Georgia Women's Press Club felt so strongly on the subject that members were in favor of withdrawing from the Federation if colored women were admitted there. Miss Corinne Stocker, a member of the Managing Board of the Georgia Women's Press Club and one of the editors of the Atlanta Journal, stated on September 19: "In this matter the Southern women are not narrow-minded or bigoted, but they simply cannot recognize the colored women socially. ... At the same time we feel that the South is the colored woman's best friend."

Southern white women's club members were most vehement in their opposition to black women joining their ranks, but northern white women also supported racial segregation. The issue of whether black women would be able to participate in the women's club movement on an equal footing with white women came to a head in Milwaukee at the General Federation of Women's Clubs conference when the question was raised as to whether black feminist Mary ChurchTerrell, then president of the National Association of Colored Women, would be allowed to offer greetings, and whether Josephine Ruffin, who represented the black organization the New Era Club, would be recognized. In both cases white women's racism carried the day. In an interview in the Chicago Tribune, the president of the federation, Mrs. Lowe, was asked to comment on the refusal to acknowledge black female participants like Josephine Ruffin, and she responded: "Mrs. Ruffin belongs among her own people. Among them she would be a leader and could do much good, but among us she can create nothing but trouble." Rayford Logan comments on the fact that white women like Mrs. Lowe had no objection to black women trying to improve their lot; they simply felt that racial apartheid should be maintained. Writing of Mrs. Lowe's attitude toward black women, Logan comments:

> Mrs. Lowe had assisted in establishing kindergartens for colored children in the South, and the colored women in charge of them were all her good friends. She associated with them in a business way, but, of course they would not think of sitting beside her at a convention. Negroes were "a race by themselves, and among themselves they can accomplish much, assisted by us and by the federation, which is ever ready to do all in its power to help them." If Mrs. Ruffin were the "cultured lady every one says she is, she should put her education and her talents to good uses as a colored woman among colored women."

Anti-black feelings among white female club members were much stronger than anti-black sentiment among white male club members. One white male wrote a letter to the Chicago Tribune in which he stated:

> Here we have the spectacle of educated, refined, and Christian women who have been protesting and laboring for years against the unjust discrimination practiced against them by men, now getting together and the first shot out of their reticules is fired at one of their own because she is black, no other reason or pretence of reason.

Prejudices white women activists felt toward black women were far more intense than their prejudices toward black men. As Rosalyn Penn states in her essay, black men were more accepted in white reform circles than black women. Negative attitudes toward black women were the result of prevailing racist sexist stereotypes that portrayed black women as morally impure. Many white women felt that their status as ladies would be undermined were they to associate with black women. No such moral stigma was attached to black men. Black male leaders like Frederick Douglass, James Forten, Henry Garnett and others were occasionally welcome in white social circles. White women activists who would not have considered dining in the company of black men welcomed individual black men to their family tables.

[...] Relationships between white and black women were charged by tensions and conflicts in the early part of the 20th century. The women's rights movement had not drawn black and white women close together. Instead, it exposed the fact that white women were not willing to relinquish their support of white supremacy to support the interests of all women. Racism in the women's rights movement and in the work arena was a constant reminder to black women of the distances that separated the two experiences, distances that white women did not want bridged. When the contemporary movement toward feminism began, white women organizers did not address the issue of conflict between black and white women. Their rhetoric of sisterhood and solidarity suggested that women in America were able to bond across both class and race boundaries—but no such coming together had actually occurred. The structure of the contemporary women's movement was no different from that of the earlier women's rights movement. Like their predecessors, the white women who initiated the women's movement launched their efforts in the wake of the 60s black liberation movement. As if history were repeating itself, they also began to make synonymous their social status and the social status of black people. And it was in the context of endless comparisons of the plight of "women" and "blacks" that they revealed their racism. In most cases, this racism was an unconscious, unacknowledged aspect of their thought, suppressed by their narcissism—a narcissism which so blinded them that they would not admit two obvious facts: one, that in a capitalist, racist, imperialist state there is no one social status women share as a collective group; and second, that the social status of white women in America has never been like that of black women or men.

When the women's movement began in the late 60s, it was evident that the white women who dominated the movement felt it was "their" movement, that is the medium through which a white woman would voice her grievances to society. Not only did white women act as if feminist ideology existed solely to serve their own interests because they were able to draw public attention to feminist concerns. They were unwilling to acknowledge that non-white women were part of the collective group women in American society. They urged black women to join "their" movement or in some cases the women's movement, but in dialogues and writings, their attitudes toward black women were both racist and sexist. Their racism did not assume the form of overt expressions of hatred; it was far more subtle. It took the form of simply ignoring the existence of black women or writing about them using common sexist and racist stereotypes. From Betty Friedan's The Feminine Mystique to Barbara Berg's The Remembered Gate and on to more recent publications like Capitalist Patriarchy and the Case for Socialist Feminism, edited by Zillah Eisenstein, most white female writers who considered themselves feminist revealed in their writing that they had been socialized to accept and perpetuate racist ideology.

In most of their writing, the white American woman's experience is made synonymous with the American woman's experience. While it is in no way racist for any author to write a book exclusively about white women, it is fundamentally racist for books to be published that focus solely on the American white woman's experience in which that experience is assumed to be the American woman's experience. For example, in the course of research for this book, I sought to find information about the life of free and slaveblack women in colonial America. I saw listed in a bibliography Julia Cherry Spruill's work *Women's Life and Work in the Southern Colonies*, which was first published in 1938 and then again in 1972. At the Sisterhood bookstore in Los Angeles I found the book and read a blurb on the back which had been written especially for the new edition:

One of the classic works in American social history, *Women's Life and Work in the Southern Colonies* is the first comprehensive study of the daily life and status of women in southern colonial America. Julia Cherry Spruill researched colonial newspapers, court records, and manuscript material of every kind, drawing on archives and libraries from Boston to Savannah. The resulting book was, in the words of Arthur Schlesinger, Sr., "a model of research and exposition, an important contribution to American social history to which students will constantly turn."

The topics include women's function in the settlement of the colonies; their homes, domestic occupation, and social life; the aims and methods of their education; their role in government and business affairs outside the home; and the manner in which they were regarded by the law and by society in general. Out of a wealth of documentation, and often from the words of colonial people themselves, a vivid and surprising picture—one that had never been seen before—emerges of the many different aspects of these women's lives.

I expected to find in Spruill's work information about various groups of women in American society. I found instead that it was another work solely about white women and that both the title and blurb were misleading. A more accurate title would have been *White Women's Life and Work in the Southern Colonies.* Certainly, if I or any author sent a manuscript to an American publisher that focused exclusively on the life and work of black women in the south, also called Women's Life and Work in the Southern Colonies the title would be automatically deemed misleading and unacceptable. The force that allows white feminist authors to make no reference to racial identity in their books about "women" that are in actuality about white women is the same one that would compel any author writing exclusively on black women to refer explicitly to their racial identity. That force is racism. In a racially imperialist nation such as ours, it is the dominant race that reserves for itself the luxury of dismissing racial identity while the oppressed race is made daily aware of their racial identity. It is the dominant race that can make it seem that their experience is representative.

In America, white racist ideology has always allowed white women to assume that the word woman is synonymous with white woman, for women of other races are always perceived as Others, as de-humanized beings who do not fall under the heading woman. White feminists who claimed to be politically astute showed themselves to be unconscious of the way their use of language suggested they did not recognize

the existence of black women. They impressed upon the American public their sense that the word "woman" meant white woman by drawing endless analogies between "women" and "blacks." Examples of such analogies abound in almost every feminist work. In a collection of essays published in 1975 titled Women: A Feminist Perspective, an essay by Helen Hacker is included called "Women as a Minority Group" which is a good example of the way white women have used comparisons between "women" and "blacks" to exclude black women and to deflect attention away from their own racial caste status. Hacker writes:

> The relation between women and Negroes is historical, as well as analogical. In the seventeenth century the legal status of Negro servants was borrowed from that of women and children, who were under the patria potestas, and until the Civil War there was considerable cooperation between the Abolitionists and woman suffrage movement.

Clearly Hacker is referring solely to white women. An even more glaring example of the white feminist comparison between "blacks" and "women" occurs in Catherine Stimpson's essay "'Thy Neighbor's Wife, Thy Neighbor's Servants': Women's Liberation and Black Civil Rights." She writes:

> The development of an industrial economy, as Myrdal points out, has not brought about the integration of women and blacks into the adult male culture. Women have not found a satisfactory way to bear children and to work. Blacks have not destroyed the hard doctrine of their unassimilability. What the economy gives both women and blacks are menial labor, low pay, and few promotions. White male workers hate both groups, for their competition threatens wages and their possible job equality, let alone

superiority, threatens nothing less than the very nature of things. The tasks of women and blacks are usually grueling, repetitive, slogging, and dirty ...

Throughout Stimpson's essay she makes woman synonymous with white women and black synonymous with black men.

[...] Whenever black women tried to express to white women their ideas about white female racism or their sense that the women who were at the forefront of the movement were not oppressed women they were told that "oppression cannot be measured." White female emphasis on "common oppression" in their appeals to black women to join the movement further alienated many black women. Because so many of the white women in the movement were employers of non-white and white domestics, their rhetoric of common oppression was experienced by black women as an assault, an expression of the bourgeois woman's insensitivity and lack of concern for the lower class woman's position in society.

Underlying the assertion of common oppression was a patronizing attitude toward black women. White women were assuming that all they had to do was express a desire for sisterhood, or a desire to have black women join their groups, and black women would be overjoyed. They saw themselves as acting in a generous, open, non-racist manner and were shocked that black women responded to their overtures with anger and outrage. They could not see that their generosity was directed at themselves, that it was self-centered and motivated by their own opportunistic desires.

Despite the reality that white upper and middle class women in America suffer from sexist discrimination and sexist abuse, they are not as a group as oppressed as poor white, or black, or yellow women. Their unwillingness to distinguish between various degrees of discrimination or oppression caused black women to see them as enemies. As many upper and middle class white feminists who suffer least from sexist

oppression were attempting to focus all attention on themselves, it follows that they would not accept an analysis of woman's lot in America which argued that not all women are equally oppressed because some women are able to use their class, race and educational privilege to effectively resist sexist oppression.

Initially, class privilege was not discussed by white women in the women's movement. They wanted to project an image of themselves as victims and that could not be done by drawing attention to their class. In fact, the contemporary women's movement was extremely class bound. As a group, white participants did not denounce capitalism. They chose to define liberation using the terms of white capitalist patriarchy, equating liberation with gaining economic status and money power. Like all good capitalists, they proclaimed work as the key to liberation. This emphasis on work was yet another indication of the extent to which the white female liberationists' perception of reality was totally narcissistic, classist, and racist. Implicit in the assertion that work was the key to women's liberation was a refusal to acknowledge the reality that, for masses of American working class women, working for pay neither liberated them from sexist oppression nor allowed them to gain any measure of economic independence. In Liberating Feminism, Benjamin Barber's critique of the women's movement, he comments on the white middle and upper class women's liberationist focus on work:

Work clearly means something very different to women in search of an escape from leisure than it has to most of the human race for most of history. For a few lucky men, for far fewer women, work has occasionally been a source of meaning and creativity. But for most of the rest it remains even now forced drudgery in front of the ploughs, machines, words or numbers—pushing products, pushing switches, pushing papers to eke out the wherewithal of material existence.

... To be able to work and to have work are two different matters. I suspect, however, that few liberationist women are to be found working as menials and un-skilled laborers simply in order to occupy their time and identify with the power structure. For status and power are not conferred by work per se, but by certain kinds of work generally reserved to the middle and upper classes. ... As Studs Terkel shows in Working, most workers find jobs dull, oppressive, frustrating and alienating—very much what women find housewifery.

When white women's liberationists empha-sized work as a path to liberation, they did not concentrate their attention on those women who are most exploited in the American labor force. Had they emphasized the plight of working class women, attention would have shifted away from the college-educated suburban housewife who wanted entrance into the middle and upper class work force. Had attention been focused on women who were already working and who were exploited as cheap surplus labor in American society, it would have de-romanti-cized the middle class white woman's quest for "meaningful" employment. While it does not in any way diminish the importance of women resisting sexist oppression by entering the labor force, work has not been a liberating force for masses of American women. And for some time now, sexism has not prevented them from being in the work force. White middle and upper class women like those described in Betty Friedan's The Feminine Mystique were housewives not because sexism would have prevented them from being in the paid labor force, but because they had willingly embraced the notion that it was better to be a housewife than to be a worker. The racism and classism of white women's liberation-ists was most apparent whenever they discussed work as the liberating force for women. In such discussions it was always the middle class "housewife" who was depicted as the victim of sexist oppression and not the poor black and non-black women who are most exploited by American economics.

[...] Feminism as a political ideology advo-cating social equality for all women was and is acceptable to many black women. They rejected the women's movement when it became apparent that middle and upper class college-educated white women who were its majority participants were determined to shape the movement so that it would serve their own opportunistic ends. While the established definition of feminism is the theory of the political, economic, and social equality of the sexes, white women liberation-ists used the power granted them by virtue of their being members of the dominant race in American society to interpret feminism in such a way that it was no longer relevant to all women. And it seemed incredible to black women that they were being asked to support a movement whose majority participants were eager to main-tain race and class hierarchies between women.

Black women who participated in women's groups, lectures, and meetings initially trusted the sincerity of white female participants. Like 19th century black women's rights advocates, they assumed that any women's movement would address issues relevant to all women and that racism would be automatically cited as a force that had divided women, that would have to be reckoned with for true Sisterhood to emerge, and also that no radical revolutionary women's movement could take place until women as a group were joined in political sol-idarity. Although contemporary black women were mindful of the prevalence of white female racism, they believed it could be confronted and changed.

As they participated in the women's move-ment they found, in their dialogues with white women in women's groups, in women's studies classes, at conferences, that their trust was betrayed. They found that white women had appropriated feminism to advance their own cause, i.e., their desire to enter the mainstream of American capitalism. They were told that white women were in the majority and that they had the power to decide which issues would be considered "feminist" issues. White women liberationists decided that the way to confront racism was to speak out in consciousness-raising groups about their racist upbringings, to encourage black women to join their cause, to make sure they hired one non-white woman in "their" women's studies program, or to invite one nonwhite woman to speak on a discussion panel at "their" conference.

When black women involved with women's liberation attempted to discuss racism, many white women responded by angrily stating: "We won't be guilt-tripped." For them the dialogue ceased. Others seemed to relish admitting that they were racist but felt that admitting verbally to being racist was tantamount to changing their racist values. For the most part, white women refused to listen when black women explained that what they expected was not verbal admissions of guilt but conscious gestures and acts that would show that white women liberationists were anti-racist and attempting to overcome their racism. The issue of racism within the women's movement would never have been raised had white women shown in their writings and speeches that they were in fact "liberated" from racism.

As concerned black and white individuals tried to stress the importance to the women's movement of confronting and changing racist attitudes because such sentiments threatened to undermine the movement, they met with resistance from those white women who saw feminism solely as a vehicle to enhance their own individual, opportunistic ends. Conservative, reactionary white women, who increasingly represented a large majority of the participants, were outspoken in their pronouncements that the issue of racism should not be considered worthy of attention. They did not want the issue of racism raised because they did not want to deflect attention away from their projection of the white woman as "good," i.e., non-racist victim, and the white man as "bad," i.e., racist oppressor.

For them to have acknowledged woman's active complicity in the perpetuation of imperialism, colonialism, racism, or sexism would have made the issue of women's liberation far more complex. To those who saw feminism solely as a way to demand entrance into the white male power structure, it simplified matters to make all men oppressors and all women victims.

[...] The emergence of black feminist groups led to a greater polarization of black and white women's liberationists. Instead of bonding on the basis of shared understanding of woman's varied collective and individual plight in society, they acted as if the distance separating their experiences from one another could not be bridged by knowledge or understanding. Rather than black women attacking the white female attempt to present them as an Other, an unknown, unfathomable element, they acted as if they were an Other. Many black women found an affirmation and support of their concern with feminism in all-black groups that they had not experienced in women's groups dominated by white women; this has been one of the positive features of black women's groups. However, all women should experience in racially mixed groups affirmation and support. Racism is the barrier that prevents positive communication and it is not eliminated or challenged by separation. White women supported the formation of separate groups because it confirmed their preconceived racist–sexist notion that no connection existed between their experiences and those of black women. Separate groups meant they would not be asked to concern themselves with race or racism. While black women condemned the anti-black racism of white women, the mounting animosity between the two groups gave rise to overt expression of their anti-white racism. Many black women who had never participated in the women's movement saw the formation of separate black groups as confirmation of their belief that no alliance could ever take place between black and white women. To express their anger and rage at white women, they evoked the negative stereotypical image of the white woman as a passive, parasitic, privileged being living off the labor of others as a way to mock and ridicule the white women liberationists.

[...] Animosity between black and white women's liberationists was not due solely to disagreement over racism within the women's movement; it was the end result of years of jealousy, envy, competition, and anger between the two groups. Conflict between black and white women did not begin with the 20th century women's movement. It began during slavery. The social status of white women in America has to a large extent been determined by white people's relationship to black people. It was the enslavement of African people in colonized America that marked the beginning of a change in the social status of white women. Prior to slavery, patriarchal law decreed white women were lowly inferior beings, the subordinate group in society. The subjugation of black people allowed them to vacate their despised position and assume the role of a superior.

Consequently, it can be easily argued that even though white men institutionalized slavery, white women were its most immediate beneficiaries. Slavery in no way altered the hierarchical social status of the white male but it created a new status for the white female. The only way that her new status could be maintained was through the constant assertion of her superiority over the black woman and man. All too often colonial white women, particularly those who were slavemistresses, chose to differentiate their status from the slave's by treating the slave in a brutal and cruel manner. It was in her relationship to the black female slave that the white woman could best assert her power. Individual black slave women were quick to learn that sex-role differentiation did not mean that the white mistress was not to be regarded as an authority figure. Because they had been socialized via patriarchy to respect male authority and resent female authority, black women were reluctant to acknowledge the "power" of the white mistress. When the enslaved black woman expressed contempt and disregard for white female authority,

the white mistress often resorted to brutal punishment to assert her authority. But even brutal punishment could not change the fact that black women were not inclined to regard the white female with the awe and respect they showed to the white male.

By flaunting their sexual lust for the bodies of black women and their preference for them as sexual partners, white men successfully pitted white women and enslaved black women against one another. In most instances, the white mistress did not envy the black female slave her role as sexual object; she feared only that her newly acquired social status might be threatened by white male sexual interaction with black women. His sexual involvement with black women (even if that involvement was rape) in effect reminded the white female of her subordinate position in relationship to him. For he could exercise his power as racial imperialist and sexual imperialist to rape or seduce black women, while white women were not free to rape or seduce black men without fear of punishment. Though the white female might condemn the actions of a white male who chose to interact sexually with black female slaves, she was unable to dictate to him proper behavior. Nor could she retaliate by engaging in sexual relationships with enslaved or free black men. Not surprisingly, she directed her anger and rage at the enslaved black women. In those cases where emotional ties developed between white men and black female slaves, white mistresses would go to great lengths to punish the female. Severe beatings were the method most white women used to punish black female slaves. Often in a jealous rage a mistress might use disfigurement to punish a lusted-after black female slave. The mistress might cut off her breast, blind an eye, or cut off another body part. Such treatment naturally caused hostility between white women and enslaved black women. To the enslaved black woman, the white mistress living in relative comfort was the representative symbol of white womanhood. She was both envied and despised—envied for her material comfort, despised because she felt little concern or compassion for the slave woman's lot. Since the white woman's privileged social status could only exist if a group of women were present to assume the lowly position she had abdicated, it follows that black and white women would be at odds with one another. If the white woman struggled to change the lot of the black slave woman, her own social position on the race-sex hierarchy would be altered.

Manumission did not bring an end to conflicts between black and white women; it heightened them. To maintain the apartheid structure slavery had institutionalized, white colonizers, male and female, created a variety of myths and stereotypes to differentiate the status of black women from that of white women. White racists and even some black people who had absorbed the colonizer's mentality depicted the white woman as a symbol of perfect womanhood and encouraged black women to strive to attain such perfection by using the white female as her model. The jealousy and envy of white women that had erupted in the black woman's consciousness during slavery was deliberately encouraged by the dominant white culture. Advertisements, newspaper articles, books, etc. were constant reminders to black women of the difference between their social status and that of white women, and they bitterly resented it. Nowhere was this dichotomy as clearly demonstrated as in the materially privileged white household where the black female domestic worked as an employee of the white family. In these relationships, black women workers were exploited to enhance the social standing of white families. In the white community, employing domestic help was a sign of material privilege and the person who directly benefited from a servant's work was the white woman, since without the servant she would have performed domestic chores. Not surprisingly, the black female domestic tended to see the white female as her "boss," her oppressor, not the white male whose earnings usually paid her wage.

[...] Resolution of the conflict between black and white women cannot begin until all women acknowledge that a feminist movement which is both racist and classist is a mere sham, a cover-up for women's continued bondage to materialist patriarchal principles, and passive acceptance of the status quo. The sisterhood that is necessary for the making of feminist revolution can be achieved only when all women disengage themselves from the hostility, jealousy, and competition with one another that has kept us vulnerable, weak, and unable to envision new realities. That sisterhood cannot be forged by the mere saying of words. It is the outcome of continued growth and change. It is a goal to be reached, a process of becoming. The process begins with action, with the individual woman's refusal to accept any set of myths, stereotypes, and false assumptions that deny the shared commonness of her human experience; that deny her capacity to experience the Unity of all life; that deny her capacity to bridge gaps created by racism, sexism, or classism; that deny her ability to change. The process begins with the individual woman's acceptance that American women, without exception, are socialized to be racist, classist, and sexist, in varying degrees, and that labeling ourselves feminists does not change the fact that we must consciously work to rid ourselves of the legacy of negative socialization.

If women want a feminist revolution—ours is a world that is crying out for feminist revolution—then we must assume responsibility for drawing women together in political solidarity. That means we must assume responsibility for eliminating all the forces that divide women. Racism is one such force. Women, all women, are accountable for racism continuing to divide us. Our willingness to assume responsibility for the elimination of racism need not be engendered by feelings of guilt, moral responsibility, victimization, or rage. It can spring from a heartfelt desire for sisterhood and the personal, intellectual realization that racism among women undermines the potential radicalism of feminism. It can spring from our knowledge that racism is an obstacle in our path that must be removed. More obstacles are created if we simply engage in endless debate as to who put it there.

DISCUSSION QUESTIONS

1. On what grounds does bell hooks contend that racism has not been adequately acknowledged and addressed by feminists?

2. According to the author, why did many Black women react negatively to invitations by white upper and middle class feminist to join the women's movement of the 1960s and 1970s?

3. What is the problem with defining women's liberation in terms of gaining greater economic status and money power?

REFERENCES

Barber, Benjamin, *Liberating Feminism*. New York: Delta, 1976.

Berg, Barbara, *The Remembered Gate: Origins of American Feminism*. New York: Oxford University Press, 1979.

Douglass, Frederick, *Narrative of the Life of Frederick Douglass*. Edited by Benjamin Quarles. Cambridge, Mass.: Belknap Press, 1969.

Eisenstein, Zillah, ed., *Capitalist Patriarchy and the Case for Socialist Feminism*. New York: Monthly Review Press, 1979.

Logan, Rayford, *The Betrayal of the Negro*. New York: Collier, 1954.

Spruill, Julia, *Women's Life and Work in the Southern Colonies*. New York: W.W. Norton, [1938] 1972. Chapter 26.

. . .

What You Can Do

1. Become familiar with the history of women of color in social movements

2. Support the work of women of color

3. Work toward inclusiveness, and remember the movement is stronger together

CHAPTER 4

Looking for Feminism

RACIAL DYNAMICS AND GENERATIONAL INVESTMENTS IN THE SECOND WAVE

By Mary Ann Clawson

In an important 1998 essay, "Whose Feminism, Whose History?" Sherna Berger Gluck pointed to "the deep investment on the part of the participants in the early days of the women's liberation movement in preserving the primacy of our particular experience and analysis." In her view, the growing recognition of feminist activism by working-class women and women of color had not been sufficient to force reconfiguration of the received paradigm. As a result, she argued, the writing of this history "might best be left to the new generation of feminist scholars ..., a generation whose understanding of historical processes is not tied up with their own direct experience and the sense of 'ownership' that this seems to have engendered."[1] Examination of five recent works on this period, one by a veteran, four by somewhat younger-generation scholars, confirms, contravenes, and complicates Gluck's provocative assertion.

Dreams of Integration

In *The Trouble between Us: An Uneasy History of White and Black Women in the Feminist Movement*, Winifred Breines, writing as both a scholar and a veteran of 1960s and 1970s radical and socialist feminist activism, looks at interactions between black and white women in the civil rights movement; the universalist assumptions of white feminists; the racially divided socialist feminist milieu(s) of Boston-Cambridge during the seventies; and the eventual accomplishment of respectful, if tentative, coalition work in which white feminists learned to accept the leadership of black women activists on issues concerning the black community. Breines interrogates her position as an early participant to examine how "white nostalgia" for the dream of an integrated society and movement shaped both her initial research agenda and the consciousness of white feminists more generally.

Gluck's charge that first-generation scholars have "settled into complacency and not tackled the problems inherent in producing a more complicated, multilayered history" is challenged by Breines's self-critical analysis of the assumptions and contradictions that informed racial thought and practice among white socialist feminists (and by implication white feminists more generally).[2] This occurs on two levels in particular: one, a thoughtful characterization of the racial attitudes that characterized post-World War II liberalism; the second, a more specific examination of white feminist activism as exemplified by the Boston socialist feminist group Bread and Roses.

In the first of these, Breines portrays a version of the form of white racial consciousness that we know as the ideology of color blindness. Although color blindness is today most often associated with conservative opposition to affirmative action and multiculturalism, Breines

Mary Ann Clawson, "Looking for Feminism: Racial Dynamics and Generational Investments in the Second Wave," *Feminist Studies* vol. 34, no. 3, pp. 526-554. Copyright © 2008 by Feminist Studies, Inc. Reprinted with permission. Provided by ProQuest LLC. All rights reserved.

Books Discussed in This Article

The Trouble between Us: An Uneasy History of White and Black Women in the Feminist Movement. By Winifred Breines. New York: Oxford University Press, 2006.

Living for the Revolution: Black Feminist Organizations, 1968–1980. By Kimberly Springer. Durham, N.C.: Duke University Press, 2005.

Separate Roads to Feminism: Black, Chicana, and White Feminist Movements in America's Second Wave. By Benita Roth. New York: Cambridge University Press, 2004.

Women of Color and the Reproductive Rights Movement. By Jennifer Nelson. New York: New York University Press, 2003.

Freedom Is Not Enough: The Opening of the American Workplace. By Nancy MacLean. New York: Russell Sage/Cambridge: Harvard University Press, 2006.

---

rightly characterizes its 1950s and 1960s version as the product of post-World War II liberalism, an "idealism in which racial difference was almost expressly denied" (8) and in which the ability to overlook race was indeed esteemed as a moral/political accomplishment. A particularly telling detail is Breines's account of her early fascination with Edward Steichen's *The Family of Man*, which used photos of families from a multitude of societies, nationalities, and racial and ethnic groups at different stages in the life cycle, to express, in Steichen's words, "'the universal brotherhood of man'" and "'the essential oneness of mankind'" through its depiction of "the universal elements and emotions in the everydayness of life." "Color-blindness, our supposed sameness," Breines comments, "moved us; it certainly did me" (10).

For white activists and supporters, the civil rights movement seemed both to articulate and fulfill the dreams of a "universal, racially integrated sisterhood and brotherhood ... where, hand in hand, we would work to create a just world" (9).[3] But color blindness, which tended to see inequality in attitudinal terms, had complex implications for this generation of white activists and the movements they participated in. At the time, Breines notes,

the early, idealistic "family of man" phase seems to have contained the assumption that upholding universalist ideals, like integration, made the one who upholds them into a newer sort of white person. ... It made us different, we thought (11).

No longer implicated, one might add, in the system of racial privilege and the divisions that accompanied it. The unspoken and deeply problematic assumption was that these "different" white people should be recognized as such by black activists.

These attitudes played out, Breines argues, in consequential ways in the development of 1960s and 1970s feminism. The ideals of 1950s liberalism and of the early civil rights movement enabled young white women to "imagine[d], naively, that our 'I' was 'we'; we thought all women were us, and we were all women" (10). The implications of such a formulation were evident in both ideology and practice, even within socialist feminist groups such as Bread and Roses that were distinguished by their recognition of class and race as systems of power within a capitalist society.

In a chapter titled "Learning about Racism: White Socialist Feminism and Bread and Roses,"

Breines points to the feminist critique of the nuclear family as exemplifying the ideological disjuncture between white and black women activists. Bread and Roses members called for the "abolition of the family as an economic unit and as the only socially sanctioned living unit of our society" (89), describing it as "an institution of privatization" (90) that should be replaced by new forms of personal life, supported by the social provision of childcare, housing, and reproductive labor. As socialists, they sought to extend social provision equally across society and thus to eradicate class and race differentials; in doing so they failed to recognize not only black women's attachment to the family as "a unique site of resistance to the ravages wrought by racism," (91) but the fact that their own "ability to cut off ties with men and families" (95) was founded on the security of class and race privilege. This point has often been made, but Breines's account is not only severe in its criticism of the tone of many of these pronouncements, terming them "mechanical and cold" (91), but insightful in its apprehension of the "blindspots of privilege" that made possible such analyses, that left these women unaware that "their middle-class whiteness inflected their politics as profoundly as race did black women's politics" (95).

Breines's sympathetic but critical portrayal of how universalist values and race-blindness shaped the worldview of white activists is courageous and compelling, as is her autocritique of "white nostalgia" for the dream of a race-blind society as an artifact of white privilege. One of Breines's preferred and distinctive ways of working, in this book as in others she's written, is to couple historical research with personal observation and remembrances.[4] This serves her well in the analysis of white feminists but less well in her discussion of black activism, where she can't rely on the use of small but telling observations to illuminate larger realities. She has worked hard to understand that black activists did not, for the most part, share the dreams of white liberals and radicals and to acknowledge that differences "enriched the movement" even as they "made trouble" (190). Yet there is a persistent disjuncture between the evidence she presents and the conclusions she draws.

This is exemplified by Breines's discussion of the civil rights movement, which identifies black-white cooperation within the Student Nonviolent Coordinating Committee (SNCC) "as moments of interracial connection," albeit "fragile" ones (49). Looking at relations between black and white women staffers and volunteers, Breines concedes that although "friendships developed, especially in the early years … on balance, the record indicates that distance prevailed" (48). More broadly, she acknowledges that black activists did not typically share in whites' "romanticization of interracial harmony in the civil rights movement," and that integration was, for most of them, more a political means to achieve equal rights than a goal of "building community with whites" (13–14).

Despite these insights, and in considerable tension with them, Breines develops a narrative arc in which black and white women "came together to create a free and racially integrated society," but "had to separate in order to find one another years later" (7). It would appear that Breines retains a vestigial attachment to the very universalist values and assumptions that her thoughtful account seeks to undermine. This is further revealed in passages that extend to both black and white feminists' goals and sentiments that more accurately characterize white women activists, as when she writes of black and white socialist feminists that "they were forced to acknowledge differences they did not know they had, did not want to have, and that nevertheless deeply divided them" (17). The idea that black women were, like white women, unaware of racial differences and that they longed to erase these differences, stands as powerful evidence of her residual investment in the universalist ideal. For Breines, the central issue is the failure of her generation to establish an interracial feminist movement, a failure she views with unambiguous regret.

The books by younger-generation scholars stand in marked contrast to Breines's approach, both analytically and evaluatively, even emotionally. All of them see difference as a source of valuable activism and fruitful theory production. Kimberly Springer, in *Living for the Revolution: Black Feminist Organizations, 1968–1980*, identifies black feminists as "the first activists in the United States to theorize and act upon the intersection of race, gender, and class" (2), thus explicitly counterposing her work to "previous women's movement histories that categorize difference and schism as disruptive and divisive" (165). Jennifer Nelson, in *Women of Color and the Reproductive Rights Movement*, intends to understand "how exactly women of color have shaped mainstream feminism" (179). Benita Roth, in *Separate Roads to Feminism: Black, Chicana, and White Feminist Movements in America's Second Wave*, differs from Breines by her insistent use of the plural, feminisms, in distinct contrast to the implication of a singular feminism in Breines's title, *The Trouble between Us*. Finally, Nelson and Nancy MacLean (*Freedom Is Not Enough: The Opening of the American Workplace*), in writing issue-based rather than organization-centered histories, focused on reproductive rights and workplace rights respectively, diversify our understanding of feminist activism by placing it in larger and more complex social movement fields.

Parallel and Multiple Feminisms: Toward a Social-Structural Analysis

Like Breines, Springer, Roth, and Nelson situate the feminism of women of color within the two-fold context of a powerful, visible, and racially un-self-conscious white feminist movement, on the one hand, and an equally forceful dynamic of racial-ethnic nationalisms, with their masculinist politics, especially pronounced in the Black Power movement, on the other. But unlike Breines, who locates the emergence of black feminism some five years after the birth of white feminism, Roth and Springer see the development of feminism among white women and women of color in the United States as both parallel and multiple, rather than sequential and reactive. In Roth's precise formulation,

Some women of color who were activists began organizing as feminists when some white women who were activists did, in the late 1960s, during a time of heightened popular protest. ... As organizationally distinct movements, these feminisms saw themselves as belonging to a different movement than white feminists did, a self-perception that should be taken seriously (11).

As a result, Second Wave feminism is best seen as "a group of feminisms, movements made by activist women that were largely organizationally distinct from one another, and from the beginning, largely organized along racial/ethnic lines" (3).

If this were the case, why has feminism been understood as a white movement? Here both Roth and Springer are distinctive in their use of more sociological approaches that emphasize the role of social structural explanation, as well as in their attention to the frameworks that have structured retrospective perceptions of feminist activism in that era. Roth points first to demography: "most feminists in the 1960s and 1970s were white because most *people* in the United States were white" (7). Most important, however, is the looking-in-the-wrong-place phenomenon, by which white scholars, conflating white feminism with all feminisms, scrutinized white feminist organizations for evidence of participation by feminists of color and, not finding them there, assumed they did not exist. "Not only were they not in white feminist organizations; there is no sense in these explanations that they could possibly have been organizing on their own" (8). Often added to this was the assumption that an authentic feminist politics was defined by a singular focus on gender oppression, so that the intersectional thinking that characterized black feminism and that was black feminism's central theoretical contribution was, for many commentators, disqualifying.

Both Springer and Roth reject the frequently advanced view that personal experiences of interactional racism are sufficient to explain the development of separate feminist movements.

Consistent with her intent to place black women "at the center of analysis in this book," Springer rejects a narrative that sees black feminist organizations "as a reaction to racism in the women's movement" (37, 3). In contrast, she argues, black feminism emerged *"from* the civil rights movement … and *at the same time as"* white feminism (4). Although specific exclusionary practices, however unintended, may have made the white women's liberation movement an environment that was at worst hostile and at best uncomfortable for women of color, it was the universalism of its "sisterhood frame" (44) and its failure to "challenge Eurocentric and classist interpretations" (3) that rendered it inadequate to address the needs of black women. Roth similarly notes that an exclusive focus on exclusionary practices posits black and Chicana feminists as primarily reactive to white initiative, with both their ideas and praxis reliant on the attitudes and actions of white feminists. Rejecting that approach, Roth and Springer argue that divisions originated in both social structural location and social movement history.

Inequalities of class and race shaped women's political understandings, assigned them to social locations and political communities, and governed their access to resources; "structural inequality was the underpinning of choices feminists of color made to construct groups that emphasized the racial/ethnic and class differences rather than gender commonalities" (Roth, 45). While self-identified feminists across the board tended to be recruited from among the college-educated middle class, such a recognition does not capture the different meanings, experiences, and levels of resources and vulnerabilities attached to middle-class status within different groups. Middle-class black and Latina women tended to be more marginally and often more recently middle class, with fewer resources and a more tenuous hold on that position. The implications of this played out in multiple ways.

Drawing on resource mobilization theory, Springer especially emphasizes that black feminist activists typically made less money, had fewer family resources, and were in general unable to call on the kinds of monetary and time resources to which white feminists often had access. Roth too points to the scarcity of economic resources as at least a partial explanation for why a group like the National Black Feminist Organization (NBFO) was unable to sustain itself as a national organization that could capitalize on the grassroots enthusiasm its establishment invoked. In a literature that emphasizes the explanatory value of ideological factors, this attention to the importance of paying the rent and answering the mail is an important reminder of the role played by resources in sustaining activism.

Different class and racial locations also shaped perceptions of political interest and collective identity. Because of their acute awareness of the role that structural inequalities of class and race had played in their own lives and those of their communities, an awareness often made palpable by the "marginalization and social isolation" they had experienced as students in predominantly white colleges and universities, feminists of color, Roth argues, simply "did not see [white feminists] as natural allies in the struggle for gender, racial/ethnic, and economic justice" (39, 45). Rather, "white feminists, as white women, were a group to be challenged for unfair advantage, just as white men were" (44). Although negative interpersonal interactions with white feminists might confirm and intensify these views, "this different vision occurred because structural inequalities mattered on the ground" (45). This was a perception that white feminists, with their focus on the universality of gender oppression, their unawareness of themselves as raced and classed people, and their assumption of the commonality of women's experience did not, with a few exceptions, grasp. The structurally based idea that "inequalities created barriers between groups of feminists from the start of their movements" (45) represents a very different model than the universalist one that sees or saw all women as potential and logical allies unless specific obstacles such as racist episodes or systematic exclusionary practices intervened to disrupt the assumed trajectory of common self-interest and unproblematic unity.

Their locations in a divided society also meant that women activists had been politically formed in different oppositional movements—the white New Left, the civil rights and Black Power movements, the Chicano movement. Equipping them with "organizing skills and social networks," these organizations were the sites of their ideological formation, investing them with core political perspectives that continued to shape their thinking, and loyalties that were "particularly acute for feminists of color" (Roth, 5). In each case, women first sought equality in mixed-gender groups, and in each movement, male activists derided their demands. But women's responses to men's attacks differed considerably as they struggled, over a period of time in each case, to reconcile conflicting demands.

White women's liberation, for example, emerged from an attempt to refashion gender relations within the New Left, as women increasingly decried their relegation to movement "housewifery," their vulnerability to sexual exploitation, and their exclusion from leadership. Initially, then, their assumed constituency was an internal, movement-specific one, but New Left men's antagonistic response led emerging women's liberationists to see the movement as a microcosm of the larger society and to conclude that radical men were incapable of reform, no different from any other men. As a result, women's liberationists expanded their target constituency to include "all women" who suffered from the oppression of "all men" and thus opened the way for an autonomous mass movement based on the concept of the universality of gender oppression, a concept that placed white feminism in opposition to the opposing claims of intensified racial and ethnic nationalisms. Thus the universalist option claimed by racially unmarked white feminists was not available to women of color, even had they wished to claim it.

Like that of their white peers, black feminists' activism was motivated by gender dynamics internal to their racially grounded movement. The political shift from civil rights to black nationalism entailed a masculinism that equated black empowerment with masculine empowerment, placed increasing limits on women's movement activism, and prescribed a patriarchal family model in which women's greatest contribution to the revolution was to support their men and care for their children. Exacerbating this, and even shaping it, were influential public policy discourses, most notably the Moynihan Report, with its focus on "black matriarchy" as a principal explanation for the persistence of racial inequality. Reinforced by popular media representations, the report not only pathologized the black family but seemed to make black women responsible for that pathology and thus complicit in the oppression of their community.

The inclusion of Chicana feminism in Roth's comparative framework gives added analytic leverage, as well as contributing to that movement's incorporation into the broader narrative of both women's and Chicano activism. Like early white and black feminists, Chicanas characterized gender equality as a way to enhance the effectiveness of the larger struggle and, like black feminists, they faced charges of being sell-outs to white feminism, as well as the trivialization and accusations of divisiveness that feminist women in all these movements encountered. Chicana feminists responded to such accusations by finding feminist predecessors in the history of previous indigenous and Mexican emancipatory struggles. Thus they were able to appropriate the Chicano movement's emphasis on recovering and using indigenous tradition to construct their claim of an authentically Chicana feminism and to reject charges that it was an Anglo import. Because the goal of Chicana feminism was always "greater political presence in the wider Chicano movement, in autonomous groups and in women's caucuses within mixed Chicana organizations" (130), their use of autonomous organizing was a strategy to gain power within the movement rather than an end in itself, as white feminists' autonomous organizing quickly became.

Like their Chicana peers, black feminists resisted "calls to choose" between affiliation with white feminism and loyalty to their own racial movement. And, like other black activists, they accepted racial authenticity as the principal standard of a meaningful black politics.

What they did not accept was the charge that feminism—their feminism—was "white." Accordingly, they sought to maintain their own racial authenticity by turning the tables on their nationalist critics, charging black men with an uncritical acceptance of the Moynihan Report and arguing that in espousing the patriarchal family as a political ideal, black nationalists had adopted a white bourgeois model inimical to black tradition.

Despite such efforts, it is clear that the penalties within the radical black community for self-identification as a feminist, even an explicitly black feminist, could be substantial and must be figured into our understanding of the movement's development. The NBFO's 1973 Eastern Regional Conference is a case in point. While white feminist reporting, grounded in a combination of universalist assumptions and personal unease, was largely clueless about the conference's emerging articulation of black feminism, the major account to appear in a black publication, Brenda Verner's *Encore* article "Women's Lib Has No Soul," presented a "scathing" denunciation that asserted the "mission of feminism" was "to convert black women to lesbianism and make them handmaidens of white supremacy" (Springer, 99). "Verner's article," Springer observes, "belied an investment in maintain[ing] the idea that black feminists were unauthentically [*sic*] black and traitorous to black liberation" (100–101). In effect, both white feminists and black nationalists portrayed black women as incapable of articulating an independent feminist vision.

As a result, black feminism seems to have operated as a political tendency that was organizationally distant not only from the white feminist movement but from black nationalism as well, in distinct contrast to Chicana feminism's closer relationship to the Chicano movement. Owing in part to the burden of the Moynihan Report, their strategic options seem to have been more limited than those of Chicana feminists. In particular, the Chicana strategy of validating feminist organizing within their nationalist movement by placing it in a historical tradition of indigenous women's activism was less available to black

feminists insofar as black nationalist politics rested on a repudiation rather than a reclaiming of previous black struggles and frequently a view of those struggles as feminized, for example, the civil rights movement's use of nonviolence as well as its integrationist rhetoric. Springer's use of the term "interstitial" (2), that is, inhabiting a small narrow space in the cracks between two larger entities, captures this sense of detachment quite precisely.

Pluralisms and Continuities in the Protest Field

Springer, writing as a "next generation black feminist" (6) with an eye to current and future mobilization, emphasizes the pluralism of black feminism. Analysts, she argues, should avoid essentializing black women and treating black feminism as "monolithic" (171). Black feminist groups, in *Living for the Revolution: Black Feminist Organizations, 1968–1980*, represented by the Third World Women's Alliance (TWWA), the NBFO, the National Association of Black Feminists (NABF), Black Women Organized for Action (BWOA), and the Combahee River Collective, differed from one another in their goals, organizational structures, identity constructions, and boundary formations.

TWWA, for example, growing out of SNCC's northern branch, operated as a kind of cadre organization, its title signifying an identification with Third World liberation movements in the United States and the world. Within this milieu, Frances Beal's widely circulated 1970 essay "Double Jeopardy" was an early theorizing of black women's dual oppression, later expanded to include class, as *Triple Jeopardy*, the title of TWWA's newspaper, proclaimed. In contrast, NBFO aspired to be a national organization, addressing a wide range of black women's issues, while NABF, based in Chicago, espoused something of a self-help orientation, reserving consciousness raising sessions for black women while offering classes for women and men of all races on topics including feminist history, black female-male relationships, assertiveness training, drug awareness, and discussions of beauty standards and body image. BWOA, a San Francisco Bay-area group, emphasized leadership training to enable black women to advance women's issues and assert their presence in local black political mobilization. Finally, the Combahee River Collective is best known for its classic theorizing of the "interlocking" character of "racial, sexual, heterosexual, and class oppression" (quoted in Springer, 117). Because it saw writing and theory production as an important form of activism, Combahee did not seek to become a large membership organization, focusing primarily on movement analysis and support for members' individual activism in coalition work. Composed predominantly of lesbians, it was the first black feminist organization to elaborate a theory of black feminist identity that explicitly incorporated sexuality in its intersectional vision.

In critiquing the notion of a monolithic black feminism, Springer emphasizes that difference was played out within as well as between the organizations, especially as regards class and sexuality. Inequalities of class background, current economic resources, and educational level posed the question of whose needs would be met and which black women the organizations aimed to empower. Within NABF, for example, tensions emerged between highly educated women who saw the organization as providing resources for further economic and social mobility and lower-income women who wanted it to focus on the "material concerns" of "the grassroots woman" (127–28).

Combahee, a much smaller organization, did not include the broad expanse of class and educational differences that characterized NABF. Yet, despite its greater homogeneity and socialist feminist politics, Springer's interviewees identified a tension between those who emphasized writing and intellectual work as forms of activism and those who favored grassroots community work. For some within the group, this was not simply a political disagreement about how to define and prioritize activism, but also a class divide insofar as theory production might become a means of individual advancement. At the crux of Combahee's class conflicts, Springer

comments, "were differences over how educational aspirations fit into collective ideas of class struggle" (129). In general, she concludes, class was marginalized in the practice of black feminist organizations despite its theoretical centrality.

Sexuality was an even more problematic division. Interactionally, it appeared in tensions between lesbian and heterosexual women and expressions of homophobia, especially in NABF and NBFO. In a larger political sense, Springer charges, it represented a failure to recognize and theorize the meaning of sexuality to black feminism more generally. Heterosexual women in NABF, including the organization's leadership, saw lesbians as a separate interest group, deserving perhaps of tolerance but irrelevant to a feminist agenda: "a category separate from *feminist*" (135). Unlike TWA A and the Combahee River Collective, the NABF, NBFO, and BWOA "did not interpret heterosexism as an oppressive force in black women's lives, regardless of sexual orientation" (130), and even Combahee, "at the frontlines of black lesbian struggle in the 1970s," did not, Springer charges, "specify the ways black communities were complicit in perpetuating heterosexism" (130). Their critique was "strategically … underarticulated in the interest of establishing the foundational basis of solidarity between Combahee's black feminism and black communities" (130–31).

The conclusion Springer draws from this history is that the assumption of a "uniform oppositional consciousness," with its failure "to recognize the multidirectional flow of power and privilege inside as well as outside their organizations" (14) was as unfeasible, and undesirable, for black feminists as for feminists more generally. "White feminists," she observes, "were not the only ones guilty of universalizing tendencies in defining the categories of *women* and *sisterhood*; African American women activists also underestimated the limits of defining the category *black womanhood* by ignoring the heterogeneity of black women and their communities" (171).

If Springer looks productively inward, depicting heterogeneity within a black feminism too often seen as monolithic, Roth expands her gaze outward to emphasize commonalities as she places white, black, and Chicana feminisms within a larger protest field, the "particularly vibrant extra-institutional political milieu … that structured [feminists'] choices about how to organize and with whom" (179). This moment, she argues, was characterized by a distinctive and widely held ethos of organizing, stretching across race and gender lines, and by an intense competition for symbolic and practical resources. Both factors had significant implications for the formation and trajectory of women's activism.

Roth defines the influential "ethos of organizing one's own" as "a generalized, consensual, and specific instruction on how to organize as authentic leftists" (200), usually understood as a mandate to organize within one's own racial/ethnic group. SNCC's 1965 decision to exclude white participation was particularly influential in making explicit the widely held belief that, in women's liberationist Kathie Amatniek's words, "'the most radical thing to do was to fight against your own oppression'" (quoted in Roth, 204), a sentiment later echoed by the Combahee River Collective's statement that "we believe that the most profound and potentially the most radical politics come directly out of our own identity, as opposed to working to end somebody else's oppression."[5] In Roth's view, the "organize one's own" ethos authorized the universalizing claims of white women's feminism while strengthening already existing organizational and communal divisions through the promotion of a "consensus whereby feminists agreed among themselves that it was impossible for them to organize across lines of race and ethnicity" (207).

One of Roth's most original insights is that women's self-organizing, in a crowded and competitive social movement sector, challenged an existing "economy of social movement activism" (179). Because women were responsible for much of the day-to-day labor of organizational maintenance in all of the mixed-gender oppositional movements of the period, feminist organizing threatened the loss of female labor. Consequently, Roth argues, male activists' antipathy to feminism rested as much on practical self-interest as on ideological disagreement. Male opposition to feminist claims may have

been framed ideologically, because "ideological arguments were more accepted responses to the emerging feminist challenge than admitting that it was not as much fun to type one's own minutes and make one's own dinner" (184). For the black and Chicano movements, domesticity was ideologically central in a way it was not for whites, because of the dominant view of "traditional roles as a means of reconstructing the community for revolution (the Black Liberationist emphasis) or preserving culture from Anglo domination (the Chicano version)" (184); but for all these groups, the loss of women's labor was an immediate threat to organizational stability and men's own convenience.

Finally, Roth sees the era's crowded social movement sector as intensifying what Deborah H. King, in an important 1988 essay, termed "monism."[6] In jockeying for power and recognition, movements sought to legitimate and differentiate themselves, as well as to claim public attention, by focusing on single axes of oppression, deemed to be the most "fundamental." Roth thus sees monism as the product, at least in part, of inter-movement competition for resources and allegiances, an insight that is original and compelling, yet incomplete insofar as it neglects the powerful influence of Marxism on these late-1960s to early-1970s movements. Feminists, like black nationalists, may have rejected the Marxist privileging of class, but they freely embraced a larger Marxist problematic. In this vein, the Redstockings, and others, identified women as a class and "'male supremacy'" as "'the oldest, most basic form of domination'" such that alleviating it became "the key revolutionary force" (193). Black feminists asserted a politics of multiple oppressions, but retained the Marxist emphasis on identifying a single historical agent who stood at the center of universal emancipation: "'If Black women were free,'" wrote the Combahee River Collective, "it would mean that everyone else would have to be free since our freedom would necessitate the destruction of all the systems of oppression'" (quoted in Roth, 121).[7]

In situating these movements in a larger field, Roth places competition at the center of her analysis—competition for women's labor, competition for moral authority and revolutionary credibility. Her consistent emphasis on feminists and other social movement activists as strategic in their decision making and responsive to political opportunities and drawbacks offers an original and compelling perspective on a history, especially a feminist history, that is most often told in purely ideational terms. Yet at times it confines her, it seems to me, within an overly rationalistic model. For example, she sees white feminists' universalizing claims about gender oppression, at least originally, as largely defensive and "strategic" in their motivation. To combat New Left men's charge that women's interests were "narrower than those of the working class (or of Third World peoples)," and thus unworthy of serious attention, white feminists needed to insist that "gender oppression was as fundamental and widespread as racism and class domination" (188). Similarly women's exodus from the mixed-gender white Left is seen as primarily a response to bad treatment at the hands of male peers, with an emphasis on the push away from the New Left rather than the pull in the form of the increasingly visible incentives of autonomous feminist organizing.

Most simplistically, this could include the considerable psychic rewards to be gained from claiming the mantle of "most oppressed group" and, for some, the key to historic agency [who gets to be the vanguard of history?] "'What a relief it is to discover that we too are oppressed,'" remarked Pam Allen (and quoted in Roth, 197), perhaps the most insightful white feminist regarding the interaction of race and gender. In a larger and more lasting sense, Roth's emphasis on rationality and strategic response downplays, if not ignores, the revelatory (albeit, in retrospect partial) insights—intellectual, political, personal—that came from using the lens of gender to name and comprehend women's subordination. Missing is the emancipatory pull of the emerging movement and the vision of community it offered white women in particular. Similarly, Roth's parsing of men's opposition to feminism is simultaneously original and insightful but ultimately incomplete insofar as male activists appear more as employers with a labor

recruitment problem than as people with profound intellectual, political, cultural, material, and emotional investments in their masculinity and the privileges that accompanied it.

Formal Implications of Informal Mobilization: The Limits of Social Networks

The important role of social networks in mobilization has long been a central theme in the sociological study of social movements. In this view, social movements do not commonly emerge as aggregations of previously unconnected strangers; rather they build on pre-existing networks of acquaintanceship, whether informal or organizationally based, that allow for rapid communication, social bonding, and mutual accountability. Most famously, the civil rights movement relied on the networks of the black church and of students at historically black colleges, while the women's liberation movement emerged among student, New Left, and civil rights movement veterans. An implicit corollary to this is that the more movements can rely on pre-existing networks, the more spontaneous and self-motivating they will be and the less they will need to depend on infusions of external resources for their inception and functioning.[8]

The greater spontaneity and creativity associated with informal, non-hierarchical groups is often observed and almost as frequently celebrated.[9] The formation and multiplication of consciousness raising groups, the site for the development of so many key Second Wave feminist insights and initiatives, exemplifies a method of informal, network-based social movement mobilization that has typically been seen as more democratic and authentic, as well as more innovative than more bureaucratic organizations such as the National Organization for Women (NOW).

The works discussed here suggest as well the limits of this model in a society divided by race and class. Roth makes this point in her structural analysis of the demographics of U.S. society, while Breines simply observes that "most [young Northern whites] knew no black people" (10), certainly, one might speculate, not as age peers, friends, or political collaborators, as opposed to employees or other racial subordinates.

The problems associated with informal, network-based organizing are exemplified by Bread and Roses' efforts at the antiracist work their socialist feminist commitments mandated. According to Breines, this most often took the form of support actions for the Black Panther Party, which meant, in practice, working with that organization's predominantly male leadership. This approach to interracial cooperation may have been motivated in part, as she notes, by the Panthers' visibility and prestige within the white Left. But it is also likely that the Panthers, as an organized group with a visible leadership structure, offered a visible and available opportunity for political collaboration, whereas the paucity of pre-existing informal ties between black and white women was a significant obstacle to the kind of work with black women that some Bread and Roses members, troubled by the authoritarianism and male chauvinism of the Panther leadership, would have found more ideologically and personally congenial. Nelson's account of more concerted longer-term efforts by white socialist feminists in the Committee for Abortion Rights and against Sterilization Abuse (CARASA) to establish political ties with black and Latina women activists around reproductive rights issues in the early 1980s suggests that a lack of networks continued to be an obstacle to joint work by white feminists and women of color even when accompanied by basic agreement on the issues.

Thus the lack of peer-based networks proved to be crucial in limiting movements so heavily reliant on personal acquaintanceship (and indeed, as Francesca Polletta has pointed out, on the model of friendship as the basis for social movement activism). Although this model proved difficult to sustain even within internally homogenous groups as they grew larger, it was especially problematic insofar as it called upon black and Latina women to embrace the idea of *friendship* with white women as a precondition

for alliance.[10] Yet examination of issue-based politics suggests that political ideas frequently crossed racial, ethnic, and organizational boundaries.

Issues versus Organizations

In seeking a more concrete understanding of "how exactly women of color have shaped mainstream feminism" (179), Nelson departs from the more frequently encountered model of the organizational history, here exemplified by Springer and Roth, to craft an issue-based study of reproductive rights activism. Examining the perspectives of white radical feminists, black and Puerto Rican nationalists (both female and male), black feminists, and predominantly white socialist feminists reveals "how essential women of color were to the transformation of the abortion rights movement of the late 1960s and early 1970s into a more inclusive movement for reproductive freedom" (179). In its most expansive formulation, the idea of reproductive choice would come to include not just equitable access to birth control and abortion, not just protection from sterilization abuse, but the demand for basic human-needs provision (adequate income, employment and educational opportunities), such that women could make unconstrained decisions about having and rearing children.

Nelson is especially judicious in identifying and contextualizing the contributions of various political groups and tendencies. For example, despite her obvious commitment to a broader reproductive rights agenda, she gives a cogent and sympathetic explanation of why early white radical feminists, as exemplified by the Redstockings, saw the right to abortion on demand as a central condition for gender equality: "without the fundamental right to control reproduction in every instance, women remain subject to men" (15). As this formulation suggests, the Redstockings conceived reproductive rights as the right not to bear children. "With the ability to terminate a pregnancy would come the freedom to transform traditional womanhood" (27–28). Although cognizant of the radical particularity of this perspective, with its confident universalizing of women's needs, Nelson is equally sensitive to the significance of the Redstockings' insistence that "women needed to be central to any discussion of abortion laws" (15). It was their insistent naming of abortion as a woman's decision, rather than the domain of medical and legal professionals, that helped move the debate out into a broader political arena.

Similarly, in discussing black nationalist characterizations of birth control and abortion as genocidal, Nelson recognizes their profound masculinist bias while simultaneously placing them within a well-founded critique of both contemporary population control programs and of earlier traditions of eugenics directed against the poor and communities of color. The race-based pro-natalism of the early Black Panther Party combined opposition to abortion, birth control, and sterilization with demands for improved healthcare in poor communities. By the mid 1970s, however, Black Panther Party thinking had shifted to support for "safe, legal abortion provision in the black community as part of a larger system of social provision" (108–9), a shift that reflected the growing input of women in the party as well as the influence of black feminists who "combined the fight for abortion rights with an anti-sterilization abuse movement" (108). Panthers ultimately emphasized "that improved access to total health care, a living wage, adequate housing, and subsidized child care all needed to be present before a woman could know she had total control over her fertility" (57). Thus Nelson's account suggests that black feminist ideas may have exerted an influence despite the black nationalist antipathy to autonomous black feminist organizing.[11]

The controversial 1973 sterilization of a black twelve-year-old in a federally funded clinic was an important catalyst for mobilization against sterilization abuse in communities of color, but critiques had been voiced among black women activists as early as 1968 by the National Welfare Rights Organization (70) and in 1970, by Tony Cade Bambara's influential 1970 collection *The Black Woman*, which "laid the groundwork for a black women's reproductive rights discourse

that departed from both black nationalist and mainstream feminist reproductive politics up to that point" (80). Black women, Beal wrote in "Double Jeopardy,"

> have the right and the responsibility to determine when it is [in] the interests of the struggle to have children or not to have them. ... It is also her right and responsibility to determine when it is in her own best interests.... The lack of availability of safe birth control methods, the forced sterilization practice, and the inability to obtain legal abortion are all symptomatic of a decadent society that jeopardizes the health of black women (and thereby the entire Black race). (Quoted in Nelson, 80)

Melding individual and communal self-determination, these black women writers, intellectuals, and activists argued that black women's empowerment was central to the black struggle, in distinct contrast to the black nationalist perspective that made masculine empowerment the centerpiece of racial advance.

Most remarkable is Nelson's identification of Puerto Rican women activists who advanced a comprehensive reproductive rights agenda within the framework of a mixed-gender nationalist organization, New York's Young Lords. "For the first time," she observes, "a nationalist organization, composed of people of color, made an explicitly feminist position central to their political ideology" with a "reproductive rights agenda [that] ... encompassed access to voluntary birth control, safe and legal abortion, a quality public health system, free day care, and an end to poverty" (114). Moreover, the Young Lords' formulation of reproductive rights, based on a "politics of multiple identity positions" (115), became an important influence on the thinking of the predominantly white socialist feminist activists who in 1977 formed CARASA, an organization that combined the defense of abortion rights, opposition to sterilization abuse, and support for welfare rights, subsidized child-care, and reproductive safety in the workplace.

Given the volatile and rapidly shifting arena of 1960s-1970s social movements, Nelson's strategy of writing a history of reproductive rights activism is a particularly fruitful one that enables her to identify a wider range of key players and influential positions, to place them in dialogue with one another, and to show how they contributed to transforming a narrowly defined "movement for the legalization of abortion into a movement for reproductive rights to address the broad health care needs of all women, and particularly the need of women of color and poor women to be free from reproductive abuses" (16–17). Equally important, however, is her recognition of how important feminist practice and theory production could be developed within the framework of a mixed-gender, nationalist organization, a recognition that raises significant questions about the models we use to identify feminist practice more generally.

Looking for Feminism

To the extent that scholarly definitions of authentic feminist practice have been grounded in continued investment in the particular ideological and strategic choices made by an earlier generation of white radical women, they have worked to render alternative organizational forms and activist practices indistinct, if not altogether invisible. Although the activism of black, Latina, Asian American, and white working-class women is increasingly acknowledged, it is too often bracketed, as these authors suggest, rather than prompting a needed rethinking of larger analytic models. At major issue here are questions about how to define Second Wave feminist activism and when and where to look for it.

As noted earlier, Roth responds to what she calls the whitewashing question by asserting a full temporal parallelism. Springer takes a somewhat different tack, differentiating between "the black feminist *movement,* black feminist *organizations,* and black feminist *activists*" (4). For Springer, the movement encompasses not only black feminist organizations, but the analyses, critiques, and polemics that preceded them. Important

black feminist texts such as *The Black Woman,* for example, "provided black women with a very public, if controversial, forum to air grievances" (Springer, 38). This more expansive conception of social movement challenges a white feminist model in which organization, especially the consciousness raising group, was necessarily either coterminous with or prior to theory production and suggests one of the ways the narrative of the white feminist movement has been paradigmatic in defining feminist activism.

Similarly, scholarly model-making, consistent with the political investments and strategic decisions of the first generation of women's liberationists, has tended to identify autonomous, women-only organization as a principal requisite for discerning authentic feminist activism. The effect of this is to equate particular organizational forms and boundary constructions with feminist practice more generally. In doing so we reproduce, rather than interrogate, the political assumptions and practices of forty years ago. Early women's liberationists, for example, organized women-only groups, called themselves feminists, and opposed themselves to "politicos"—women who chose to continue their involvement in mixed-gender Left groups and who were often derided as women who placed loyalty to men over their feminist commitments. Among white women activists, the politicos have been regarded as a tendency that was both short-lived and retrograde. But Roth's, and especially Nelson's, analyses suggest that for black and Latina activists, the feminist-politico opposition is not so easily maintained.

Chicana feminists formed autonomous women-only groups to advance feminist demands within the movement, but continued to see their groups as intrinsically part of the larger Chicano movement rather than as the starting point for a separate, autonomous Chicana feminist identity. The case of the New York-based Young Lords, whose Puerto Rican women leaders, working within a mixed-gender nationalist organization, developed an important formulation of reproductive rights, takes this a step further; yet strict use of the autonomous women's movement standard would preclude their recognition as feminists. By showing the distinctive contributions of these women, Nelson's work suggests the need to distinguish between feminist *organizations* and feminist *practices* in order to be able to comprehend the full range of feminist activism in this period. An exemplification of Roth's point that where we look, and using what lens, determines to some degree what we can find; it also suggests that the continued use of autonomous organization as a defining principle of feminism may have had the effect of erasing feminist practices and articulations that occurred in other locations and by other means.

A broader framing of feminist practice will also enable us to see the engagement, indeed the leadership, of women of color within the more bureaucratically organized sphere of equal rights feminism. Early liberal feminist activism grew out of networks formed through professional and political association between white and black women, in the YWCA, under the auspices of the U.S. Department of Labor's Women's Bureau, and especially in progressive labor unions, that is, out of relationships fostered through formal, institutional positions rather than the informal personal ties that characterized radical feminist mobilization.[12] Organizations like the National Women's Political Caucus (NPWC), characterized by Sara Evans as the most diverse of the liberal feminist groups, operated with a conception of formal representation that established regularized means of input through the incorporation of minority caucuses into governance structures and through the early, influential involvement of women of color in planning processes and leadership positions. As a result, Evans observes, "The leadership of minority women in NOW and NWPC contrasts with the near absence of women of color in early meetings of women's liberation."[13]

The struggle against gender discrimination in employment is a case in point, as MacLean's recent book, *Freedom Is Not Enough: The Opening of the American Workplace*, makes clear. Her research, a study of both race and gender activism, reveals the disproportionate leadership of black women

in developing strategy following the enactment of Title VII of the 1964 Civil Rights Act outlawing workplace discrimination: black women attorneys (Pauli Murray, Eleanor Holmes Norton); economists (Gloria Tapscott Johnson, a longtime researcher for the International Union of Electrical Workers); and policy activists (Phyllis Wallace, the Equal Employment Opportunity Commission [EEOC]'s top researcher, and Aileen Hernandez, a former union activist who was one of the first EEOC commissioners as well as the second president of NOW, following Betty Friedan). MacLean argues that feminist employment activism took a number of forms, including individual complaints to the EEOC, legislation, litigation, and an insufficiently recognized wave of grassroots workplace activism, principally women's caucuses, among both working-class and middle-class women employees. Above all she emphasizes the dynamic, interactive character of these practices, as well as the race and class diversity of their practitioners.

Title VII, for example, did not enact change, but rather galvanized it, serving as a resource for activists and as the starting point for a long process of understanding and organizing around an emergent recognition of employment discrimination as a systemic phenomenon built into the very structure of the labor market. Consider, for example, the emergent understanding of sexual harassment as a form of job discrimination. Black women played a leading role in the development of the very concept, given Carrie Baker's finding that "African-American women brought most of the early precedent-setting sexual harassment cases." Baker speculates that it is precisely their experiences with racially coercive employment relationships that made black women more likely to see sexual harassment as a systemic rather than an individual problem.[14] Here as well, Baker argues, awareness of black women's involvement and of the distinctive insights they brought has not been significantly incorporated into a theoretical model that, as noted earlier, has tended to see black feminism as primarily reactive to trends initiated by white women activists.

The recognition of sexual harassment as a form of discrimination exemplifies the multidirectional processes that characterized feminist activism at its peak in this period. In the midst of a rapidly exploding movement, MacLean and Baker demonstrate, litigation could operate as a social movement practice that both relied on and stimulated more broadly based activism rather than standing apart from it or dampening it down.[15] Again, the experience of black women with the use of litigation in the civil rights movement may help explain their disproportionate influence within and orientation to this mode of feminist activism. It may also be the case that black women's activism focused disproportionately on influencing state policy because of their more visible reliance on state provision, as clients and recipients (thus the welfare rights movement), and because of the fact that black professional women were historically concentrated in government and non-profit employment because of greater discrimination in the private sector, further confirming Roth's point that structural location and previous social movement history are crucial in shaping the targets, character, and location of activism.

Like Nelson's work on reproductive rights, *Freedom Is Not Enough* is an issue-based history, written on the most ambitious scale of any of these works. MacLean expands our conception of social movement and feminist activism and in doing so enables us to recognize the extensive participation and leadership roles of black women, which would remain invisible within a more constrained conception of activism. Chapter 4, "Women Challenge 'Jane Crow,'" along with a later discussion of the frustrating efforts to open up skilled working-class employment to women, are the most obviously relevant to the focus of this essay, as MacLean argues that "the movement looks more diverse and more attentive to bread-and-butter needs ... when the focus of inquiry turns from the youthful women's liberation activists ... to the older working women who mobilized around issues of employment" (118). But by identifying "civil rights at work" as her subject of inquiry, a subject that encompasses

the black community's development of models for challenging employment discrimination; the crucial importance of this model for other groups; the interactions, both cooperative and rivalrous, among different constituencies, including African Americans, women, and Mexican Americans; and the shifting formulations of conservative response to these mobilizations, MacLean has constructed a truly intersectional history that widens and diversifies our vision of feminist activism by placing it in a much more expansive terrain of struggle.

CONCLUSION

Taken together, what do these books contribute to the reformulation of our models of feminism during the period of the Second Wave? What resources do they offer us and what kinds of limitations do they continue to reproduce?

Roth and Springer demonstrate the importance of bringing social structural factors more fully into the analysis, not just in terms of identifying the demographic characteristics that signify difference but in looking at how economic, social, and cultural factors united and divided women within the frameworks of everyday life, constructing networks and boundaries and shaping perceptions of individual self-interest and collective affiliation. Yet despite structural divisions, political ideas often crossed back and forth across racial, ethnic, and organizational boundaries, enriched and complicated by the stimulus of different social, cultural, and economic contexts. Issue-based histories, as typified by Nelson's and MacLean's work, are thus one important way to expand the scope of our vision.[16] At the same time it is important to recognize that "sympathies," when unsupported by shared social networks or collective identities, did not, as Roth observes, "dictate association" (171).

Finally, the conceptual models we use to comprehend Second Wave feminism need to encompass a fuller understanding of its character as a mass social movement. Breines argues that although black feminism, especially the black socialist feminism of the Combahee River

Collective, "transformed feminist thinking" (149), it "was never a grassroots movement" (133) on a massive scale. But if black feminist organizations remained small, failing to achieve the status of a mass movement in their communities, it is equally the case that the socialist feminism chronicled in such a valuable way by Breines also remained a relatively small tendency, one that arguably paralleled black feminism insofar as its theoretical insights have tended to overshadow its on-the-ground activist accomplishments.

To a significant extent, all the works discussed here confine their gaze to the generation of feminists that emerged directly from, and were politicized within 1960s oppositional movements—white, black, and Latina. But Second Wave feminism became a mass movement, as Nancy Whittier argues in *Feminist Generations*, through its appeal to a much larger cohort of women who were politicized directly by feminist ideas. Like much else about it, the racial dynamics of that transformation are yet to be fully explored.[17] In expanding our vision of what constitutes feminism, these studies of first generation black, Latina, and white feminisms offer a useful starting point for that effort.

NOTES

1. Sherna Berger Gluck, "Whose Feminism, Whose History? Reflections on Excavating the History of (the) U.S. Women's Movement(s)," in *Community Activism and Feminist Politics: Organizing across Race, Class, and Gender,* ed. Nancy A. Naples (New York: Routledge, 1998), 33, 54.

2. Ibid., 54.

3. It should be noted that such sentiments were, for many, a response to the fact that racial difference had most often been used to justify racial hierarchy and denigration, used in the United States and elsewhere to deny basic human rights and used, not that long before, to justify the wholesale slaughter of European Jews and others deemed "different."

4. See, for example, Wini Breines, *Young, White, and Miserable: Growing Up Female in the Fifties* (Boston: Beacon Press, 1992).

5. The Combahee River Collective, "A Black Feminist Statement," in *The Second Wave: A Reader in Feminist Theory,* ed. Linda Nicholson (New York: Routledge, 1997), 65.

6. Deborah H. King, "Multiple Jeopardy, Multiple Consciousness: The Context of a Black Feminist Ideology," *Signs* 14 (Autumn 1988): 42–72.

7. See also the earlier statement by Marianne Weathers of the Third World Women's Alliance that "forming a Black women's movement was the correct strategy for building an all-encompassing movement that would liberate men, women, and children, a movement that would be pro-human for all peoples." Quoted in Benita Roth, *Separate Roads to Feminism: Black, Chicana, and White Feminist Movements in America's Second Wave* (New York: Cambridge University Press, 2004), 92.

8. See, for example, Jo Freeman, "On the Origins of Social Movements," in *Waves of Protest: Social Movements since the Sixties,* ed. Victoria Johnson and Jo Freeman (Lanham, Md.: Rowman and Littlefield, 1999), 7–24; Aldon D. Morris, *The Origins of the Civil Rights Movement: Black Communities Organizing for Change* (New York: Free Press, 1984). The Internet now makes movements composed of previously unconnected strangers much more feasible. But while the Internet excels in rapid communication, it's not clear how it allows for more sustained social bonding and mutual accountability.

9. Nonetheless, scholars also find that such groups tend to disintegrate more quickly than more explicitly structured, and often better financed, groups do. See especially, Suzanne Staggenborg, "Stability and Innovation in the Women's Movement: A Comparison of Two Movement Organizations," *Social Problems* 35 (February 1989): 75–92; and Staggenborg, "The Consequences of Professionalization and Formalization in the Pro-Choice Movement," in *Waves of Protest*, 99–134.

10. Francesca Polletta, *Freedom Is an Endless Meeting: Democracy in American Social Movements* (Chicago: University of Chicago Press, 2002), esp. chap. 6.

11. Despite a host of well-known abuses, the Black Panther Party was arguably the most gender-egalitarian of black nationalist organizations. Perspectives on this complex history include Tracye Matthews, "'No One Ever Asks What a Man's Role in the Revolution Is': Gender and the Politics of the Black Panther Party, 1966–1971"; Angela D. LeBlanc-Ernest, "'The Most Qualified Person to Handle the Job': Black Panther Party Women, 1966–1982"; and Regina Jennings, "Gender Dynamics: Why I Joined the Party: An Africana Womanist Reflection," all in *The Black Panther Party Reconsidered,* ed. Charles E. Jones (Baltimore: Black Classics Press, 1998); and Elaine Brown, *A Taste of*

Power: A Black Woman's Story (New York: Anchor Books, 1994).

12. Sara M. Evans, *Tidal Wave: How Women Changed America at Century's End* (New York: Free Press, 2004), 26, 72; Dorothy Sue Cobble, *The Other Women s Movement: Workplace Justice and Social Rights in Modern America* (Princeton, N.J.: Princeton University Press, 2004).

13. Evans, *Tidal Wave,* 116. The point here is not to privilege bureaucratically organized liberal feminist organizations but rather to suggest an expansion and diversification of the models we use to identify feminist practices. For such a broadening at the other end of the organizational spectrum, see Anne Enke's analysis of women's more informally organized, often impromptu struggles to control public space as still another form of feminist activism in the 1960s and 1970s in her *Finding the Movement: Sexuality, Contested Space, and Feminist Activism* (Durham, N.C.: Duke University Press, 2008).

14. Carrie N. Baker, "Race, Class, and Sexual Harassment in the 1970s," *Feminist Studies* 30 (Spring 2004): 7–27. These included "the first successful Title VII cases in the federal district court (Dianne Williams), the federal courts of appeals (Paulette Barnes) and the Supreme Court (Mechelle Vinson), and the first successful cases involving harassment of a student (Pamela Price), coworker harassment (Willie Ruth Hawkins), and hostile environment harassment at the appellate level (Sandra Bundy)," 9.

15. Litigation obviously played a similar role in the civil rights movement throughout much of the twentieth century.

16. Nancy Matthews, *Confronting Rape: The Feminist Anti-Rape Movement and the State* (London: Routledge, 1994) is an earlier example of an issue-based history that does an excellent job of tracing interactions of gender, race, and ethnicity.

17. Nancy Whittier, *Feminist Generations: The Persistence of the Radical Women's Movement* (Philadelphia: Temple University Press, 1995).

■ ■ ■

Discussion Questions:

1. What did women of color see as reproductive justice?

2. Why do you think the differences varied so much between women of color and white women?

3. Do you think these differences are still true today?

What You Can Do

- Support women of color by attending events, volunteering, and asking what you can do
- Recognize women of color have a separate struggle in addition to feminist identity
- Be aware of making presumptions or suggestions based on your own goals for feminism
- Listen, understand, and stand in solidarity

Legal Movements and Social Change

This section will focus on legal issues addressed during the second wave. Through activism and political action, women reformed rape and domestic violence laws and created battered women's shelters and hotlines. Issues outside of personal safety, such as employment discrimination, were also addressed for the first time in court. The second wave saw the first class-action lawsuit brought for gender discrimination. Through sheer bravery and determination, the women of *Newsweek* stood up for women everywhere when they challenged the sexist atmosphere of the corporate world.

CHAPTER 5

Moving onto the Terrain of the State

THE BATTERED WOMEN'S MOVEMENT
AND THE POLITICS OF ENGAGEMENT

By Claire Reinelt

Undoubtedly the most pressing work before us is to build our own autonomous institutions. It is absolutely crucial that we make our visions real in a permanent form so that we can be even more effective and reach many more people.

Barbara Smith, *Home Girls* (1983)

Where we have not yet succeeded as a movement is in the structural arena. We have not brought this vast, decentralized revolution of consciousness and the small projects characteristic of the women's movement into sufficient engagement with the political structures to create lasting structural changes that would institutionalize some of the new possibilities for life that we seek.

Charlotte Bunch, *Passionate Politics* (1987)

Is it possible to build and nurture autonomous feminist institutions and at the same time engage with mainstream institutions? Or are these two strategies politically contradictory? Historically, feminist activists have tended to emphasize one strategy over the other, depending upon their political beliefs. Radical feminists, who were skeptical about transforming the existing system, favored creating alternative, autonomous institutions (Echols 1990). Liberal feminists, by contrast, sought legal reforms within that system. These divergent political strategies characterized much feminist activism throughout the 1960s and early 1970s.

By the late 1970s the boundary between liberal and radical feminism had blurred (Taylor 1983). Feminist activists within alternative institutions increasingly attempted to transform the politics and practices of mainstream institutions.[1] Women within mainstream institutions began organizing collectively to challenge institutional forms of gender inequality.[2] Self-defined feminists were moving into positions of power within bureaucratic structures (H. Eisenstein 1991a). And liberal feminist organizations, such as NOW, adopted proposals that required more than legal reform (Z. Eisenstein 1981; Taylor 1983).This blurring of movement and institutional boundaries transformed feminist political strategies.

In this essay I focus on the meaning of these changes for feminists within an alternative institution: I discuss how feminists in the Texas battered women's movement moved onto the terrain of the state by creating the Texas Council on Family Violence, hereafter referred to as the Council. Council activists brought a feminist movement agenda to local shelter activists, state agency employees, and legislators, among others. The Council is of particular interest because it has been instrumental in the funding, evaluation, and administration of state funds to battered women's shelters through a series of contracts with the state.

State-level shelter activists in Texas practice what I call *a politics of engagement*. A politics of engagement is based on a belief that long-term social change depends on mobilizing and educating women in their communities by creating autonomous institutions, and on establishing relationships and structures of communication with those who work in and set policy for mainstream institutions. This political approach starts with the insight of radical feminists that autonomous institutions are essential for women in a patriarchal society. At the same time, it views mainstream institutions as absolutely necessary terrains of political struggle.

Moving onto the terrain of the state is full of political contradictions for movement activists. On the one hand, there are new political opportunities for organizing and education; on the other hand, there are increased opportunities for divisions within the movement and for co-optation of the movement's agenda. The challenge for state-level feminist activists is to negotiate a path that provides support for services to battered women and at the same time promotes a feminist program for change. The case study of actual feminist practice presented here can help us understand how some feminists are defining and implementing a politics of engagement in the 1990s.[3]

Moving onto the Terrain of the State

During the 1960s and 1970s, radical feminists created alternative institutions such as battered women's shelters, rape crisis centers, and feminist health centers. One of the most vexing problems for these institutions was funding. At issue was whether an alternative institution could maintain its autonomy and political commitments if it received money from the very structures it was seeking to change, such as local and state governments. The debate over funding was particularly heated in the literature on the battered women's movement (Ahrens 1980; Johnson 1981; Morgan 1981; Sullivan 1982b; Tierney 1982).

In the 1980s there was a rapid increase in the number of battered women's shelters because large amounts of money from local governments and foundations were made available to fund local shelters. This influx of money was in many ways a mixed blessing. Shelters were more financially secure and could concentrate on building their programs to meet the needs of battered women, but funding also brought such changes as increased specialization, more hierarchy, and less autonomy for shelter residents (Schechter 1982). Resisting the depoliticizing effects of increased funding has been an ongoing political struggle.

Forming state coalitions of battered women's shelters (Schechter 1982) is one strategy feminists used to define and institutionalize a collective political vision. State organizations play a critical role in sustaining and building the battered women's movements nationwide. They are often organized by veteran shelter activists to engage in political and educational activities that local shelters find little time to pursue. Their vision and political perspective is likely to be explicitly feminist.

Most of the literature on the battered women's movement has focused on the creation, transformation, structures, and practices of local shelters (Ferraro 1981, 1983; Wharton 1987; Rodriguez 1988). Little attention has been paid to the state coalitions of shelter activists that operate now in almost every state.[4] State organizations act as a network for and provide assistance to local shelter activists by developing public education and outreach programs; producing manuals and newsletters; and holding conferences. Since state organizations are not involved in providing direct services to battered women, they do not face the same pressures to concentrate on service instead of politics; nonetheless, they confront many of the same issues that arise in local shelters. They make choices about organizational structure, political goals, values, and strategies for changing attitudes and structures that support violence against women.

During the time of my research in Texas, feminist activists mobilized to shape state legislative decisions and institutional practices that had an impact on battered women. They secured the passage of funding legislation in 1981 that created the Family Violence Program and thereby structurally solidified a set of relationships between local shelters, the Council, and the state. This process of politically engaging with the state opened up possibilities for political activism but at the same time created its own set of contradictions.

Historically, feminists have approached the state as either a neutral arbiter of competing interests or as a site of gender inequalities originating elsewhere.[5] Liberal feminists have tended to accept the structures and processes of the state as democratic and just, even though they recognized inequities. These they sought to redress primarily through existing political means, believing that their interests would prevail because they were politically consistent with democratic values. Radical and Marxist feminists have not considered the state a primary site for political struggle, believing its policies and practices to reflect inequalities structured either in the family or the workplace. Both these conceptions treat the state as a unified entity.

I suggest that the state itself is a contradictory and uneven set of structures and processes that are the product of particular struggles. The state is neither a neutral arbiter of gender nor simply a reproducer of existing gender inequalities. It is a site of active contestation over the construction of gender inequalities and power. Legislative decisions and institutional practices are made in historically specific social, political, and economic contexts that shape, by either perpetuating or altering, particular social formations of gender.[6] With this conception of the state, we can understand state policy outcomes for battered women as the result of social processes that include feminist mobilization.

Feminist Mobilization and Organizational Practice

During the 1970s and early 1980s, shelters for battered women formed all across the country. They had diverse organizational beginnings. Some were neighborhood-based (for example, Casa Myrna Vasquez in Boston). Others emerged from consciousness-raising groups (such as Women's Advocates in St. Paul, Minnesota). Still others were organized by formerly battered women (Boston's Transition House). In some locations women's centers became de facto shelters, as did the Women's Center South in Pittsburgh (Schechter 1982), or shelters were integrated into existing treatment programs (Johnson 1981). Many of the early organizational efforts were grassroots; many of them were also feminist, although this was not always a term that the women involved used to describe themselves.[7]

Many who did describe themselves as feminists embraced radical feminism,[8] Radical feminist ideology profoundly influenced the politics and practices of many early shelters.[9] It defined violence against women not as a personal or family issue but as a political issue; it argued that existing institutional practices were male-dominated and perpetuated violence against women. What women needed was a safe space of their own where they could escape the violence and begin to rebuild their lives. Shelters became those spaces.

Organizing local shelters was in many instances both exhilarating and frustrating. For many radical feminists, it offered opportunities to create nonbureaucratic, nonhierarchical organizations based on collective, collaborative work, consensus decision-making, and respect for the expertise that women have about their own lives. Even though actual shelter practices did not always measure up to such ideals, these ideals profoundly influenced the movement. Many shelter activists are committed to empowering battered women to take control of their own lives, rather than solving problems for them. There is a widespread belief that battered women are victims of male violence who primarily need practical and personal support, not therapy. Many shelters take seriously the need to be grassroots community organizations whose primary support comes from community members who volunteer time and money. Many shelters are committed to involving battered women in an ongoing way in shelter activities. Organizationally, many shelters create structures and practices that value collective consensus decision-making, ethical communication, and group empowerment. Institutionalizing radical differences in knowledge, status, and power is discouraged (Rodriguez 1988).

Despite their widespread influence on the politics and practices of shelters, radical feminist values have been difficult to sustain and implement. Some radical feminists have argued that this failure is political and ideological. Too many shelter activists, they say, are not committed to feminist ideology. They lose touch with communities through creating boards that are white and professional; they opt for hierarchical structures and job descriptions that make them more legitimate; and they engage in lesbian-baiting in order to secure their positions of power (Ahrens 1980).

Radical feminist values and practices have been difficult to sustain for economic and political reasons as well. Very few shelters can or choose to remain entirely autonomous and disengaged from existing institutions, whether those be funding agencies, state and local governments, law enforcement, welfare bureaucracies, or the courts. The considerable costs of running a shelter and working to end violence against women make fund raising a high priority. Many shelters rely on community support for both money and volunteer staff, but these are often not enough to cover expenses. Most shelters turn to foundations, corporations, or local and state governments to fund their programs. For some shelter activists this is done reluctantly, since it often can mean a loss of autonomy and control over the politics and organization of shelter practices; other activists believe that governments and foundations *should* be financially responsible for supporting work that aims to end battering and provide a better life for women and their children. Whatever the reason, most shelters devote considerable time and energy to fund raising, and as the literature makes clear, outside funding sources often have a depoliticizing effect (Johnson 1981; Morgan 1981; Ristock 1990).

Shelter activists engage with outside institutions for other reasons as well. A battered woman has numerous encounters with outside institutions, from the police officer she calls when her partner beats her to the courts that preside over her assault case or divorce proceeding. Hospitals, welfare offices, social workers, and housing authorities also have contact with battered women while they are at the shelter. These institutions operate with practices and values radically different from those of shelters; nonetheless, because they provide essential resources for women to rebuild their lives, shelter activists often find themselves challenging the institutional practices they see as unfair or discriminatory. Shelter activists have trained law enforcement officials, lobbied for legislation that will protect battered women, and provided technical assistance to programs that are working with abusive men. These are time-consuming and often frustrating activities, but few shelter activists refuse to engage in them.

In addition to the ideological, economic, and political forces that have made it difficult to implement radical feminist political practices fully, there are problematic aspects to radical feminist practice itself. Consensus decision-making, a hallmark of radical feminist practice, may empower group members and challenge hierarchical structures of decision-making, but as early as 1972 feminists also identified negative aspects. Resolving conflict is difficult (Mansbridge 1980); participation is very demanding and time-consuming (Wharton 1987; Rodriguez 1988), and homogeneity is fostered (Freeman 1972). Many shelter organizations have thus moved away from pure consensus-based decision-making.

Collectives, the defining organizational form of radical feminist practice, minimize the division of labor, specialized knowledge, and status differences between participants (Rothschild-Whitt 1979; Ahrens 1980; Schechter 1982), but pure collective forms have been difficult to sustain. Collectives often have no mechanism for ensuring worker accountability (Schechter 1982). Without a formal structure, informal power structures develop that are often more difficult to negotiate than formal ones (Freeman 1972). Intense face-to-face relationships among collective members personalize conflicts that make them emotionally painful (Rothschild-Whitt 1979; Mansbridge 1980). Thus, most shelter organizations today operate with some form of "modified collective" or "modified hierarchy" (Schechter 1982).

Radical feminist shelter organizations have worked toward eliminating professional hierarchies. Some shelters made commitments to hire primarily former residents (Rodriguez 1988); others tried to minimize differentials in status by paying everyone the same salary. Formal education and training were not considered relevant criteria in hiring decisions. By rejecting professional status, feminists were trying to create alternative systems of value and power that did not depend on institutional legitimation. For many working-class women who wanted the skills, money, and control over their work that professional status offered, this rejection was incomprehensible (Schechter 1982). By hiring only formerly battered women, shelters maximized group bonding but often created barriers between themselves and the rest of the women's movement (Rodriguez 1988). As shelters gained community legitimacy, more professionals (social workers, mental health workers, lawyers and other criminal justice workers) staffed battered women's shelters. For some feminists this signaled the depoliticization and co-optation of the battered women's movement (Ahrens1980).

Practicing a Politics of Engagement

The question of whether the movement has become depoliticized and co-opted is a complex one. In part, the answer depends on the conceptual framework used to understand processes of social change and political transformation. During the 1960s and 1970s, blacks, students, and women pursued a politics of confrontation and protest. Underlying this political strategy was the belief that the state and mainstream institutions were the mechanisms through which the powerful maintained and managed the oppression of subordinate groups. Subordinate groups were outsiders whose only source of power was mobilization and protest against the establishment. The profound sense of being simultaneously outside political organizations and structures and oppressed by them shaped a political ideology and strategy of confrontation.

The battered women's movement in its early years drew its political strength and energy from defining itself in opposition to patriarchal and hierarchical institutions. By constructing itself as outside the political and institutional structures of mainstream society, the movement had the political space to experiment with and create new organizational forms. It was critical for the emergent movement to define what constituted radical, feminist, and transformative practices.

In part this was achieved by reifying and dismissing what were considered masculinist, mainstream, and hegemonic practices. Creating an "us" versus "them" opposition was essential to this process.[10] The following sets of practices and values were grouped together and opposed in order to provide a basis for judging whether a shelter or movement organization was feminist or not.

feminist	patriarchal
collective	hierarchy
democratic participation	bureaucracy
empowerment	power
grassroots	professional
confrontation	co-optation
political	institutional
outside	inside
people	state

If a shelter or a movement organization was organized collectively to empower people at the grassroots level by engaging in political confrontation against patriarchal institutions, then it could be considered feminist. If it worked with mainstream institutions, developing hierarchical or bureaucratic organizational structures, then it was co-opted.[11]

Several assumptions underlying this conceptual framework are problematic for understanding a politics of engagement.[12] First, this framework assumes that an organization or a movement is either feminist or patriarchal, collective or hierarchical, and so on. There is no way of conceptualizing the politics of a movement that may include both collective and hierarchical processes, participatory and bureaucratic elements, outside and inside political strategies, grassroots mobilization and organizing within institutions. Second, this framework assumes that whatever is collective, participatory, and grassroots is open, democratic, and responsive to people's needs, while all hierarchies and bureaucracies are oppressive, static, and unresponsive. There is no room within this framework to explore the oppressive, unresponsive elements in

collective practices or the democratic impulses in hierarchical practices. And third, this framework assumes that if the terms on the left come into contact with the terms on the right, the right will win; therefore, the left must maintain a rigid boundary between itself and all that is on the right. It is not possible within this framework to understand feminist mobilization within institutions, feminist engagement with existing institutions, and the formalization of feminism within alternative institutions.

As these forms of feminist politics grow in significance, we need a conceptual framework that allows us to understand how feminists are using institutional and state resources to build their movements and to open up terrains of political activism and education (Freeman 1975; Simon 1982; Matthews 1989). We need to explore new forms of feminist consciousness within institutions and look at how feminists are transforming institutional structures and practices (Katzenstein 1990). Toward that end I turn to the political strategies and practices of the Texas Council on Family Violence.

Building a Statewide Battered Women's Movement

In 1977, feminist activists from around the country met in Houston for the International Women's Year Conference. At this conference, shelter activists held several workshops. It was the first time so many women from that movement had gathered in one place. They shared information, traded stories, and felt empowered by being together. This conference was instrumental in the formation of the National Coalition Against Domestic Violence (NCADV).

It was also out of this conference experience that shelter activists in Texas decided to form the Texas Council on Family Violence. They moved quickly to define an agenda and a workable structure for the new organization. A working board of eight people was set up. Each board member was responsible for coordinating

Council activities in one of several areas such as legislation, fund raising, membership, and research. Like many shelters, the Council decided on a modified collective structure. The board had a chair who was responsible for running board meetings, but decisions were made by consensus.

In 1979 the Council coordinated the passage of a bill to establish a pilot project that would provide state funds for six Texas shelters. This was the beginning of the Council's effort to involve the state in funding local shelters. Its decision to seek state funding was uncontroversial; in fact, the Council had formed in large part for this purpose. State funding was seen as a means to create a more stable funding source for local, community-based shelter programs.[13]

The legislation that Council activists drafted to increase state funding was carefully written to ensure that shelter programs continued to be autonomous, local, community-based programs with primary funding coming from community sources. State contracts were to be awarded only to those shelters that had been "in actual operation offering shelter services 24 hours a day with a capacity for not less than five persons for at least nine months before the date that the contract [was] awarded." This provision was designed to discourage those who might form a shelter solely for the purpose of getting state funds, reflecting the Council's belief that such shelters were less likely to be grassroots, community organizations. This commitment to community-based organizations, however, though consistent with feminist practice, does not acknowledge that some communities, particularly those that are poor, may find it extremely difficult to organize without state funds (Matthews 1989).

The law further provided a declining scale of state support over a six-year period so that after six years no more than 50 percent of a shelter's funding could come from the state. By limiting state support, the Council sought to encourage local shelters to continue raising funds in their communities in order to build acceptance and support for their work. Community support is one of the strongest guarantees that a shelter

will continue to survive. Shelters that lack community support lose touch with the population and are not as responsive to community needs. Strong local shelters that have broad community support also strengthen the statewide movement. A legislator is more likely to back the Council's legislative and funding agenda if there is a community-supported shelter in his or her district. In addition, those shelters that are well established in their communities have more staff resources to contribute to political and educational work organized through the Council.

Council activists saw the state as a potential resource for their own activities as well. The enabling legislation they wrote required the Department of Human Services (DHS), which would administer the funds, to "contract for the provision of training, technical assistance, and evaluations related to shelter and service program development." This provision was meant to ensure that the Council would be actively involved in carrying out the mandate of the legislation. Its role was further reinforced by another section of the bill: "In implementing this chapter, the department shall consult with individuals and groups having knowledge of and experience in the problems of family violence."

The legislation was passed in 1981. Soon afterward the Council received a contract from DHS to visit every shelter in order to prepare them all for state funding. DHS contracted with the Council because they perceived it in their interest to do so. When DHS received the legislative mandate to administer the Family Violence Program, the staff had no knowledge of family violence or shelters. The legislation required that they contract for technical assistance, and the most knowledgeable source on family violence and shelters was the Council. In addition, the Council's community and legislative support made it highly unlikely that DHS would choose to contract with another organization.

This first contract marked the beginning of a contractual relationship with DHS that in 1991 generated $260,000 for movement-building activities, in addition to the money that local shelters received. DHS contracts funded a toll-free technical assistance hotline, a resource library, the Council's newsletter, training conferences, an information database, site visits, a statewide public education campaign, and Council members' active participation in shaping the DHS administration of the Family Violence Program (Texas Council on Family Violence 1990). The initial contract, along with a grant from the Levi-Strauss Foundation, made it possible for the Council board to hire a staff: two shelter activists from the Austin Center for Battered Women who had been instrumental in obtaining the grant and contract.[14] Under the new contract, they began visiting every shelter that qualified for state funding.

When an advocacy group contracts with the state for funding, it raises the possibility of conflict of interest. Whom does the Council represent: the state? shelters? itself? The potential for conflicts of interest was not very great under this first contract, since its purpose was purely informational. With this limited state agenda the staff was able to spend a lot of time talking with shelter directors about their programs and about the Council's agenda. The context for the visits was in fact very favorable, since it was the Council that had been instrumental in securing state funds for the shelters.

Evaluating Local Shelters

The potential for conflict of interest increased significantly with the next contract. In 1982 the Texas Council on Family Violence contracted with DHS to evaluate shelter services. It did this for several reasons. First, members were interested in developing a "competency-based evaluation system" that would be used as a basis for allocating funds to shelters. The idea behind this system was to encourage shelters to develop their programs in the direction of more public education and advocacy work. Second, knowing that DHS would want some form of evaluation to ensure that shelters complied with their contracts, the Council wanted to have input into how

the state conceptualized these evaluations and, if possible, use the state's authority to implement its own ideas. Third, they saw the evaluation contract as a way to shape the state's perception of its relationship to local shelter programs. And fourth, they saw the evaluations as a means of learning about shelter programs, assisting shelter staff with problems, and encouraging them to take risks and innovate. This diverse agenda proved very hard to negotiate.

When the Council sought the evaluation contract, members were aware that some local shelters might misperceive their relationship with the state. Not all shelters were equally aware of the Council's history: when it first formed, there were only six shelters in existence; at the time of the evaluations there were twenty-nine.[15] Those shelter activists who had been involved in the formation of the Council had a very different relationship to it than did those whose shelters were established afterward. Having a part in creating a movement organization from scratch is a much different experience from coming into an already established organization. Some of the new shelters were formed through the active nurturance of Council members; others developed on their own. Most shelters were members of the Council, but some perceived it as a professional organization for shelter providers rather than a movement organization. Others did not feel that feminism spoke to their communities.

The evaluations took place during a day-long visit to each shelter.[16] The Council staff conducted the visits with the shelter staff in the presence of the DHS regional contract managers. The participation of the contract managers was required by the Council, which saw in such participation a political opportunity to educate state employees about battering and shelters, as well as a chance to define the state's relationship to local programs.[17] If during evaluation visits contract managers referred to the shelter program as a state program, the Council staff would correct them in no uncertain terms, pointing out that these were locally based community programs that the state was helping to fund. Often a conversation would ensue about the difference between the state's relationship to shelters and its relationship to other DHS-administered programs. The substance of the conversation was always that while DHS "owned" other welfare programs, it "funded" family violence programs. The consistency with which the Council staff corrected DHS misconceptions underscores the strategic importance they placed on maintaining the autonomy of local shelters. If DHS began to perceive shelters as "their" programs, then the shelter movement would lose a significant tactical edge. By maintaining the autonomy of local shelters, the movement strengthened its claim vis-à-vis the state to define how shelter would be provided.

The evaluation instrument that the Council designed had several purposes.[18] First, it met the needs of DHS by assessing whether shelters were complying with the law. Second, it provided a mechanism for the Council to gather information about how shelters handled batterers, children, staff-board relations, budget planning, personnel policies, and general organization. With this information, Council activists hoped to be better able to advise and consult with shelters. Finally, the evaluation instrument was designed to open up dialogue—on issues such as advocacy versus counseling, the use of volunteers, public education, developing community resources, and shelter accessibility—that would give the Council staff an opportunity to discuss shelter philosophy and politics with both shelter staff and DHS contract managers.

Most shelter directors actively engaged with the Council staff during the evaluation visits, using them as a resource and seeing them as allies. Engaging in practical, philosophical, and political discussions was a learning experience for both the Council staff and shelter directors. This was particularly evident in one South Texas shelter run by the Catholic Charities. The director, a middle-aged Hispanic woman, operated the shelter with a philosophy of "charity" that included viewing battered women as victims who primarily needed therapy. She was very reticent

about doing public outreach. As she explained, this is "macho country," by which she meant that it was dangerous for women to challenge male power by discussing the rights of women—including the right not to be beaten.

The Council staff conducting the evaluation visit had never provided shelter in a hostile environment. Their experiences had been in a liberal, urban city where politicians and community leaders were generally receptive. The visit to South Texas caused the staff to reflect on how regional, racial, and cultural differences shape the way a community provides shelter. The Council staff worked hard to empower the Catholic Charities shelter staff to take the political risk of raising the issues of violence against women in their communities, pointing out that not only would a public presence build community support, but it would also increase their opportunities for diversifying their funding base. The two direct service staff (also Hispanic) responded positively to the Council staff's suggestions, but the shelter director was still afraid to "rock the boat."

The success of the battered women's movement in the 1990s will depend on how it handles issues of diversity and difference (Ristock 1990). At the time of these evaluations the Council's philosophy statement did not include any mention of how culture, race, and sexuality impact on battering relationships and on the movement's political agenda. They were afraid early on to raise issues of homophobia and racism because they believed such a focus would weaken their efforts to pass funding legislation for battered women's shelters, to transform the way police officers view battered women, and to encourage all shelters to become members of the Council. More recently the Council has taken on these issues through a series of training workshops aimed at new shelter staff. These include a work session on homophobia and lesbian battering, and one on racism and women of color.[19] The Council's willingness to confront these contentious and emotional issues signals its own greater feelings of political strength and recognition that understanding and working across differences are essential political work in the 1990s.[20]

Local Shelter Resistance

Some shelter directors were unhappy with the Council's approach to the evaluations. One shelter director said in a letter to the Council that she felt "the evaluators tended to impose themselves into the internal operations of a private agency, well beyond the scope of the [DHS] contract under evaluation." She considered any discussion of philosophy, politics, personnel policies to be inappropriate. Part of her resistance came from very real philosophical differences between herself and the Council staff. This director was neither a feminist nor a movement activist. At one point in the evaluation report, the Council staff objected to the shelter's policy of "limiting women's activities and problem-solving during the first three days of their stay." This, they argued, was "incongruous with accepted shelter practices." The shelter director objected by invoking her own "experts" and arguing that women in crisis experience "cognitive, behavioral and affective disequilibrium and need a three day waiting period to regain their sense of equilibrium" (personal correspondence). The Council staff, consistent with their approach, tried to engage the shelter director in a discussion about this policy, but without much success. The director was particularly angry that the Council's assessment of this policy was included in the evaluation report sent to DHS.

In writing up the evaluation reports, the Council staff included a full assessment of all the shelter's policies and practices. These reports were used simultaneously to give feedback to the shelter and to report to DHS. Such mixed goals were problematic. Feedback is an internal movement activity aimed at strengthening and supporting local shelters; to be useful, it should include frank assessments about the strengths of the program and the areas where improvement is needed. Reporting to DHS is an official act that can have consequences for the local shelter's share of state funding. By not distinguishing these two activities, the Council placed itself in an extremely contradictory position. Some local shelters protested that "their" organization was divulging negative information about them to their funders. Feedback from local shelters on the evaluation visits led the Council to reevaluate this strategy.

The Council wanted to maintain a mechanism for discussing philosophical issues and providing technical assistance to shelters but did not want to be in a position of providing DHS with knowledge about these discussions, thus adversely affecting their relationship to local shelters. As the Council's director said to me, "We have become much more circumspect about what we reveal to DHS." Consequently, the Council made a decision not to continue evaluating shelters for DHS. It does still engage in evaluative activities by investigating complaints or questionable practices engaged in by shelter staffs. But although DHS may ultimately be asked to intervene if a complaint or grievance is not resolved internally, the goal is to create internal processes for handling problems.

Re-visioning Feminist Politics in the 1980s and 1990s

I have discussed the politics of the evaluation contract at some length because it points to both the potential benefits and the contradictions of engaging with the state. Once the state is viewed as a terrain of political struggle, some form of political engagement is likely. Defining the parameters of this engagement in a way that maximizes autonomy for the movement and effectively challenges institutional practices is a major feminist challenge.

Successfully pursuing this dual agenda requires not only a more complex understanding of the state but also a revised understanding of the dynamics of power. Earlier movement activists understood power as the ability of the state, institutions, and those who held positions of authority to impose their will on others. Power was competitive, individualistic, and zero-sum. If some had it, then others did not. As feminist politics changed, power was redefined as the ability to act, the ability to transform oneself and the world. Power was no longer defined only as something that others possessed and wielded over you. Through working together collectively, creating organizations, and challenging patriarchal practices, feminists began to experience their own power, based on energy, strength, effectiveness, not domination and control (Hartsock 1979).

Andler and Sullivan, in an article that is quite skeptical about the possibilities of transforming and engaging with mainstream institutions, describe eloquently this sense of power within the battered women's movement.

> We can mobilize countless unpaid women whose commitment keeps numerous shelters operating and whose work is building a national movement to end women abuse. Bureaucracies are in awe of this because it is not within their experience. There is power in the knowledge that it is our groups that are providing the correct answers about issues of our work. Government agencies and funding sources recognize this, and that gives us clout. As recognition of our expertise increases, our political power will increase and we will be able to make demands and set directions within these same institutions. We should never lose the sight and ability to set directions for them. (Andler and Sullivan 1980, 14)

This sense of power is very different from control and domination. It is a collective power that is experienced by movement activists as they mobilize and gain recognition for their work .

Empowering movement activists to challenge bureaucratic and institutional practices has been one of the important political contributions of the Texas Council on Family Violence. During one regional meeting that I attended with local shelter activists, the Council staff spent a good deal of time demystifying the power of the state. Local shelter activists were angry that their contract manager was slated to be changed during a bureaucratic reshuffling. Feeling powerless to influence the DHS decision, much of their anger was directed toward the Council for not protecting their interests. The Council staff redirected the focus of local activist anger to the DHS decision and empowered those activists to work collectively to change it. This turned what began as a hostile encounter between the Council staff and local shelter staffs into a common struggle to find effective ways to challenge oppressive bureaucratic practices. Feelings of powerlessness that had caused anger and resignation were replaced by feelings of collective power.

Empowering others to act and take responsibility for their decisions is a political strategy that Council activists have also used with those in mainstream institutions. One of the most frustrating aspects of engaging with mainstream institutions is the bureaucratic and hierarchical processes that delay action and derail communication. From the beginning of its relationship with DHS, the Council sought to create structures and patterns of communication that held DHS personnel accountable for both decisions and indecisions. Through a joint Council-DHS advisory committee, extensive written correspondence, and regular phone calls, Council activists have been more effective than other advocacy organizations in demanding timely, honest, and open consideration of issues that affect the Family Violence Program.

In the beginning the Council's approach was particularly awkward for some DHS staff people because they were being asked to engage with the Council staff in ways that were highly unusual for agency personnel. In one case a DHS staff person responsible for the Council's contracts with the agency was initially quite antagonistic toward the Council and felt threatened by its power and its approach to dealing with the agency.

Through extensive and persistent communication, Council activists gradually developed a relationship of trust and understanding with her, until she actually became an active advocate for the movement within DHS.

Is such a staff person a movement activist? What about the shelter director who has been active in the battered women's movement for years who takes a job with DHS working with the Family Violence Program? Has she been co-opted, or is she an advocate on the inside? In both cases the boundaries between the movement and mainstream institutions have been blurred. While this blurring has political risks, it also creates political opportunities for transforming institutional practices and furthering a feminist agenda using the resources and power of the state.

CONCLUSION

The blurring of boundaries between who is and is not a movement activist, between hierarchical and collective processes, and between movement and mainstream institutions leaves many feminists feeling shaky about the ideological ground they stand on. If firm determinations cannot be made about who is a movement activist and what constitutes feminist practice, then how can we know with any clarity whether our work is contributing to women's liberation or simply to more sophisticated forms of oppression? I believe that it is impossible to know for sure. Such uncertainty, however, should not be resolved by assuming that engagement is antifeminist.

Engaging with the state is a strategy that has risks. It is risky because state funding is contingent on economic and political forces that one does not control. It is risky because state engagement can threaten movement solidarity. But any strategy that has risks also has benefits. Funding for movement activities, access to policymakers, and opportunities for educating many people about the issues of violence against women are not trivial. Risks and benefits are present in any political choice. Organizations that acknowledge this are better able to cope with the uncertainty.

Feminism is a dynamic process. It is guided by values that include nurturance, democracy, cooperation, empowerment, inclusion, transformation, maximizing rewards to all, and ending oppression (Martin 1990a). These values provide a moral framework for action but do not entail specific organizational forms or political strategies. Because the process of social change is neither predetermined nor linear, all activism is historically contingent and shifting, replete with its own contradictions. Instead of denying this reality, many feminists in the 1990s accept this as the condition of their activism.

The battered women's movement has changed but this change cannot adequately be characterized as either a radical break from the past or a quiet slippage toward ever greater bureaucratization. Instead feminists continue to move into more and more arenas of political activism; they are developing innovative organizational and communicative structures and strategies; and they are continually challenging the structure and practices of mainstream institutions. While many of these changes may appear less radical than the early feminist organizing efforts of the 1970s, they may in the long run result in more profound and long-lasting transformation.

NOTES

Acknowledgments: I thank Carmen Sirianni, Mary Katzenstein, Shulamit Reinharz, Richard Alterman, Mindy Fried, Kamini Grahame, George Ross, and anonymous reviewers for giving me valuable feedback on this work. I also thank Myra Marx Ferree and Patricia Yancey Martin for their encouragement and support. A big thank-you also goes to Debby Tucker and Eve McArthur, who made this work possible.

1. For a discussion of how the battered women's movement has attempted to transform mainstream institutional policies and practices, see Schechter 1982.

2. See Katzenstein 1990 for a discussion of women organizing within the U.S. military and the Catholic Church.

3. Dobash and Dobash (1992) describe in some detail feminist efforts to define and implement an antiviolence agenda at the federal level in both Britain and the United States. Leidner (1991) provides an excellent analysis of feminist practice by looking at the internal

organizational process of defining what it means for a feminist organization to be inclusive and representative.

4. Two exceptions are Andler and Sullivan 1980; and Schechter 1982.

5. For a thorough discussion of feminist approaches to the state, see Franzway, Court, and Connell 1989, chap. 2. For a summary of socialist feminist debates on the state see Barrett 1980. For earlier socialist feminist discussions of the state, see Wilson 1977; and McIntosh 1978. For a radical feminist theory of the state, see MacKinnon 1982. Liberal feminists have not articulated a distinct theory of the state, but for a discussion of liberal feminism and the state, see Z. Eisenstein 1981.

6. Australian feminists have been in the forefront of defining a feminist theory of the state that understands the state as a historically constituted set of social processes. "The state cannot be analyzed in abstraction from history. It does not exist as a reflex of the functional needs of a system, whether a class system or a gender system. It is the product of specific, historically located social processes. Quite specifically, the shape of the state is the outcome of particular social struggles. What kind of state we have depends on who was mobilized in social struggle, what strategies were deployed, and who won" (Franzway, Court, and Connell 1989). For further case studies and theoretical developments on feminism and the state, see Watson 1990.

7. For some women, defining themselves as feminists emerged through their work with battered women. One of the founders of Women's Advocates says, "Personally, I didn't call myself a feminist when we started, it sort of snuck up and embraced me as I lived it." Women of color often did not describe themselves as feminists because of the racism they encountered in the women's movement. Racism took the form of being excluded from leadership positions, being ignored when concerns that predominantly affected women of color were raised, and by an unwillingness to examine the interconnectedness of oppressions, in effect forcing women of color to choose between gender and racial struggles. This racism has made it difficult for women of color to self-define as feminists even though many of them espouse feminist beliefs. See Moraga and Anzaldua 1981; and Hooks 1984.

8. The definition of radical feminism has been and continues to be highly contested. For a history of radical feminism, see Echols (1989); see also Douglas's (1990) review of Echols' book and Echols's (1990) response.

9. I base this claim both on my personal knowledge and on my reading of Susan Schechter's account of the emergence of the battered women's movement.

She states that "in many programs, locally and nationally, radical feminists organized first, setting the style and practice that continues to dominate in much of the battered women's movement" (Schechter 1982, 45). For a comparison of shelter organizing by radical feminists in both the United States and West German y, see Ferree 1987.

10. Ristock (1990) notes in her discussion of feminist collectives that this political strategy allowed collectives to feel united and strong but it also assumed a false unity. Anyone who was different was considered a threat to that unity and had her feminism called into question.

11. This assessment has been particularly widespread in the literature on the battered women's movement (Martin 1990b).

12. Works that explore the need for a new conceptual framework for understanding feminist organizational practice include Simon 1982; Taylor 1983; Staggenborg 1988; Katzenstein 1990; Martin 1990b; and Sirianni 1993.

13. For more positive accounts of the impact of state funding on organizations and movements, see Simon 1982; and Matthews 1989. For more critical or pessimistic accounts, see Andler and Sullivan 1980; and Morgan 1981. For a more recent critical account, see Fraser 1989.

14. Both women are White, college-educated feminists with a long history of community activism, including anti-rape work and shelter organizing .

15. Most of the evaluation visits were held during 1983.

16. I accompanied the Council on eight shelter visits in the south and central Texas regions as a participant observer. The Council staff arranged my participation. I was introduced as a researcher interested in the evaluation process.

17. During the week I traveled with the Council staff in south Texas, one contract manager attended all five evaluations. At the beginning of the week he spoke continually about state requirements and seemed uneasy about the Council staff's approach to evaluations. By the end of the five days his bureaucratic concerns had been replaced by an interest in the programmatic issues shelters faced. He began to assume the role of an advocate, discussing strategy with shelter directors much as he had heard the Council staff do earlier in the week. In other words, he became an active participant in the evaluations on the terms that the Council had defined.

18. The instrument was developed and used in 1982–83.

19. There has been active resistance by some attendees at the sessions on homophobia and lesbian battering,

primarily from women in the shelter community who are fundamentalist Christians. For a discussion of feminism and fundamentalism, see Stacey 1990.

20. There is a growing literature that addresses battering in the African American community (White 1985), in the Latino community (Zambrano 1985), and among lesbians (Lobel 1986).

∎∎∎

Discussion Questions

1. Why was the funding of domestic abuse shelters troubling for radical feminists?

2. What are some reasons to engage with outside institutions?

3. In chapter five, the question is asked: "If firm determinations cannot be made about who is a movement activist and what constitutes feminist practice, then how we can we know with any clarity whether our work is contributing to women's liberation or simply to more sophisticated forms of oppression?" What do you make of this conundrum?

What You Can Do

- Learn the phone number of the local shelter and share it often
- Volunteer at a shelter and donate needed items
- Withhold all judgment and refer victims and survivors to the hotline and shelter numbers
- Volunteer to care for the victim/survivor's pets while she finds safe housing
- Accompany a victim/survivor to court for hearings, filings, and trials to show support
- Raise awareness around your campus

CHAPTER 6

Confronting Rape

THE FEMINIST ANTI-RAPE MOVEMENT AND THE STATE

By Nancy A. Matthews

Today, rape crisis centers are ubiquitous in the U.S. and many other countries. Found in cities of all sizes and in many rural counties, they offer counseling and other services to survivors of sexual assault. Although their funding may be precarious in times of shrinking social service spending, they have nevertheless gained recognition as legitimate, necessary social services. But it was not always so. The rape crisis services we see today developed from a social movement, and many of the providers of rape crisis services still see themselves as part of a movement. This means that even if a person is employed doing rape crisis work, their commitment to "the cause" goes beyond it being just a job, and a person doing volunteer rape crisis work may see their work as contributing to social change, even if it is by helping one victim at a time. The anti-rape movement is a good example of the process of institutionalization in social movements.

The anti-rape movement was born in the wave of collectivist, radical feminist activism that occurred at the end of the 1960s and through the 1970s. The feminist anti-rape movement generated new ideas about violence against women and invented a new service, rape crisis work. The activists who began the anti-rape movement combined feminist politics with providing services to individual victims. As the movement matured, new opportunities arose, and rape crisis centers became more integrated into existing social service networks. Becoming part of the constellation of social services in a city, county, or state, was not an accident or a "natural" outgrowth of a good idea. It was the result of years of struggle, through persistent lobbying and advocacy by a movement toward the state and the state responding with new policies. In the language of social movement scholars, it is the result of *challengers* making successful demands on the state (Tilly 1978). Challengers are those who are *outsiders* to the groups who wield power (that is, government and its agencies and representatives), control resources (for example, tax money that is granted to various groups for specific purposes), and make policy. Challengers, or social movement activists, influence the public agenda by pushing the government to address new issues (Baumgartner and Mahoney 2005). This is what the anti-rape movement did so successfully. As Baumgartner and Mahoney point out, "Perhaps the greatest long-term impact of social movements ... is that as SMOs [social movement organizations] develop, they must interact more closely over time with established professional communities, especially among service providers, be they social workers, medical researchers, environmental engineers, or the manufacturers of pollution abatement equipment. Eventually, most groups then become much more closely a part of the ... policy process, despite their 'pure' social movement roots" (2005, 81). This *institutionalization* of social movements, includes developing more formal organizational structure, gaining access to regular financial support, shifting to more moderate goals, and adoption of a more conventional action repertoire (Kriesi 1996).

The survival and maturation of rape crisis services exhibits this pattern. In this excerpt from *Confronting Rape* you will read about the establishment of one rape crisis center in California in the 1970s and its struggles to survive and eventual institutionalization. The whole story is more complex: *Confronting Rape* encompasses six anti-rape organizations and is enriched by comparisons and contrasts. But the story of the Los Angeles Commission on Assaults Against Women (recently renamed Peace Over Violence) offers a window on transformation in a social movement organization. You will see how more formal organization came about, and goals and action repertoires shifted with the opportunities to secure funding. I argue that the kind of work the early activists chose—work that combined service provision to victims of violence with their feminist goal of changing gender relations—shaped their demands on the state, primarily for resources to support the services. Yet for many of these early activists, accepting money from the state was fraught with contradictions. Coming out of the 1960s counter-culture critique of the state, they initially wanted little to do with it.

Why examine a social movement about sexual violence in the first place? I chose to do this research because I was interested in how people make history as social actors and the dynamic ways that their actions are constrained by the historical, political and social context, and the ways that their actions shape the future context. In the anti-rape movement, I found a movement and its organizations that posed compelling questions. In studies of violence, women are commonly conceived of as victims, both of individuals and of social forces; my study approaches them as social actors, resisting and reshaping the social relations that constitute their lives. Thus, I was interested in what people did in those communities about the issue of rape, what

happened as a result of what they did, and how it was affected by events and processes outside and within those communities. I studied these events through in-depth interviews with participants in the movement and officials of the Office of Criminal Justice Planning. I also examined archival materials from the six organizations I studied, and conducted field research, attending meetings, special events, and conferences related to the movement.

A Changing Movement and the State

The anti-rape movement was founded on two notions: first, the radical political insight that violence against women is a fundamental component of the social control of women, and second, that women could empower each other by helping *victims* become *survivors*. Early activities included confrontations with individual rapists, street theater, and confronting the police in public forums. The early movement tended to be anti-establishment and anti-state, stemming from its roots in the leftist counter-culture of the period and also activists' outrage about the particular violations of rape victims by the police and criminal justice system. Yet an important strand in this story is the anti-rape movement's changing relationship to the state.

Feminists' anger about inadequate law enforcement action on behalf of women victims of male violence led to an ambiguous stance toward the state. From the beginning, the failure of law enforcement effectively to prevent, control, or punish rape was a target of the movement's activity, but at the same time, many feminist anti-rape activists saw their work as an alternative to relying on or being involved with the criminal justice system. Skepticism toward the state extended to careful scrutiny of possible funding sources—early activists often refused money that required too close a relationship with suspect state agencies, particularly law enforcement.

Despite their outsider, anti-establishment tactics, anti-rape groups became increasingly oriented toward providing services to individual women. Doing that effectively required financial support and organization. Government funding was the most consistent available source of financial support, as long as the movement was able to persuade policy makers that the services were needed. The political context of this movement's struggle was the transition from the widespread movements of the sixties to the increasing conservatism of the seventies. Feminism made some political inroads, and succeeded in gaining attention for the issue of rape, aided by the wider societal focus on violent crime. Eventually, some members of the movement become the policy makers and government bureaucrats who make decisions about financial support for these activities. Meyer, Jenness, and Ingram (2005) note the ways that social movements and government entities interpenetrate each other, with the boundaries between movement and the state not so firm. This eventually occurs in the story of the anti-rape movement.

Over time, increased reliance on state funding had a contradictory effect on the movement, both effectively promoting the movement's survival and contributing to its transformation from grassroots activism to professionalized social service provision. The distinctive organizational form of countercultural feminism in the early 1970s was the collective. Many early rape crisis centers were egalitarian, non-hierarchical, and attempted to operate by consensus. But conventional organizational structure supplanted the early collectives, due in large part to requirements of various types of funding. Today rape crisis centers have a variety of organizational forms. Pat Martin's analysis of rape work (2005) outlines the variety: some are part of larger institutions, including hospitals, community mental health centers, and even district attorneys' offices; some are located in YWCAs or other community organizations, others are in women's centers on college campuses, or are projects of battered women's shelters; some are free-standing organizations. The common structure, though, is some version of the not-for-profit corporation. They usually look more like social service agencies than social movement organizations. Thus, the institutionalization of the movement is closely connected to its changing relationship to the state.

Rape Crisis Services Today

Rape crisis services have evolved considerably since they were first started, but the core activities have remained constant. Although rape crisis centers vary in their organizational location quite a bit, they are associated with a surprisingly consistent set of services (Martin 2005; Byington, Martin et al. 1990; Gornick, Burt, and Pittman 1985). The rape crisis centers I studied had the following kinds of services in common: they offer crisis intervention through a 24-hour telephone hotline and face-to-face counseling for rape victims and their families and friends. Trained volunteers take calls, which are forwarded to their homes, during four to six hour shifts. Women may call the hotline soon after an assault, or they may wait years before calling. The hotlines follow up after the first contact, which sometimes results in the rape survivor coming to the center for in-person counseling, being referred to a private counselor, or joining a support group organized by the center. In addition, rape crisis volunteers or staff will accompany the caller to the hospital, the police, through court-related appointments, or appointments with other agencies, and if necessary intervene with these agencies on their behalf. These advocacy services place rape crisis workers in potentially adversarial relationships with the authorities (Martin 2005).

In addition to crisis intervention services, rape crisis centers organize and provide community education about sexual assault. Members go to schools, churches, community groups, and businesses to do workshops on rape and rape prevention. Some organizations have more elaborate programs that specialize in teaching women self-defense, which can also become a conduit for including diverse communities of women. Direct services to women and community education about sexual assault are the basic activities of all free-standing rape crisis centers and larger organizations that have rape crisis programs. The uniformity in services among hotlines is a product of both the movement's evolution and specification of standards by the state funding agency.

Now we will turn to the specific history of an anti-rape organization that originated in Los Angeles in 1971. Although the focus will be primarily on one organization, at times I bring in comparative information about related organizations.

Challenges of the Early Movement—LACAAW

Despite their origins in different communities and organizing styles, the Los Angeles area rape crisis centers founded in the early to mid 1970s all faced similar challenges as they struggled to survive their early years of operation. The drama and excitement of starting new projects gave way to the hard work of sustaining the project they had invented. Internal dynamics varied with the style of leadership and decision-making practices each had developed. All had to promote their organizations' survival by recruiting new members. Their approaches to funding and relationships with other agencies, such as hospitals and the police, were influenced by ideology, the social position of the members, and particular opportunities that arose outside the groups. Their growing similarity resulted from the requirements of the work itself, an emerging process of working together in coalition, and their relationships to external agencies.

The Los Angeles Commission on Assaults Against Women (LACAAW) emerged out of an Anti-Rape Squad housed in a community based women's center. Its official-sounding name arose from a brief flirtation with ongoing city support, which did not materialize, but the name stuck for over three decades. The women who founded LACAAW were counter-cultural feminists,

meaning they were part of the overlapping leftist movements of that time (e.g., peace and justice, anti-racism) and were critical of the state, particularly law enforcement. Law enforcement had not only not done much for rape victims, but had also been used to infiltrate, spy on, and debilitate many movement organizations in Los Angeles through the FBI program COINTELPRO. They brought this political perspective to their anti-rape activism.

In this section I examine three issues that confronted LACAAW, which were typical of other organizations as well during these years: leadership and decision-making; recruitment and training; and funding. Decisions and events in each of these areas affected the possibilities and developments in the others. I discuss how the organization tackled these issues, and the incipient transformations that occurred as a result.

LEADERSHIP AND DECISION-MAKING

As is typical in social movements (Turner and Killian 1987), leadership was initially shouldered by the women who had the willingness and determination to get the organizations started. They were ideologically committed to the movement, were charismatic enough to get others involved, and had the personal resources (such as time, contacts, money, stamina) to mobilize other usable resources (such as members, money, publicity, elite support). Once established, operating the hotlines was literally a 24 hour a day job. As enough volunteers were recruited and trained, they were assigned shifts to work the telephone hotline, but leaders were commonly on call all the time, to fill in time slots that were not covered, to help handle crises, and to referee incipient conflicts over decision-making. Remember, these were the days before cell phones, so being on call meant staying by a phone in an office or at home.

The Collectivist Organization

Six friends of a rape victim started an Anti-Rape Squad in 1971 to support their friend and raise awareness about rape. They posted alerts on trees and bus stops to warn women about local rapists, performed guerilla theater skits, and sold bumper stickers with anti-rape messages. Eventually they developed a hotline for women to call. The hotline was housed in the Crenshaw Women's Center and was coordinated informally first by a social worker who got involved while doing an internship in community organizing, and later by two self-employed feminist activists. One of the early leaders recalls:

> The person who was [a] coordinator ... at that time ended up with all the [hotline] shifts. Whenever there was nobody to cover the line, they would cover the line. And whenever the counselors had a problem, they would call them. It was an enormous job.

Although someone coordinated the operation, the group as a whole operated as a collective, a form of non-hierarchical organization in which everyone is equal, rules are minimized, and decisions are reached by consensus (Rothschild-Whitt 1979). This style of organization is closely associated with a strand of the second wave women's movement (Ferree and Hess 1985). The activists soon applied for and received a small grant for innovative crisis intervention programs from the California Department of Mental Health. The selection of these two women as co-directors was practically automatic, since they had been working hard for free.

Already these decisions illuminate contradictions brewing in the organization. The untenable condition of having over-worked, uncompensated leaders coordinating intervention led them to seek what they saw as a relatively benign form of state funding, in spite of their being ideologically antagonistic to the state. (These were radical white women who hesitated to report Black men who raped to the police because they saw the racism of the police as being equally outrageous as the rape.) However, funding from mental health did not carry the same ideological baggage as law enforcement money. While having paid staff was a large step toward formalization, the manner in which the staff was chosen and their work relationship still reflected the informal, fluid, collectivist organizational style, where the norms of friendship guided the development of work styles as much as any planned program. These women were available largely because they were not in the full-time traditional labor market, but working in a sort of alternative economy of self-employment and freelance work. This would change. Having grants moved them more into the economic mainstream. Furthermore, the worsening economy in the 1970s made surviving on very little income increasingly difficult. Also, the waning of the countercultural era and the aging of the activists meant that they were less willing to live on a pittance.

Within a few years, the style of decision-making and leadership they developed became problematic as LACAAW grew, especially in 1976, when a large pool of funding increased the complexity of organizational structure. Joining with a community mental health center, the group got a grant from the newly established National Center for the Prevention and Control of Rape, a new program of the National Institute for Mental Health (NIMH). The $150,000 grant for community-based rape prevention education led to more structured work among a larger staff. As one participant explains:

> We really got structured, because it was a research and demonstration center ... we had an obligation in terms of products that we had to develop, training manual, educational manual, and we had to evaluate, do an assessment and develop the programs and then evaluate them. So we went through kind of a formal process of development, using the expertise of the people at the Commission, building on what they were already doing in the way of educational presentations, testing what we were already doing, changing it, revising it, and developed a manual

of educational presentations for adults and children.

No longer just challengers working outside the system, their grassroots work was now cast as "expertise" and staff people were paid to share it. This was a new role for women who were critical of authority and were suspicious of the whole idea of "expertise." In addition, the increase in staff numbers complicated the familiar informal work processes. A participant recounted that "Everybody went into a major crisis. You know it's the kind of thing where you expect to be happy when you get your money and everybody's totally depressed, because the change was very hard."

While the organization tried to maintain its commitment to being an egalitarian, participatory community, it faced the difficult process of integrating new participants and fitting decision-making into a more complex matrix of relationships. The LACAAW women evolved a compromise:

Well, we set ourselves up as a collective. Everybody made the same salary, everybody made decisions together. There were people who were not salaried people, but who were volunteers, who were actively involved. There was a whole process of trying to develop a decision-making process which included hotline volunteers as well as staff. It meant that every decision was agonizing. The major decisions had to be discussed at meetings of hotline volunteers as well as staff. So I think that eventually we did conduct a good portion of the business of running the hotline at staff meetings which we had every week, for the people who were on staff, and there all the time. And the major policies, the very major changes taking place in the Commission happened at membership meetings, or hotline volunteer meetings.

These years were rough ones, as the organization struggled through balancing a commitment to a collectivist structure and process with new requirements imposed by external agencies. The friendship ethic, with its assumption of shared values and concern for interpersonal ties, lost effectiveness. As a result, dilemmas that were not easily resolved through consensus-building and the tradition of informal decision-making began to create rifts in the organization. These came to a head later, when the structural and material circumstances changed again at the end of the NIMH grant.

In contrast with LACAAW's collectivist style two other rape crisis organizations founded soon after operated somewhat differently. The Pasadena Rape Crisis Center-Hotline began in 1974 as a network of social service professionals in separate agencies coordinating their services, then evolved into a distinct organization with its own identity, located under the umbrella of the Pasadena YWCA. This professional network style and working within more established agencies allowed this group to bypass some of the contentious leadership dilemmas LACAAW faced. However, leadership was still largely voluntary, based on who was most motivated, determined, and willing to add to her work-load. The third rape hotline established in Los Angeles represented a combination of the radical political activists and the professional network. East Los Angeles Rape Hotline was founded by Chicana community activists who were influenced by LACAAW but brought their Chicano movement perspective to bear in the work as well. They were based at a Community Mental Health Center, though, which made them more similar to the professionals at the Pasadena YWCA. After briefly operating as a collective, the ELARH adopted a more conventional structure in order to meet the legal requirements for non-profit status. Specifically, a board of directors had to be formed separately from the volunteers. Under the new structure, some members dropped out rather than give control to the legally recognized decision-makers, the board. Early participants felt they had lost their voice. In addition to contention over the decision-making process, there were disagreements over organizational philosophy, with tensions between a community organizing style modeled on Saul Alinsky and *La Raza* and the official bureaucratic management style of the agency. Disagreements arose over policies, especially as they related to funding from corporations such as Coors Brewery and the Playboy Foundation. ELARH reached a period of stalemate after the first several years of rapid growth.

Leadership and decision-making patterns thus varied among the organizations. Where leadership and organizational structure grew out of an egalitarian, activist relationship among participants, more conflict seemed to develop. Internal friction characterized both LACAAW and ELARH, in spite of their differing structures. The ELARH history points out that formal structures do not necessarily preclude conflict and even crises of leadership. Pasadena's relatively harmonious history stemmed from the fact that its arrangement from the beginning was more hierarchical and less political. Pasadena's founders were members of a professional network, but the volunteers they recruited were not, thus rank and file members in that organization were more socially removed from the leadership. In East LA many of the volunteers were professional women and activists, and thus were more assertive and concerned with participation.

Recruitment and Training

Operating the hotlines was labor intensive work that required a large cast of highly committed activists, so recruitment and training became a central feature of rape crisis work. New volunteers had to be recruited on a regular basis because, while many of the core group stayed involved and active for several years, there was turnover among the less involved advocates. The three organizations recruited through friendship and professional networks, radio spots and newspaper ads, and through speaking to community groups.

Once recruited, volunteers were usually put to work on the rape hotlines, but this required training. Training was intensive and incorporated the kind of consciousness-raising process that had become integral to the women's movement. Sessions covered information on rape collected by the movement (there was very little research data available, unlike the present), pointers on dealing with the police and hospitals, and training to sensitize the prospective counselor/advocate to the needs of the caller. Early members who were social workers brought in models of crisis intervention from their field. Given the inherently disempowering experience of rape, training stressed the need to put women in control of their experience. This was at the core of the empowerment model of counseling that feminists consciously adopted, a practical reflection of the political roots of the project.

An early member describes the attention given to women's personal transformation as they went through the training process and the effects it had on their lives outside the movement:

[W]e went to training two times a week for about 4 or 5 weeks and [it] involved a lot of sensitivity training. We did a lot of dyads, a lot of role playing, a lot of information sharing, I guess you would call them consciousness-raising kinds of things about what rape really was. ... The thing that I remember most about the training that I liked and that I have continued to use throughout the time that I've ever done training is giving people an opportunity to feedback. The sessions always opened with where a person was at, a kind of a check in ... what they had done in processing the information that had been given to them in the previous session.

Not all of the women who became interested in working for the rape hotline were feminists. The training was designed as a form of political education, intended to build a common understanding of rape as a product of patriarchal society among women who came in with widely differing views. Some were already feminists looking for a place to act on that commitment, while others were interested in doing good for victims of a heinous crime. And many were somewhere in between, combining an interest in women's issues with a desire to do constructive volunteer work. The rigorous training that developed over the first few years of the hotlines provided the grounds for these women to work together, both drawing on some participants' previous beliefs and structuring a "conversion" experience for others (cf. Ferree and Miller 1985). The sharing of intense emotions connected the participants, and it also produced greater homogeneity of values, viewpoints, and skills necessary for being able to count on individual members to do their part. Thus, training built membership commitment, screening out those who were not dedicated enough.

Creating homogeneity was particularly important for LACAAW, operating as a collective. Collectives depend for stability upon their members working and thinking in a similar way, in order to provide the shared meanings that enable them to reach consensus (Rothschild-Whitt 1979). But even for the non-collectivist organizations, creating shared values helped solidify the high level of commitment required. They had to be committed to pulling their weight in the organization by taking their assigned shifts on the hotline and meeting the needs of callers in ways that required emotional work as well as just the dissemination of information. After training, volunteers continued to meet in support groups and educational meetings, which helped maintain that commitment.

FUNDING

Funding is a crucial issue for social movement organizations, but became paramount for the rape crisis centers that had invented a service they wanted to provide regularly. During the five years between 1974 and 1979 the rape hotlines formalized their programs considerably and funding sources pushed them toward institutionalization.

By the late 1970s the problem of rape had gained traction outside of the grassroots movement, and was being discussed at all levels of government, which led to government funding becoming available. The activists had succeeded in getting rape on the public agenda, along with the problem of violent crime in general, which created a political opportunity for feminist anti-rape activists. Funding rape services became a particular nexus for state involvement in the movement. Early city funding had been limited. In 1978 and 1979 the California Department of Social Services provided additional funding. The establishment of the National Center for the Prevention and Control of Rape (NCPCR) as part of NIMH in 1975 brought a stream of federal money into movement-related projects. In addition, the federal Law Enforcement Assistance Administration began offering grants for rape crisis services in 1974.

Public funding, however, changed the terms of work for these organizations. ELARH, for example, applied for the Department of Social Services grants available in 1978 and 1979. Increasingly stringent demands accompanied the funding. Whereas ELARH had previously provided whatever services they could, at their own discretion, taking the modest state grants ($5000–$10,000) required providing "a whole lot of service for very little money," including 24 hour hotline coverage, accompaniment and advocacy, and community education.

Corporate funders also began to appear, but the activists were dubious about them. For example, East LA upheld the Chicano community's boycott of the Coors Company. All of the Los Angeles area organizations rejected funding from the Playboy Foundation, which was the most visible aspiring corporate donor for women's groups during these years.

Larger amounts of money for ongoing services began to be offered by criminal justice agencies in the mid 1970s. The Law Enforcement Assistance Administration (LEAA), the funding branch of the Justice Department, began to sponsor research and reports that were critical of how the criminal justice system handled rape. However, many of the feminist anti-rape activists remained hostile toward the criminal justice system. Politically oriented feminists had a theory of the state; they viewed law enforcement in particular as repressive. The LEAA's main purpose was to improve prosecution rates, and in offering funding to rape crisis groups, the agency ignored the fact that that goal was not always compatible with rape crisis goals of helping the victim (Schecter 1982: 187).

In LACAAW the question of applying for LEAA funding led to the first split in the organization, as a participant recalls:

[T]he line [had been] going for about a year on a hand to mouth kind of basis, looking for and writing proposals to whoever we could find to write them to. We tried the city, and we tried foundations, but when it came to submitting a proposal to the Law Enforcement Assistance Administration, which was a very likely source of funds for us, the membership of the Commission divided right down the middle. ... [W]e never did apply for that money, so the people who left must have been those who wanted to, and those who stayed were the ones who refused ... [W]e saw ourselves as ... an alternative to criminal justice system involvement for rape victims, because the criminal justice system was doing so badly, and ... the issue was that if we took money from the criminal justice system then we would have to participate in that system. And in fact, most of the LEAA money had with it, as a requirement, the necessity that whatever victim uses the services make a report, a police report.

And at that time we were advising women not to.

Because of their critical stance toward law enforcement, the more radical feminist anti-rape activists rejected the temptation of this "easy" source of money. Other groups accepted LEAA funds, and gained considerable budgets.

While LEAA money was controversial, government agencies were the most likely source of funding, so organizations sought funding from apparently more benign sectors of the state, such as the mental health or social service agencies. Cooptation from this direction was more subtle, involving the imposition of bureaucratic requirements and promotion of a perspective requiring social service agency intervention, downplaying the feminist political message.

The story of LACAAW's search for funding and the changes it wrought in the organization provide insight into the dynamic between participants' beliefs about how things should be done, the need for resources to do the work, and unforeseen consequences of choices made in managing these tensions. LACAAW's transformation warrants attention because it eventually became the most powerful of the hotlines in the area, and because it represents an unusual case of long-term survival of a group that maintained collectivist structure and process.

LACAAW's Funding Saga

In 1975 LACAAW succeeded in getting a small grant from the state Department of Social Services for innovative crisis intervention. Two members of the group became paid staff members for the first time. The following year LACAAW and a Community Mental Health Center (CMHC) applied together for a grant from the new National Center for the Prevention and Control of Rape (NCPCR), a program of the National Institutes of Mental Health. Their two-year project was a research and demonstration center on rape prevention education. Although the grant was earmarked for community education, it also ensured the survival of the hotline, since the same people were running both projects. The $150,000 NIMH grant lasted from 1976 to 1978 and enabled LACAAW to increase the salaries of the two co-directors and hire additional staff, which led to dramatic changes in its internal organization and decision-making process.

Other new tasks were also required: having been incorporated into the social service grant economy the activists had to meet its requirements for accountability and conduct systematic assessments of need and impact. These requirements put pressure on the organization to formalize its basic approach to work, which proved to be a source of tension for the members. Counterculture activists who never thought they would be working in "the system" found themselves doing all kinds of routine bureaucratic chores in order to continue their activist work.

Federal Comprehensive Education and Training Act (CETA) funding further exacerbated the structural and procedural changes in the organization. Many non-profit organizations gained workers they otherwise could not afford to pay through CETA positions during this period. However, they did have to meet certain standards in order to qualify for the positions. Once LACAAW had become a formal entity with a budget from the NIMH grant, it was able to pursue CETA slots. However, taking CETA money created a huge contradiction for the organization. It brought in as staff members people who had no relationship to the movement. As one member put it, "Everybody who had been there before was doing it out of the dedication and commitment that comes out of being a feminist and wanting this service to take place." Working as a collective required a fundamental shared commitment to the project. The inclusion of women who had no activist inclination and further were untrained workers, created chaos in the organization. Furthermore, the necessity of supervision, a hierarchical relationship, pressed the organization toward a more bureaucratic

structure that conflicted with its previously collectivist process.

Meanwhile, the NCPCR-NIMH grant, which by then served as the financial lifeline for the hotline, lasted only for two years. Tensions arose between the partners on the grant. The LACAAW women knew that the mental health center would go on whether the grant was renewed or not, whereas they were much more dependent on it for survival. In addition to apprehension over resources, there was an "undercurrent of distrust" over claims to expertise, with hotline staff feeling that their pioneering work would be co-opted by more socially legitimate experts.

In 1978 the second year of grant money ran out. Documents from the organization's files suggest an increasingly desperate search for funds, from the first up-scale fundraising event to an "open letter to the women's community" pleading for help. Conditions at the hotline rapidly deteriorated. The problems with money brought to the surface other dissension that had been plaguing the organization. Tensions between staff members erupted and a substantial turnover in leadership occurred for the first time since the organization's founding five and a half years earlier.

LACAAW's plight was not unique. Many of the rape crisis organizations found themselves in financial crises by 1979. The Southern California Rape Hotline Alliance, resurrected after a hiatus, increasingly focused its attention on the political fortunes of various state and federal bills that held the promise of future funding. The Pasadena YWCA announced that it no longer could support the rape crisis program, which would have to find other money or close down. ELARH was funded by an inadequate Department of Social Services grant. In the early months of 1979 the financial crisis was so severe that several groups in southern California announced that they could no longer afford their phone service, essential to operating a hotline. In March, the Southern California Rape Hotline Alliance held a press conference to inform the media and public about the crisis in funding.

Ironically, even in the midst of this crisis for the movement, new rape crisis services began to appear in more established agencies, such as hospitals. For example, the Santa Monica Rape Treatment Center at Santa Monica Hospital was quickly gaining legitimacy for its professional "treatment" of rape victims, and was squeezing out some of the support for community-based programs.

Thus, 1979 was a turning point in the anti-rape movement in California. This crisis was a watershed event in LACAAW's history, as it reconstituted itself with a different structure, and made the decision to apply for funding from the state law enforcement agency, the Office of Criminal Justice Planning. This new state funding quickly became the standard means of support for California rape crisis programs.

State funding for rape crisis services became institutionalized in a paradoxical context. California's tax revolt movement, Reagan's election, and the recession of the early 1980s all contributed to the contraction of social service spending. But this period saw the expansion of crime-related services. Quite divergent political streams merged to support funding for rape crisis services. Begun under a liberal Democratic administration, rape crisis funding continued and expanded under the subsequent Republican ones, until California's deepening fiscal crisis of the early 1990s.

The OCJP Sexual Assault Program

In 1980 California state legislation substantially increased the funding for rape crisis services and mandated ongoing support. The bill created a three-branch program including support for direct services to rape victims through rape crisis centers; training for District Attorneys about rape, and training for law enforcement. The bill was accompanied by an appropriation and the new program was to be administered by the Office of Criminal Justice Planning.

The Office of Criminal Justice Planning was founded in 1968 to administer federal LEAA block grants, which were for improving the criminal justice system and providing victim services. After the LEAA funding was phased out in 1980, California state legislation directed the OCJP to continue developing criminal justice programs. The Sexual Assault Branch was created by the Waters legislation under a Democratic governor, but programs related to victim and witness services, child abuse, crime watch, battered women's shelters, as well as rape crisis proliferated during the subsequent Republican administration.

The legislation establishing the OCJP's Sexual Assault Branch contained an unusual arrangement authored by Maxine Waters, the sponsoring legislator. Waters, an African-American state assemblywoman from Los Angeles, also sat on the State Commission on the Status of Women and made sure that State Commission on the Status of Women was given the authority to appoint more than half of the State Advisory Committee (SAC), the body set up to advise the agency on developing and implementing its program. Thus, the SAC allowed feminists (albeit officially sanctioned, moderate ones) some oversight of the OCJP sexual assault program. It insured that women as an organized group had input and represented feminists moving onto the terrain of the state (Reinelt 1995). The other members of the SAC, appointed by the OCJP, were drawn from the criminal justice system, including district attorneys, public defenders, and law enforcement officials. In addition to its composition favoring representation of women, the State Advisory Committee was given unusual authority to make actual decisions, not just recommendations, on who got the grants from the OCJP.

Finally, the first chief of the OCJP Sexual Assault Branch was a woman who had come out of the rape crisis movement. She had directed the Yolo County Rape Crisis Center for four years, coming to that from a background in social work and as a probation officer. She represented a more mainstream strand in the movement than many of the activists in Los Angeles. During her work in Yolo County (in which the state capital, Sacramento is located), she initiated organizing a statewide coalition of rape crisis centers. Shortly thereafter, she was hired by the state agency.

These arrangements suggest that feminism was beginning to have some impact in the traditional political arena, as sympathetic state leaders treated feminists as legitimate constituents. But by co-opting some of the demands and representatives of the movement, i.e., the State Commission on the Status of Women, other more radical elements of the feminist movement were marginalized, including many of the Los Angeles activists. Their continuing criticisms and suspicions of the state then appeared to be unreasonable in light of the concessions made.

Once she became head of the OCJP's Sexual Assault Program, the director's orientation to the issue of rape became a source of friction in the movement. Her hiring seemed to represent the state's legitimization of the "social service" ideological position. Later, as conflicts arose between politically oriented feminists and social service proponents, her move and those of other women from rape crisis centers to the OCJP came to signify to the radical women in the movement the dangers of cooptation. These conflicts were played out over issues as diverse as lesbians in the movement to the requirements of data collection during crisis intervention. Over the years, the fact that the OCJP tended to hire women who came from the politically moderate social service framework reinforced the perception that the state was trying to silence radicals. This magnified the schism between these strands in the movement, which was compounded in practice by the increasingly direct competition among rape crisis centers for funds from the state.

In the midst of major organizational upheaval, LACAAW finally accepted "law enforcement" money, which enabled it to survive and continue to provide services. However, that resolution was not smooth or easy. The debates within and among organizations, the emergence of a split between the "moderates" and "radicals," and the friction over required bureaucratization kept the rape crisis centers in flux for many years.

From Stopping Violence to Managing Rape?

Stopping violence against women is ultimately a project of changing gender relations, because rape, battering, incest, and other violence are rooted in the power men have over women. Both gender structures and consciousness must be changed. The feminist anti-rape movement focused on changing consciousness—redefining women's rights to their bodily and psychological integrity. Changing consciousness led to rape prevention education, along with the provision of services for victims of rape. Although more structural changes were the ultimate political goal of many in the movement, day to day crisis work became the most visible and central aspect of its work. This tendency was promoted and institutionalized by the ways in which state funding was offered and managed.

This history shows the dynamics of change within feminist movement organizations and in their relationships with the state agencies they encountered. Despite the trend toward assimilated, moderate, individualistic service provision, I found a strong thread of resistance from the feminist political elements in the movement.

In this excerpt I have focused on the processes of institutionalization in social movement organizations. The story of LACAAW, with some comparison to other organizations, allows us to see how the internal dynamics and conditions of founding of SMOs interact with external context and pressures. The trend toward a social service agency orientation was promoted by the anti-rape movement's choice of an action repertoire that included service provision. The organizations' consequent reliance on state agencies for funding consolidated this shift in orientation, and was the most prominent characteristic of the changes in the movement during its first fifteen years. Involvement with the state began early, but escalated in California when most rape crisis organizations became reliant on OCJP funding for survival. The resulting shift in orientation encompassed both ideological challenges to the movement and reduced autonomy. Rape crisis organizations changed their work in response to state agencies' application of everyday bureaucratic processes, backed up by the ultimate threat of lost funding.

But state policy was also changed by the movement. The anti-rape activists of the 1970s named a problem and helped set an agenda that the state responded to through new laws, policies and money. Despite their distaste for becoming enmeshed with the state, and particularly a law enforcement agency, activists chose to continue their agenda of turning rape victims into survivors, and working for changing gender relations to the extent that they can.

Feminist demands and state responses converged at the point of what happens after the fact of violence: having rape taken more seriously, having laws that do not blame the victim, having fairer standards of judging "facts" in sexual assault cases, having stricter punishment of attackers, and the subject of this study, providing services to victims. The state funds rape prevention services, but at much lower levels than it funds crisis intervention. In the context of the pervasive social construction of gender the limited rape prevention work represents a very modest effort to change gender relations. This suggests that the state incorporates feminist goals only in limited ways.

I argued in *Confronting Rape* that the institutionalization of state funding for rape crisis services constituted a move toward merely "managing" rape, i.e., helping women after the fact. However, social life is never that simple.

In the years since *Confronting Rape* was published, some of the organizations I studied have continued to transform themselves as their definitions of confronting violence evolves. LACAAW, one of the oldest rape crisis centers in the US, is now called Peace Over Violence, and has a broad range of programs that represent its identity after 35 years of activism. The Peace Over Violence mission statement still expresses the goal of transforming society: "Building healthy relationships, families and communities free from sexual, domestic and interpersonal violence." And the organization's website contains a "Manifesto" that captures the spirit of the organization's roots in social movement, both providing services and changing consciousness.

DISCUSSION QUESTIONS:

1. What were the sources of transformation in the anti-rape movement?

2. What do we mean by the *institutionalization* of social movements? Can you think of other examples?

3. What do you think collectivist organization offers participants, compared to more conventional, hierarchical or bureaucratic organizations?

4. How does interacting with the state transform social movement organizations?

REFERENCES

Baumgartner, Frank R. and Christine Mahoney (2005) "Social Movements, the Rise of New Issues, and the Public Agenda" in David S. Meyer, Valerie Jenness, and Helen Ingram, eds., *Routing the Opposition: Social Movements, Public Policy, and Democracy*, Minneapolis: University of Minnesota Press.

Burt, Martha R., Gornick, Janet C. and Pittman, Karen (1984) *Feminism and Rape Crisis Centers*, Washington, D.C.: The Urban Institute.

Byington, Diane B., Martin, Patricia Yancey, DiNitto, Diana M. and Maxwell, M. Sharon (1991) "Organizational Affiliation and Effectiveness: The Case of Rape Crisis Centers," *Administration in Social Work* 15: 83–103.

Ferree, Myra Marx and Hess, Beth B. (1985) Controversy and Coalition: The New Feminist Movement, Boston: Twayne Publishers.

Kriesi, Hanspeter (1996) "The Organizational Structure of New Social Movements in a Political Context" in Douglas McAdam, John McCarthy, and Mayer Zald (eds.) Comparative Perspectives on Social Movements, Cambridge: Cambridge University Press.

Martin, Patricia Yancey (2005) Rape Work: Victims, Gender, and Emotions in Organization and Community Context, New York: Routledge.

Martin, Patricia Yancey, DiNitto, Diana, Byington, Diane and Maxwell, M. Sharon (1992) "Organizational and Community Transformation: The Case of a Rape Crisis Center," Administration in Social Work 16: 123–45.

Meyer, David S., Valerie Jenness, and Helen Ingram, eds. (2005) Routing the Opposition: Social Movements, Public Policy, and Democracy, Minneapolis: University of Minnesota Press.

Reinelt, Claire (1994) "Moving onto the Terrain of the State: The Battered Women's Movement and the Politics of Engagement," in Myra Marx Ferree and Patricia Yancey Martin (eds) Women's Organizations: Harvest of the New Women's Movement, Philadelphia: Temple University Press.

Rothschild-Whitt, Joyce (1979) "The Collectivist Organization: An Alternative to Rational-Bureaucratic Models," American Sociological Review 44 (August): 509–27.

Schecter, Susan (1982) Women and Male Violence: The Visions and Struggles of the Battered Women's Movement, Boston: South End Press.

Tilly, Charles (1978) From Mobilization to Revolution, Reading, Massachussetts: Addison-Wesley.

Turner, Ralph and Killian, Lewis (1987) Collective Behavior, Third Ed, Englewood Cliffs, New Jersey: Prentice-Hall, Inc.

...

What You Can Do

- Raise awareness on your campus
- Volunteer at the local shelter
- Attend police interviews, court hearings, and trials with victims to show support
- Do not question victims about the circumstances—just show support
- Promote and support Title VII
- Know your university's policy on sexual assault, and ask for the university resources required in all class syllabi and class websites.

CHAPTER 7

HOW 'ROE V WADE' STARTED WITH STUDENTS, BIRTH CONTROL, AND A PAY PHONE

By Rachel Brown

https://rewire.news/article/2018/01/19/how-roe-started-pay-phone/

■ ■ ■

Discussion Questions

1. How did the unique way in which the women organized contribute to the success of their efforts?

2. The University of Texas took extreme measures to stop the publication and distribution of the *Rag*. Are you surprised a university tried to limit free speech? What about the *Rag* was threatening to the University?

3. What did the students' win against the university ultimately lead the women to do?

What You Can Do

- Familiarize yourself with local women's health clinics
- Follow state and federal legislation to keep up-to-date on laws related to reproductive rights
- Know your advocacy organizations, and support them
- Volunteer at a women's health clinic
- Identify and support the legislators who support women's reproductive rights
- Vote
- Determine the health care available to women at your own university

Feminist Art as an Instrument of Social Change

This section introduces the use of art as activism and political speech. Feminist art made a fundamental change to the art world during the second wave by addressing oppression and sexism. No longer content to paint and create what was deemed "gender appropriate," women began pushing back and created art meant to be as much of a political statement as a work of art. This type of activism changed the way the art world saw women artists, ushering in a new level of respect and acknowledgment.

CHAPTER 8

Frontiers in Feminist Art History

By Jill Fields

If we can bring in women's history, we can bring in women's future.

Judy Chicago, 1976

In the televised reality competition series *Work of Art: The Next Great Artist*, young artists compete each week in various challenges testing their abilities to make art on demand within a limited time. I just watched the recently concluded second season's episodes over a couple days while recovering from the flu. Over and over again the contestants' enthusiastic and affluent art auctioneer mentor, the series' stylish and wealthy art and fashion scene host, and the show's successful and at times perceptive art world judges—a critic, a gallery owner, and a guest who is often an artist him- or herself—encouraged the artists to make work based upon their personal experiences; to experiment with a range of materials and methods, including performance art; and to challenge themselves by confronting emotional obstacles to their work. Those who did so were rewarded with prize money, "immunity" from being dispatched in the next week's episode, and appreciative praise from the judges during their "crit." Not surprisingly, the final three contestants in their last challenge to determine who would win the grand prize of one hundred thousand dollars and a solo exhibition at the Brooklyn Museum of Art all made art that centered on explicitly represented personal feelings

and experiences, especially mourning, loss, and longing.

Women artists have done well on *Work of Art*, which has as one of its executive producers Sarah Jessica Parker of *Sex and the City* fame. Though I've yet to see a challenge for the artists to create feminist art as the show has done for pop art, confrontational art, and portraiture, some of the female contestants have focused on gender issues and the body—often their bodies—in the work they make on the show. The Brooklyn Museum of Art's extraordinary Sackler Center for Feminist Art may go unmentioned despite the museum's prominent role in the series, but the feminist art movement's influence is clearly present in the aesthetics and approaches upheld in this reality show and the serious attention given to its female contestants.[1]

The absence of explicit acknowledgment of feminist art's impact upon contemporary artwork and practices is a wider phenomenon. Judith Brodsky and Ferris Olin fear with reason that "feminist innovations have become so thoroughly embedded in contemporary perspectives that their role in introducing these ideas is in danger of being erased."[2] Though relatively ignored as a movement by high-profile museums for a long period, during the past five years a number of major exhibitions in the United States and Europe have reassessed the innovations, impact, and legacy of the feminist art movement that began in the 1970s. In 2007 *WACK! Art and the Feminist Revolution* at the Museum of Contemporary Art in Los Angeles and *Global Feminisms*—along with the permanent installation of Judy Chicago's *The Dinner Party* (1974–79)—at the Sackler Center for Feminist Art gave feminist artists and their movement a renewed and enhanced level of recognition from coast to coast. Subsequent feminist art retrospectives were held in the Netherlands, Russia, and Spain, and exhibitions of women artists' work that had languished in museum basements followed at the Pompidou in Paris and the Museum of Modern Art in New York City. Despite the pleasures viewing these shows afforded, whether or how such exposure transforms standard narratives of modern and contemporary art history remains to be seen.[3]

These recent feminist art exhibitions have coincided with emerging studies of the US women's movement that provide new evidence and reconsiderations of its history. Some of this research explores the efforts of activists outside major centers like New York City to explain more fully how the far-reaching effects of feminism were initiated and enacted across America in places like Dayton, Ohio, and Gainesville, Florida. The personal and political achievements of the women's movement necessarily took place not only in big cities but in homes, schools, public spaces, and workplaces nationwide. The feminist art movement developed in conjunction with the wider women's movement because female artists faced discrimination in pursuing professional careers and because art depicting women's subjective experiences was discouraged and disparaged by the art world establishment. Feminist artists challenged the exclusion of women artists from galleries and museums; created new aesthetic practices; and developed innovative forms, styles, and subjects of representation to portray female experiences and critique a range of gendered restraints on women's agency from trivialization to violence. They also

built new institutions to support women making and exhibiting their art. Understanding how feminist aims were achieved and also thwarted requires investigating the many localities, both large and small, in which goals were formulated, articulated, and fought for in addition to their appearances on national agendas and arenas.[4]

The essays exploring feminist art history collected in this special issue of *Frontiers* are part of that effort. They similarly provide new information and suggest new ways to consider both the political and the cultural history of the women's movement, as well as the history of feminist art more specifically. Michelle Moravec's study of the internationally active yet locally based West East Bag, better known as WEB, Joanna Gardner-Huggett's investigation of the Artemisia gallery in Chicago, Kathleen Wentrack's assessment of the first international feminist art exposition in Amsterdam, Tal Dekel's overview of feminist artists in Israel, and Jennie Klein's review of the 2011 *Pacific Standard Time* exhibit at Otis College of Art and Design on the Woman's Building speak in varying ways to the issues of collective work and feminist identity, in addition to broadening the geographic scope of feminist art inquiry that is necessary for fuller understanding of this movement and its effects.

Political histories typically emphasize large urban centers and government capitals; art histories can be even more narrowly focused on artists who work in cultural capitals. For example, the dozens of *Pacific Standard Time* exhibitions mounted in museums and galleries in Los Angeles and Southern California from fall 2011 to spring 2012 focusing on art created in that region from 1945 to 1980 point out that even artistic achievements in Los Angeles have generally been considered, when not ignored entirely, far less important than those that took place in New York City.[5] Feminist art history has been more inclusive geographically not only because the field began in defiance of traditional narratives that excluded and denigrated women artists but also because the 1970s achievements of artists and art historians in California were so extraordinary and significant to the movement's foundational moments and trajectories. They include the launching in 1970 by Judy Chicago and her students of the first Feminist Art Program at Fresno State in Central California; the creation of the first major feminist art installation, *Womanhouse* (1972), in Hollywood by Judy Chicago and Miriam Schapiro and their students in the second Feminist Art Program at CalArts; and the opening of the unprecedented Woman's Building in Los Angeles in 1973 by cofounders Judy Chicago, Arlene Raven, and Sheila Levrant de Bretteville.[6]

Feminist art history thus has been distinct from traditional art history in its origins, content, and purpose since its beginnings. Early forays in feminist art research were motivated by political, personal, and academic goals. Judy Chicago aimed early on in the collective work of the Feminist Art Program to reclaim the lost history of women artists to restore—if not create—a truer picture of women's artistic contributions, find sources of inspiration for herself and her students, and bolster their belief in their own artistic potential. As they broke from conventional artistic subjects, methods, and pedagogy to find new ways to represent female experiences and make it more possible for female art students to succeed as professionals, Chicago and her students scoured libraries and used bookstores to locate information about and create slide libraries of women artists who were absent or dropped from conventional historical narratives. Linda Nochlin's virtually simultaneous, though more individual, activities on the East Coast produced one of the first undergraduate women's art history courses in the United States and the germinal 1971 essay "Why Have There Been No Great Women Artists." The title suggests the problem women artists faced, that is, the widespread view that women had never before produced great art and were thus unlikely ever to become capable of doing so. However, Nochlin's central purpose was to point out the institutional and discursive barriers that had stymied female artists' careers. The essay also launched feminist art history as a field of study within an academic discipline and, in tandem with protests by artists against Los Angeles and New York City museums' failure to equitably exhibit work by women and artists of color, led to Nochlin curating with Ann Sutherland Harris the first major historical survey of women artists at the Los Angeles County Museum of Art in 1976. Corresponding efforts by art critic Lucy Lippard drew attention to contemporary art by women in essays and also exhibits she curated that transcended academia and the (alternative) art scene and enriched the terms upon which women's artistic production could be analyzed.[7]

As feminist art history—like women's studies—took on a life of its own distinct from the broader mobilizations of the women's movement, scholars in this active field developed theories regarding feminist aesthetics; deployed gender as a category of analysis to assess artistic production by men and women across a wide spectrum of time and space; engaged in archival research to recuperate the work and lives of women artists of the past; focused wider attention on diverse women artists of the present; and interrogated disciplinary structures and categories from the perspective of gender, including the very notion of art.[8] The huge outpouring over the past four-plus decades of books and articles appearing both in new journals emerging from this field and in established art history venues is testament to the richness of this arena of investigation and its methodologies and to the energies unleashed by the feminist perspectives on art first articulated in the early 1970s. The activism of the women's movement and the feminist academics who supported the creation of women's studies programs also made it more possible to pursue these projects in university settings. Perhaps, too, the integration of the feminist art movement's innovations into contemporary art generally that Brodsky and Olin reference also contributed to the legitimization of feminist art inquiry.[9]

As it became a significant movement and arena for scholarship, debates within feminist art history and among feminist artists paralleled developments in feminist theory. A school of thought emerged that discounted some earlier innovations and perspectives by categorizing them as essentialist. Anti-essentialists focused on the distinction between sex and gender, finding the latter a socially constructed, historically situated phenomenon. They criticized feminists such as Mary Daly and Adrienne Rich for purportedly making assertions about shared female identity and sisterhood based on an unchanging, ahistorical female biological "essence" that mirrored and therefore sustained anti-feminist ideologies and inequitable gender structures. However, Mira Schor has noted that essentialism "was a category created by its opposition," and others have found that few 1970s feminists actually engaged in such reductive thinking. More often, such feminists distinguished—however problematically—between their radical revaluation of female experience and harmful "biological determinism."[10]

The anti-essentialist argument was bolstered by an increasing interest across academic disciplines in poststructuralism that began in the 1980s and at times eclipsed feminist theory outside of women's studies. Poststructuralism directed attention to the operations of language and mobilization of discursive strategies and thus provided theoretical frameworks for intensified questioning of gendered categories and their constructions and for explaining why oppositional movements had faltered. Yet in directing attention away from fixed centers of power and authorial/artistic intention, some strains of poststructuralism undermined or set aside as passé the work undertaken by women and people of color to represent their subjective experiences, imagine social and cultural transformations, create alternative institutions, and articulate standpoints against inequitable and what often appeared to be immovable hierarchies. Nonetheless, feminists continued to analyze and depict how gender operated in all spheres on a broad scale and in daily life, both historically and in the contemporary moment.[11]

Debates about essentialism among feminist art historians and artists differed from those in other disciplines because they were grounded in discussions of particular works of art and artists' statements explaining their work. For example, Judy Chicago and Miriam Schapiro's advocacy of "central core" imagery, a term that named their quest to represent distinctive aspects of the female body in new ways as a feminist revisioning that also challenged the primacy of the phallus in Western iconography and built environments, could be read about but also seen in paintings like Schapiro's *Big OX No. 2* (1968) and Chicago's *Through the Flower* (1973). Some anti-essentialists feared calls for such imagery promoted a new orthodoxy that would limit the definition of feminist art and squelch the creativity of female artists just as they were finding new forms of expression and opportunities for making and showing their art. However, art historians Norma Broude and Mary Garrard instead found the "crippling prohibition against essentialism" more oppressive.[12]

More pointed feminist critiques of anti-essentialism emerged in the late 1980s. Diana Fuss, Teresa di Lauretis, Linda Alcoff, and others explained how some form of essentialism was intrinsic to any discussion of difference and identity. According to Fuss, "While a constructionist might recognize that 'man' and 'woman' are produced across a spectrum of discourses, the categories 'man' and 'woman' remain constant" and therefore are relied upon as essential terms of analysis. Furthermore, "the strength of the constructionist position [in] its rigorous insistence on the production of social categories like 'the body' and its attention to systems of representation … is not built on … essentialism's demise [but] … by displacing it … onto the concept of sociality." Thus, strategic deployment of essentialism—a concept suggested by Gayatri Spivak and understood not as an inherent and fixed biological quality but in relation to women's experiences, habits, practices, and positionality—remains a necessary "risk" to challenging the status quo.[13]

Growing attention to the female body by feminist activists, scholars, and artists as a category of analysis and site upon which the workings of discourse, structures of power, sexuality, and resistance could be read and traced transcended aspects of the essentialist–social constructionist binary. Artists and historians who rejected the concept of female imagery still upheld the centrality of feminist art practices that reclaimed the representation of the female body from its central role in Western art as an object of spectatorship and evidence of male artists' professional skill.[14] Aspects of essentialism also cannot be fully disengaged from the feminist art movement's successful challenge to the divide between (masculine) high art and (feminine) craft, the influential but still necessary call for more equitable inclusion of works by women in museums and galleries, the rejection of viewing artists as singular (male) geniuses, and the emphasis on collaborative projects involving only women.

Despite the problematics of anti-essentialism, some poststructuralist critiques spoke to the real difficulties of organizing on behalf of women and in the name of a universal sisterhood, which were more than evident by the end of the 1970s. Efforts to create a stronger women's movement in and outside the academy that acknowledged differences among women and was therefore more inclusive had mixed results.[15] These struggles continue to reverberate. Yet even as feminist activists and their organizations faced internal struggles and conservative backlash, they never ceased fighting for greater opportunities for women in work, politics, art, and education; for reproductive rights; to end violence against women; to challenge cultural stereotypes and unequal domestic responsibilities; and to enforce hard-won gains such as Title IX, among other aims. Efforts at consciousness-raising continued, though in formats different from the small groups that had fueled the movement—and feminist art education—across the country in the early 1970s. In addition to marches, rallies, and political campaigns, women who were not activists per se encountered feminist ideas in a range of separatist locations (at least through the early 1990s), such as health collectives, book stores, and art galleries, and from mass-market and feminist-press novels, plays, poetry, and nonfiction, in addition to films and television. Historian Jane Gerhard terms women's access to widely available cultural forms of feminism, in which she includes Judy Chicago's *The Dinner Party*, popular feminism.[16]

The 1996 exhibition *Sexual Politics: Judy Chicago's Dinner Party in Feminist Art History*, co-curated by historian Amelia Jones at the Hammer Museum in Los Angeles, was a turning point in the reassessment of 1970s feminist art. Chicago's iconic installation, Jones argues, "came to be seen ... as paradigmatic of all that was problematic about certain strands of 1970s feminism." Identifying herself in her introduction to the exhibition catalog as a poststructuralist, Jones is nonetheless critical of anti-essentialist claims. Since the 1960s, Jones asserts, many works by feminist artists, such as Hannah Wilke, Lynn Hershman, Karen LeCocq, Carrie Mae Weems, Lauren Lesko, and Marlene McCarty, referenced the body in diverse ways, including varying approaches to "cunt art," a term Chicago and her Feminist Art Program students pioneered and popularized. In considering such works together, Jones's analysis broke apart reductionist characterizations not only of the 1970s but also of rigid generational breaks in modes of representation. Doing so further destabilized the 1980s linkage between poststructuralism and anti-essentialism, at least in the field of feminist art.[17]

In the broader public sphere of feminist discourse, however, the 1990s rise of "post-feminist" best-sellers reinvigorated caricatures of 1970s feminists as strident, politically correct opponents of all things fun. In addition, conceptions of generational feminist divides were bolstered by the assertion of a "third wave" at the same time mainstream media reports asked once again whether "feminism is dead." Self-identified third wave feminists and their contemporaries who were "not feminists ... but" grappled with post-feminism's self-defeating claims while still facing discrimination and the expectations that accompanied supposedly being able "to have it all." Such contradictions, according to third wave feminists Leslie Heywood and Jennifer Drake, marked their generation's "desires and strategies." They embraced "second wave critique as a central definitional thread" and emphasized "cultural production and sexual politics" located in alternative music scenes and icons as "sites of struggle."[18]

Some third wave feminists hoped to reenergize a movement by and for younger women that would capture the nation's attention like feminism had in the 1970s and yet speak to diverse women's contemporary concerns.[19] Acknowledging contributions by women of color and lesbians, they looked toward a new direction in feminist theory based on intersectionality, a term introduced by Kimberle Crenshaw in 1989 to address multiple and overlapping constructions of gender, race, class, and sexuality. Advanced initially by women of color, intersectionality stimulated thinking about a wealth of topics across disciplines. In addition, new tropes emerged that sparked research and analysis beyond their fields of origin, such as the concept of borderlands articulated by Gloria Anzaldúa and Chicana feminists, the closet and queer perspectives from gay and lesbian studies, and the rethinking of the body offered by feminists working in disability studies. Additional tropes already in use, such as the diaspora, which had long been used to reference first the Jewish and then the African experience of traumatic dispersal, became more widely applied in feminist analysis of the transnational.[20]

Artist Suzanne Lacy defines feminist art as "investigations of gender identity and the relationship of art practice to public life," grounded in "activist traditions within ethnic communities, ... media deconstruction, and ... political art," and produced in collaborative projects that aim to shift "power relationships in *daily* life." Indeed, it is impossible to imagine the feminist art movement's impact occurring to the degree that it has without such collective work, whether

this meant smaller groups of performance artists such as The Waitresses, the larger group of artists who ran the institution they came out of, the Woman's Building, or specialized groups who worked on, for example, the large-scale public performance projects organized by Lacy.[21] The articles collected in this special issue of *Frontiers* assess artists' work on a range of collaborative projects—including the building of the feminist art movement itself—in familiar and less well-known locations that engaged the public, challenged entrenched institutions, created new forms of representation, and opened up greater opportunities for women to make and exhibit their art. Together, the articles offer new evidence and perspectives that augment understandings of how and why feminist artists came together and drifted apart, formed organizations and developed feminist practices, shared their work and debated definitions of feminist aesthetics, and in the process created and sustained a movement that profoundly changed the course of feminism as well as contemporary art history.

Moravec's article, "Toward a History of Feminism, Art, and Social Movements in the United States," offers the first detailed study of West East Bag (WEB), a self-described "International Liaison Network for Women Artists" founded in September 1971 by Judy Chicago, Lucy Lippard, and Miriam Schapiro and perhaps also Grace Glueck, Ellen Lanyon, and Marcia Tucker. Utilizing the social science framework of "diffusion," Moravec explains how the artists who started this important early organization made connections to artists in other cities in this pre-Internet era when doing so required mailing postcards; sending out newsletters; and traveling for visits, lectures, and conferences. Moravec also uses this evidence to consider the feminist art movement as a social as well as an aesthetic movement that functioned within the wider context of women's liberation.

Diffusion theory points toward "the activist networks, organizational brokers, and communication channels that facilitate the spread" of a movement.[22] Diffusion can occur by direct personal contact, by indirect mechanisms such as texts, and through "mediated mechanisms [that] involve a third party" (23). Moravec especially finds these distinctions useful as she sifts through archival evidence—such as the organization's newsletters—because conflicting stories or gaps in the record make it difficult to determine decisively how WEB began. Moravec further contextualizes these origins by describing how the group's founders were inspired by and had participated in art activism already under way that challenged museums in New York City and Los Angeles to include more work by women and artists of color. In creating their own network for women artists, they sought to break down barriers for women in art schools, museums, and galleries. Overcoming the isolation women artists often experienced was a critical and at times exhilarating first step. As networks were established in New York, Los Angeles, and Chicago, meetings in which slides of work by women artists were shared and critiqued might last for hours and became opportunities to develop ideas about just what constituted feminist art practice.

Moravec traces the relationship between artists and women's liberation activists by relating, for example, newsletter suggestions for reading books like Shulamith Firestone's *The Dialectic of Sex*. A fascinating section of this article details how consciousness-raising (CR) techniques were defined by and diffused among WEB members and thus is a welcome contribution to understanding more fully how CR quickly spread nationwide and was so effective in sparking activism of all kinds. The nonhierarchical organizational structure of WEB, which included rotating editorship of the newsletter to different localities for each issue, was aligned with CR and women's liberation practices. Yet in a telling incident that suggests the tensions that would emerge later among feminists, a Bay Area chapter of the National Organization for Women (NOW) organized a protest in 1972 against an exhibit at the University Art Museum in Berkeley of E. J. Bellocq's photographs of New Orleans prostitutes because its members found them offensive. Local WEB members initially were reluctant to join the protest because they didn't agree with the cause. However, they decided to picket the museum anyway to protest the absence of art by women exhibited by the museum. Though subsumed in this case, conflicting views about whether particular representations upheld or undermined feminist perspectives—especially those artworks referencing female sexuality and depicting the female body—became central to movement debates and art criticism. Highlighting specific examples of how such conflict played out in practice illuminates understandings of theoretical concerns.

Moravec counts among the achievements of WEB the slide registries that members put together and archived. The first newsletter noted work by one thousand artists. She concludes, however, that though individual artists benefited from such efforts, institutions remained largely unchanged. However, in addition to the greater though not fully equitable exhibition of work by women and artists of color, two of the goals articulated by art activist groups like WEB have been instituted, though not universally: payment to artists when their work is resold for larger sums and the institution of guidelines that protect curators from the financial pressures of the art market. Though Moravec wonders whether "the goal of WEB [was] to help women achieve greater visibility and success in the art world or ... to raise the consciousness of women artists about sexism and patriarchy in the context of the art world ... [and] in the larger society," she concludes, "feminist artists across the United States would take up a range of approaches for both of those ends" (42).

Joanna Gardner-Huggett's article, "Artemisia Challenges the Elders: How a Women Artists' Cooperative Created a Community for Feminism and Art Made by Women," explores one of those sites, the Artemisia Gallery in Chicago. Inspired by a summer WEB conference presentation in Chicago by Harmony Hammond, a member of the women's cooperative gallery AIR (Artists in

Residence) in New York City, Artemisia was established in September 1973 after Chicago Art Institute student Joy Poe returned from a visit to AIR. In fact, there was so much enthusiasm for the concept that another women's gallery, ARC, opened in Chicago within a week. Poe had enlisted the help of several other artists to recruit members by visiting 150 women artists in their studios. Signaling the intention to challenge women's exclusion from dominant institutions and assert that women could indeed be professional artists, the gallery opened its doors across the street from the Museum of Contemporary Art.

By naming their gallery in honor of Italian painter Artemisia Gentileschi (1593–1692), whose work prior to feminist art scholarship interventions had been both underappreciated and in some instances attributed to her artist father, the founders also signaled their interest in recuperating the history of women artists and inserting themselves into an alternative narrative of Western art history that included women. Art critics also took the name to indicate a militant stance, due to Gentileschi's paintings of women committing violence against men, such as *Judith Decapitating Holofernes* (c. 1618), some of which were used for gallery flyers.[23] Gardner-Huggett points out a crucial difference between the defiant acts of individual women depicted in Gentileschi's paintings and the gallery project, in that the artists were joining together to collectively resist the status quo by creating a separatist space for art and action. She is particularly interested in how the gallery formed a feminist community for women artists in Chicago.

Gardner-Huggett acknowledges the larger context of women's liberation groups in Chicago as critical for articulating feminist aims and instigating feminist struggle that also inspired the founding of a women's art gallery. Like WEB, Artemisia's structure was intended to be nonhierarchical in the mode of women's liberation organizations. As a result Artemisia became a place where women first encountered a feeling of sisterhood and felt that they had truly engaged with feminism. Gallery members, like those at the Woman's Building and the Feminist Art Programs before, rotated tasks to learn the necessary skills for professional careers, from installing to promoting exhibitions. The gallery also sponsored art education in public events, such as workshops and lectures by visiting artists. Judy Chicago spoke in 1974 about *The Dinner Party* project that she had just begun, Arlene Raven and Ruth Iskin discussed feminist art education in 1977, and Lucy Lippard curated a show in 1979.

Though the gallery engaged in feminist process, members did not seek to define feminist aesthetics. Nonetheless, the issue came to a head when Joy Poe staged a controversial performance on rape in 1979 that many members found offensive. Poe and almost half the gallery's members resigned due to deeply held disagreements among the artists about the intention, effect, and meaning of Poe's work despite their shared identification as feminists. More prosaic problems included the perennial search for sufficient resources and the difficulties inherent in voluntary efforts regarding time commitments. Gardner-Huggett also thoughtfully explores the absence of racial diversity in the gallery that haunted women's separatist institutions nationwide. Artemisia instituted a minority recruitment effort with some success, but not until the late 1980s. In that decade the gallery, like other arts organizations, faced the declining funding and increasing real estate costs fostered by the culture wars and Reaganomics. Under these conditions, and with some modest success for women artists in infiltrating mainstream arenas, separatist galleries found survival more difficult. Gardner-Huggett concludes that Artemisia's history "can reveal where activist tactics in the arts are effective and where they are likely to fail when attempting to create inclusive communities" (69). In addition, adding Chicago to the map of feminist art activism emphasizes the importance of regional scenes and the complex variations they produced.

Kathleen Wentrack's article, "What's So Feminist about the *Feministische Kunst Internationaal*? Critical Directions in 1970s Feminist Art," assesses the impact of this exhibition of European and American feminist art held in Amsterdam in 1978 and 1979 "to reveal how feminist art was understood" at the time (76). To do so, she addresses central questions about the definition and purpose of feminist art, a major concern of exhibition organizers, and describes in detail a number of artworks. Known as *FKI*, this exhibition is largely unknown to feminist art historians in the United States, though considered "the most important feminist art exhibition of the decade in Europe" (79). It was mounted in two parts, both of which emphasized the new media and performance art that feminists embraced because they were free from male-dominated artistic styles and traditions and provided flexibility in expressing the artists' subjectivity and experiences. As in the United States artistic practice often grew out of consciousness-raising.

In setting the scene, Wentrack explores distinctions between feminist art's status in the United States and in Europe. For example, Europe lacked the close-knit feminist art communities that women in the United States, as Moravec and Gardner-Huggett demonstrate, had worked so hard to establish. A few small groups did emerge in Europe during the early to mid-1970s, and German artist Ulrike Rosenbach established a feminist art school in 1976 in Cologne after teaching in the Feminist Art Program at CalArts. However, European artists also faced more skepticism about the potential of feminist art to be seen as politically important, even by leftists. Yet the organizers of *FKI* insisted that work included in the show be explicitly feminist, whether or not the artist was an activist in the more conventional sense. This criterion, of course, led to fascinating debates about what that meant.

Wentrack defines feminist art as "artwork that exposes the prejudices against women in society, challenges representations of women in art, engages feminist issues or theory, critiques … femininity, develops new media … , or presents new ways of working with traditional art materials" (77). Themes developed in the exhibition include a "critique of traditional roles, a search for women's true desires and feelings, and a proposal of alternatives to what constitutes woman" (80). In addition, questions about the existence of a feminist aesthetic were intertwined with reconsiderations of just what that constituted and how one should assess quality in art by women. Debates about the representation of beauty and the nude female body were inseparable from concerns about the reappropriation of feminist art by the male gaze and how the status of female artists could be undermined as a result. Yet the focus on the body, particularly the artist's body, was crucial, especially to performance or "action" art, as it was known in Europe. Art exhibited at *FKI* also attended to women's work in and outside the home, alternative role models, collaborative feminist practice, and sexuality.

The critical reception of *FKI* was mixed, with some critics appreciating the innovative art on display and others dismissing feminist art as political statements rather than works of art. One critic missed the point entirely, protesting, "who wants to see art about household drudgery?"[24] Yet in assessing the legacy of *FKI*, Wentrack finds that many of the themes it presented continued to reverberate in feminist art exhibitions that followed. In the 2009 Dutch exhibit *Rebelle: Art & Feminism 1969–2009*, pieces from the 1960s and 1970s were juxtaposed with those made after 1990, reaffirming the groundbreaking role of *FKI*.

Tal Dekel's article, "Feminist Art Hitting the Shores of Israel: Three Case Studies in Impossible Times," provides insight into the status of feminist art in Israel by focusing on three artists associated with the movement who were all born in the 1940s: Yoheved Weinfeld, Miriam Sharon, and Pamela Levy. Dekel situates their lives and work in the wider context of Israel's unique history as a country established in 1948 in the wake of the Holocaust. The founding principles of the state included equality for women and their conscripted service in the army, which suggested that "women in Israel were already emancipated" (112). However, the work of building a haven for the thousands of refugees who arrived in the 1940s, plus the waves of Jewish immigrants who followed, while enduring periodic wars, did not always bear out this utopian vision. Yet as women's status and opportunities continued to improve in education and the workplace in the 1970s, and feminist activism emerged in that decade, the movement primarily looked to the United States for inspiration. According to scholar Hannah Safran, conflicts about whether to focus strictly on issues of concern to women or to address all forms of discrimination hampered the movement's effectiveness.

The prevailing view within the art scene in Israel in the 1970s was that separate consideration of female artists' work was not necessary. In addition aesthetic objections were made to the concept of "women's art." Nonetheless, female artists engaged with a range of feminist art practices and interacted with feminist artists in the United States. Yoheved Weinfeld began in the 1970s to make autobiographical and conceptual work and also performance art that explored female sexuality, bodily detritus, menstruation, and the female body as object of the male gaze in work that corresponds to that of Judy Chicago, Faith Wilding, and Hannah Wilke. When Miriam Sharon returned to Israel in 1977 after an exhibit of her work with Ana Mendieta's at AIR in New York City, she initiated an energetic agenda of egalitarian feminist art activism, including mounting group exhibitions and founding a magazine. In her artwork she celebrated women's relationship with nature, the revaluation of the materials and methods of feminized crafts, and reverence for the Great Goddess. She also upheld the artistic traditions of indigenous peoples from the Sinai Desert, with whom she collaborated. Pamela Levy, an immigrant to Israel from the United States who arrived in 1976, initially produced textile collages made from ordinary and secondhand fabrics along the lines of the Pattern and Decoration Movement, associated with Miriam Schapiro.

She explored the artistic practices of women in diverse cultures, particularly the widespread use of wooden stamps by women in Asia and Africa.

Dekel does not explore in this article (as she does elsewhere) how these artists' Jewish identity figured in their art, though she mentions in reference to Weinfeld that this was an important theme of her work. Intersectional analysis could be helpful in doing so. According to Yael Guilat, there was no lack of "women artists, critics, or curators" in Israel, though few of them identified as feminists in the 1970s and 1980s.[25] Thus, rather than viewing Israeli feminists and female artists' work as a "delayed reaction" to innovations that began elsewhere, perhaps Israeli women's agency may be more richly understood in relation to the experience of women in minority communities in the United States whose feminist identity emerged on a "separate road." As Dekel's article suggests, fuller evaluation of Israeli women's encounters with feminism and feminist art on their own terms and in their historical contexts engenders new insights about feminism in Israel and also of multivalent feminist trajectories relevant to minority group experiences and diverse global feminist perspectives.[26]

The special issue ends with Jennie Klein's review of *Doin' It in Public: Feminist and Art at the Woman's Building*, an exhibition at the Ben Maltz Gallery, Otis College of Art and Design, that opened in October 2011 as part of *Pacific Standard Time: Art in L.A., 1945–1980*, an unprecedented set of exhibitions held in over sixty museums in Southern California between October 2011 and March 2012. Klein finds collaboration a key concept in this comprehensive survey. The Woman's Building rejected dominant art world standards across the board, focusing instead, as curator Meg Linton writes in the catalog, on the "collaborative creative energy and output [that] challenged the prevailing, patriarchal concept of the lone artistic genius."[27] Klein assesses the many documents and artworks on display in the exhibition to consider the larger impact of the Woman's Building. The work completed and shown there, the feminist art education it sponsored, and the existence of the institution itself inspired women both nationally and internationally "to become feminists and artists" (129). Engaging with political issues and injustice was central to the definition of feminist art projected by the Woman's Building and the many performance groups and art collectives it fostered. In that Klein also points to the importance of cultural feminist ideas at the Woman's Building, its history suggests possibilities for reconsidering the divide often drawn between cultural and political feminism.[28]

All of the articles in this special issue describe separatist institutions that functioned either briefly, such as WEB and the organizations created by Miriam Sharon in Israel, or for extended periods, such as Artemisia and the Woman's Building. *FKI* in a sense also operated for a few years as a separatist space for feminist art in Europe. The themes that emerge from these studies—the centrality of collaboration, the debates over process, the concerns over the role of the individual artist, the struggles over defining feminist art, the search for funding, and the embrace of new forms of media and art making—resonate with what has been asserted previously about the movement's history. However, considering the distinct experiences, innovations, accomplishments, and difficulties of artists working in varied locations enriches our understanding of feminist art as a social and aesthetic movement that transformed people's lives and perceptions on a global scale. The opening of spaces outside New York City and Los Angeles provided opportunities for female artists in greater numbers of locations to engage with, learn about, and produce feminist art and, indeed, to diffuse feminist perspectives and practices. In addition these new localities on the feminist art map provided opportunities for higher-profile artists like Judy Chicago, Harmony Hammond, and many others to travel to present their ideas and art and also to meet new artists and view their work. This meant not only increased possibilities for including regional artists' work in gallery exhibitions in larger venues but also further occasions for Los

Angeles– and New York City–based artists to articulate their vision and engage in discussion with like-minded artists. Doing so surely aided the development of the theories and practices of feminist art nationwide. Incorporating local perspectives provides a fuller picture of how the feminist art movement became so influential and offers greater possibilities for wider and lasting acknowledgment of its achievements.

NOTES

I am grateful to Andrea Pappas for her comments on an early draft of this essay and for conversations about it I was lucky to have with Loretta Kensinger and Jennie Klein. I also benefited from Gayle Gullett's close reading of this essay, perceptive comments, and editorial expertise.

1. *Work of Art: The Next Great Artist*, season 2 (Bravo, 2011).

2. Judith Brodsky and Ferris Olin, "Stepping Out of the Beaten Path: Reassessing the Feminist Art Movement," *Signs* 33, no. 2 (2008): 330. Amelia Jones similarly expects, despite the recent attention, feminist art "to be rendered obsolete once again." See Amelia Jones, "1970/2007: The Return of Feminist Art," *X-TRA: Contemporary Art Quarterly* 10, no. 4 (2008), http://www.x-traonline.org/past_articles.php?articleID=184. See also Mira Schor, "Backlash and Appropriation," in Norma Broude and Mary Garrard, eds., *The Power of Feminist Art: The American Movement of the 1970s, History and Impact* (New York: Abrams, 1994), 248–63. Schor compares the critical reception and career trajectories of feminist artists to male artists who were influenced by the Feminist Art Program while they were students at CalArts.

3. Cornelia Butler and Lisa Gabrielle Mark, eds., *WACK! Art and the Feminist Revolution* (Los Angeles: Museum of Contemporary Art, 2007) (exhibition catalog); Maura Reilly and Linda Nochlin, eds., *Global Feminisms: New Directions in Contemporary Art* (New York: Merrell, 2007); Camille Morineau, *Women Artists: elles@centrepompidou* (Paris: Centre Georges Pompidou, 2009) (exhibition catalog); Cornelia Butler and Alexandra Schwartz, eds., *Modern Women: Women Artists at the Museum of Modern Art* (New York: Museum of Modern Art, 2010); Joanna Isakk, Gaia Cianfanelli, and Caterina Iaquinta, "Curatorial Practice as Collaboration in the United States and Italy," in Jill Fields, ed., *Entering the Picture: Judy Chicago, the Fresno Feminist Art Program, and the Collective*

Visions of Women Artists (New York: Routledge, 2012), 294.

4. Judith Ezekiel, *Feminism in the Heartland* (Columbus: Ohio State University Press, 2002); Carol Giardina, "Origins and Impact of Gainesville Women's Liberation, the First Women's Liberation Organization in the South," in Jack E. Davis and Kari Frederickson, eds., *Making Waves: Female Activists in Twentieth-Century Florida* (Gainesville: University Press of Florida, 2003), 312–21. For overviews of the women's movement see Ruth Rosen, *The World Split Open: How the Modern Women's Movement Changed America* (New York: Viking, 2000); Myra Marx Ferree and Beth Hess, *Controversy and Coalition: The New Feminist Movement across Four Decades of Change*, 3rd ed. (New York: Routledge, 2000); Estelle Freedman, *No Turning Back: The History of Feminism and the Future of Women* (New York: Ballantine, 2002); Sara Evans, *Tidal Wave: How Women Changed America at Century's End* (New York: Free Press, 2003).

5. *Pacific Standard Time* catalogs include Chon Noriega, Terezita Roma, and Pilar Tompkins Rivas, eds., *L.A. Xicano* (Los Angeles: UCLA Chicano Studies Research Center Press, 2011); C. Ondine Chavoya and Rita Gonzalez, eds., *ASCO: Elite of the Obscure, A Retrospective, 1972–1987* (Ostfilderrn, Germany: Hatje Cantz Verlag, 2011); Kellie Jones, ed., *Now Dig This: Art and Black Los Angeles, 1960–1980* (New York: Prestel, 2011); Rebecca McGrew and Glenn Phillips, eds., *It Happened at Pomona: Art at the Edge of Los Angeles, 1969–1973* (Pomona: Pomona College of Art, 2011); and Rebecca Peabody, Andrew Perchuk, Glenn Phillips, Rani Singh, and Lucy Bradnock, eds., *Pacific Standard Time, Los Angeles 1945–1980* (Los Angeles: Getty Research Institute, 2011).

6. Fields, *Entering the Picture*; Sondra Hale and Terry Wolverton, eds., *From Site to Vision: The Woman's Building in Contemporary Culture* (Los Angeles: Otis College of Art and Design, 2011); Meg Linton and Sue Maberry, *Doin' It in Public: Feminism and Art at the Woman's Building* (Los Angeles: Otis College of Art and Design, 2011) (exhibition catalog); Alex Donis, curator, *Collaboration Labs: Southern California Artists and the Artist Space Movement* (Santa Monica, CA: 18th Street Arts Center, 2011); Laura Meyer and Faith Wilding, *A Studio of Their Own: The Legacy of the Fresno Feminist Experiment* (Fresno: CSU Fresno Press, 2009); Amelia Jones, ed., *Sexual Politics: Judy Chicago's* Dinner Party *in Feminist Art History* (Berkeley: University of California Press, 1996); Broude and Garrard, *Power of Feminist Art*.

7. For more on the research into women's art history undertaken during the Feminist Art Program, see sources cited in previous note and Gail Levin, *Becoming Judy Chicago: A Biography of the Artist* (New York: Harmony Books, 2007). Nochlin taught "Women and Art" at Vassar College in 1969; see Linda Nochlin, "Starting from Scratch: The Beginnings of Feminist Art History," in Broude and Garrard, *Power of Feminist Art*, 130–37; Linda Nochlin, "Why Have There Been No Great Women Artists," *Art News* 69 (Jan. 1971); Linda Nochlin and Ann Sutherland Harris, *Women Artists: 1550–1950* (Los Angeles: Los Angeles County Museum of Art, 1976). Lucy Lippard, *The Pink Glass Swan: Selected Feminist Essays on Art* (New York: New Press, 1995), includes essays written from 1970 to 1993.

8. Hilary Robinson, ed., *Feminism-Art-Theory: An Anthology, 1968–2000* (Oxford: Blackwell, 2001), offers a wealth of readings. The three volumes edited by Norma Broude and Mary Garrard—and their introductions—gauge changes in the field over time. See Norma Broude and Mary Garrard, eds., *Feminism and Art History: Questioning the Litany* (New York: Harper and Row, 1982), *The Expanding Discourse: Feminism and Art History* (New York: Harper Collins, 1992), and *Reclaiming Female Agency: Feminist Art History after Postmodernism* (Berkeley: University of California Press, 2005). For more on feminist aesthetics see, e.g., the special issue *Feminism and Traditional Aesthetics, Journal of Aesthetics and Art Criticism* 48, no. 4 (1990); Hilde Hein and Carolyn Korsmeyer, eds., *Aesthetics in Feminist Perspective* (Bloomington: Indiana University Press, 1993); Peggy Zeglin Brand and Carolyn Korsmeyer, *Feminism and Tradition in Aesthetics* (Philadelphia: Pennsylvania State University Press, 1995). For a survey of women's art history that synthesizes much important scholarship see Whitney Chadwick, *Women, Art, and Society*, 4th ed. (New York: Thames and Hudson, 2007) (1st ed. published in 1990).

9. The 1987 opening of the National Museum of Women in the Arts (NMWA) in Washington, DC, and its research library is another significant accomplishment. Like the establishment of NMWA, the activities I am summarizing here refer primarily to feminist art scholarship in the United States.

10. Mary Daly, *Gyn/Ecology: A Metaethics of Radical Feminism* (Boston: Beacon Press, 1978); Adrienne Rich, *Of Woman Born: Motherhood as Experience and Institution* (New York: Norton, 1976); Wendy Kolmar and Frances Bartkowski, "Lexicon of the Debates," in Wendy Kolmar and Frances Bartkowski, eds., *Feminist Theory: A Reader* (Mountain View, CA: Mayfield Publishing Company, 1999), 39–40; Schor,

"Backlash and Appropriation," 254; Broude and Garrard, *Reclaiming Female Agency*, 2; Arlene Raven, "Women's Art: The Development of a Theoretical Perspective," *Womanspace Journal* 1 (Feb.–Mar. 1973): 14, quoted in Amelia Jones, "The 'Sexual Politics' of *The Dinner Party*: A Critical Context," in Broude and Garrard, *Reclaiming Female Agency*, 417.

11. Linda Alcoff, "Cultural Feminism versus Post-Structuralism: The Identity Crisis in Feminist Theory," *Signs* 13, no. 3 (1988): 405–36; Joan Scott, "Deconstructing Equality-Versus-Difference: or, The Uses of Poststructuralist Theory for Feminism," *Feminist Studies* 14, no. 1 (1988): 32–50; Linda Nicholson, ed., *Feminism/Postmodernism* (New York: Routledge, 1990). See also the extensive bibliography in Robinson, *Feminist-Art-Theory*.

12. Judy Chicago, "Woman as Artist," *Everywoman* 2, no. 7 (1972): 24–25, excerpt reprinted in Robinson, *Feminism-Art-Theory*, 294–95; Judy Chicago and Miriam Schapiro, "Female Imagery," *Womanspace Journal* 1 (1973): 11–17, excerpt reprinted in Amelia Jones, ed., *The Feminism and Visual Culture Reader*, 2nd ed. (New York: Routledge, 2010), 53–56; Barbara Rose, "Vaginal Iconology," *New York Magazine* 7 (Feb. 11, 1974), excerpt reprinted in Robinson, *Feminism-Art-Theory*, 575–77. Opposing views include Pat Mainardi, "A Feminine Sensibility?" *Feminist Art Journal* 1, no. 1 (1972): 4, 25; Judith Stein, "For a Truly Feminist Art," *Big News* 1, no. 9 (1972), excerpts reprinted in Robin-son, *Feminism-Art-Theory*, 295–98. Broude and Garrard find the concept of essentialism more useful when analyzing "*masculinist* essentialisms" (italics in original); see Broude and Garrard, *Reclaiming Female Agency*, 2.

13. Diana Fuss, *Essentially Speaking: Feminism, Nature and Difference* (New York: Routledge, 1989), 3–4, 6, 20. Fuss also discusses Luce Irigaray's "strategic use of essentialism" in chap. 4, "Luce Irigaray's Language of Essence." See also Teresa de Lauretis, "The Essence of the Triangle; or, Taking the Risk of Essentialism Seriously: Feminist Theory in Italy, the U.S., and Britain," in Naomi Schor and Elizabeth Weed, eds., *The Essential Difference* (Bloomington: Indiana University Press, 1994), 1–39. See also Naomi Schor's introduction to that book. Gayatri Chakravorty Spivak references strategic essentialism in *The Post-Colonial Critic*, ed. Sarah Harasym (New York: Rout-ledge, 1990), 11, and in her earlier work *In Other Worlds: Essays in Cultural Politics* (New York: Methuen, 1987). See also Alcoff, "Cultural Feminism." For anti-essentialist perspectives see Chris Weedon, *Feminist Practice and Poststructuralist Theory* (Oxford: Blackwell, 1987); Judith Barry and Sandy Flitterman-Lewis, "Textual Strategies: The Politics of Art-Making,"

LIP: Feminist Arts Journal (1981–82), reprinted in Hilary Robinson, ed., *Visibly Female: Feminism and Art: An Anthology* (New York: Universe Books, 1988), 106–17. Griselda Pollock, "Women, Art and Ideology: Questions for Feminist Art Historians," *Woman's Art Journal* 4, no. 1 (1983): 39–47, includes anti-essentialist critiques that also offer important frameworks for research and analysis of women's art history. The book Pollock coauthored with Rozsika Parker, *Old Mistresses: Women, Art and Ideology* (New York: Pantheon Books, 1981), provides greater detail in terms of argument and evidence. Amelia Jones's review of *The Power of Feminist Art* points out problems with both the anti-essentialist perspective and its opposition. See Amelia Jones, "Power and Feminist Art (History)," *Art History* 18, no. 1 (1995): 435–43. For a recent examination of these issues see Jennie Klein, "Goddess: Feminist Art and Spirituality in the 1970s," *Feminist Studies* 35, no. 3 (2009): 575–602.

14. Lynda Nead, *The Female Nude: Art, Obscenity and Sexuality* (London: Rout-ledge, 1992); Kristen Swinth, *Painting Professionals: Women Artists and the Development of Modern American Art, 1870–1930* (Chapel Hill: University of North Carolina Press, 2001).

15. bell hooks addresses essentialist thinking and difference in *Feminist Theory: From Margin to Center* (Boston: South End, 1984).

16. Jane Gerhard, "Judy Chicago and the Practice of 1970s Feminism," *Feminist Studies* 37, no. 3 (2011): 591–618. Gerhard cites her forthcoming book, *Judy Chicago, The Dinner Party, and the Rise of Popular Feminism, 1970-2007* (Athens: University of Georgia Press).

17. Amelia Jones, "Sexual Politics: Feminist Strategies, Feminist Conflicts, Feminist Histories," in A. Jones, *Sexual Politics*, 20–38; A. Jones, "'Sexual Politics' of *The Dinner Party*, 415.

18. Rebecca Walker coined the term "third wave" in the 1992 *Ms.* article "Becoming the Third Wave," which she wrote in the wake of the Clarence Thomas Supreme Court nomination hearings. See also Jennifer Pozner, "The 'Big Lie': False Feminist Death Syndrome, Profit, and the Media," in Rory Dicker and Alison Piepmeier, eds., *Catching a Wave: Reclaiming Feminism for the 21st Century* (Boston: Northeastern University Press, 2003), 31–56; Leslie Heywood and Jennifer Drake, "Introduction," in Leslie Hey-wood and Jennifer Drake, eds., *Third Wave Agenda: Being Feminist, Doing Feminism* (Minneapolis: University of Minnesota Press, 1997), 4, 7–8. See also Astrid Henry, *Not My Mother's Sister: Generational Conflict and Third-Wave Feminism*

(Bloomington: Indiana University Press, 2004). *Bitch* editor Lisa Jervis rejects the term in "The End of Feminism's Third Wave," in *Ms.* (2004), http://www.msmagazine.com/winter2004/ thirdwave.asp. Recent studies critiquing the wave metaphor include Nancy Hewitt, *No Permanent Waves: Recasting Histories of U.S. Feminism* (New Brunswick: Rutgers University Press, 2010); Kathleen Laughlin et al., "Is it Time to Jump Ship: Historians Rethink the Waves Metaphor," *Feminist Formations* 22, no. 1 (2010): 76–135; Kathleen Laughlin and Jacqueline Castledine, *Breaking the Wave: Women, Their Organizations, and Feminism, 1945–1985* (New York: Routledge, 2011).

19. Heywood and Drake, *Third Wave Agenda*; Jennifer Baumgardner and Amy Rich-ards, *Manifesta: Young Women, Feminism, and the Future* (New York: Farrar, Straus, and Giroux, 2000); Dicker and Piepmeier, *Catching a Wave*. The editors' "Introduction," in Stacy Gillis, Gillian Howie, and Rebecca Munford, eds., *Third Wave Feminism: A Critical Exploration*, 2nd ed. (New York: Palgrave/Macmillan, 2007), provides a helpful overview of third wave discourse, including criticisms of third wave feminism as overshadowing feminists of color. See also Kimberly Springer, "Third Wave Black Feminism?" *Signs: Journal of Women in Culture and Society* 27, no. 4 (2002): 1059–82; Daisy Hernández and Bushra Rehman, eds., *Colonize This! Young Women of Color on Today's Feminism* (New York: Seal Press, 2002).

20. Kimberle Crenshaw, "Demarginalizing the Intersections of Race and Sex: A Black Feminist Critique of Antidiscrimination Doctrine, Feminist Theory, and Antiracist Politics," in Joy James and T. Denean Sharpley-Whiting, eds., *The Black Feminist Reader* (Oxford: Blackwell, 2000). Vivian May sketches out a longer history of the concept in African American women's thought in her essay "Intersectionality," in Catherine Orr, Ann Braithwaite, and Diane Lichtenstein, eds., *Rethinking Women's and Gender Studies* (New York; Routledge, 2012), 155–72. Representative works that disseminated new tropes of analysis include Gloria Anzaldúa, *Borderlands: The New Mestiza = La Frontera* (San Francisco: Aunt Lute Books, 1987); Eve Kosofsky Sedgwick, *The Epistemology of the Closet* (Berkeley: University of California Press, 1990); Rosemarie Garland-Thompson, "Integrating Disability, Transforming Feminist Theory," *NWSA Journal* 14, no. 3 (2002): 1–31; Chandra Mohanty, "Under Western Eyes: Feminist Scholarship and Colonial Discourse," in Chandra Mohanty, Ann Ruso, and Lourdes Torres, eds., *Third World Women and the Politics of Feminism* (Bloomington: Indiana

University Press,1991), 51–80; Jana Evans Braziel and Anita Mannur, eds., *Theorizing Diasporas* (Oxford: Blackwell, 2003).

21. Suzanne Lacy, "Affinities: Thoughts on an Incomplete History," in Broude and Garrard, *Power of Feminist Art*, 264, 269, 270.

22. Rebecca Givan, Kenneth M. Roberts, and Sarah A. Soule, "The Dimensions of Diffusion," in *The Diffusion of Social Movements*, ed. Rebecca Given et al. (Cambridge: Cambridge University Press, 2010) 3, quoted in Moravec, "Toward a History of Feminism, Art, and Social Movements in the United States," 23.

23. Chadwick, *Women, Art and Society*, 102, 105–13; Mary D. Garrard, "Artemisia and Susanna," in Broude and Garrard, *Feminism and Art History*, 147–72.

24. Tim Guest, "Not Demanding Enough," *Fuse* 4, no. 2 (1980): 125, quoted in Wentrack, "What's So Feminist about *Feministische Kunst International*?," 98.

25. Yael Guilat, "Where Have You Been and What Have You Been Doing? Gendered Discourse in the Early 1990s and Its Place in Ha'Aretz Art Criticism," *Israel* 9 (2006): 197, quoted in Dekel, "Feminist Art Hitting the Shores of Israel," 125.

26. Benita Roth, *Separate Roads to Feminism: Black, Chicana, and White Feminist Movements in America's Second Wave* (Cambridge: Cambridge University Press, 2004). For articulations of this perspective see the Combahee River Collective, "A Black Feminist Statement" (1977), and the important anthologies Gloria Hull, Patricia Bell-Scott, and Barbara Smith, eds., *All the Women Are White, All the Men Are Black, but Some of Us Are Brave* (New York: Feminist Press, 1982), and Cherrie Moraga and Gloria Anzaldúa, eds., *This Bridge Called My Back: Writings by Women of Color* (New York: Kitchen Table, Women of Color Press, 1983).

27. Meg Linton, "Foreword: Doin' It in Public: Feminism and the Art of the Woman's Building," in *Doin' It in Public: Feminism and Art at the Woman's Building*, ed. Meg Linton and Sue Maberry (Los Angeles: Otis College of Art and Design, 2011), 16, quoted in Klein, "Doin' It in Public," 131.

28. See, e.g., Alice Echols, *Daring to Be Bad: Radical Feminism in America, 1969-1975* (Minneapolis: University of Minnesota Press, 1989).

• • •

Discussion Questions

1. Think about how art and creativity shapes your own views on social issues. What type of creativity affects you most (i.e., music, movies, TV, paintings, plays, etc.)?

2. How do art and creativity play into your understanding of social movements?

3. Music, TV, and movies, for example, often address current issues, as do paintings and other artistic mediums. Which do you prefer? Are they all equally meaningful? What about political/social graffiti? Is it art or simply graffiti?

What You Can Do

- Attend women art events, and show support, when possible, by purchasing pieces, music, or tickets to events
- Host an event
- Include women artists in feminist activist events like marches, protests, conferences, and other activities
- Check the promotion of female artists in your area and university. If you feel women are not equally represented, find out why they are excluded, and demand change.
- Promote female artist events via social media

CHAPTER 9

All Representation Is Political

FEMINIST ART PAST AND PRESENT

By Josephine Withers

The year 2008 is an exhilarating and challenging moment to be reflecting on feminist art, feminist artists, their impact on our culture, and their place at the table. In the past two years, two major exhibitions circulated in Los Angeles, New York, and Washington, D.C., museums, assessing the history of Second Wave feminist art and presenting a global view of contemporary art: WACK! Art and the Feminist Revolution; and Global Feminisms: New Directions in Contemporary Art. Judy Chicago's monumental *Dinner Party* (1979) opened in its now-permanent location at the Brooklyn Museum as the centerpiece of the new Elizabeth A. Sackler Center for Feminist Art. Both WACK! and Global Feminisms in their turn were riding a long wave with other ambitious retrospective feminist shows stretching back to the Inside the Visible exhibition of the mid-1990s.

In the past five years alone, three other exhibitions assessed the legacy of 1970s feminist art, and two others connected that legacy to the work being done by young artists today.[1] One of these, Claiming Space: Some American Feminist Originators, at American University, was explicitly intended as a counterpoint to the WACK! exhibition being shown concurrently in Washington, D.C. More on that later in this essay.

Depending on what critic or journal you read, feminism is thoroughly imbricated in

---

Principal Exhibitions Discussed in This Essay

- Global Feminisms: New Directions in Contemporary Art (Brooklyn Museum of Art; Wellesley College, 2007). Opening concurrently with the permanent installation of Judy Chicago's *Dinner Party* (1979) in the Elizabeth A. Sackler Center for Feminist Art, Brooklyn Museum of Art.

- WACK! Art and the Feminist Revolution (Museum of Contemporary Art, Los Angeles; National Museum of Women in the Arts, Washington, D.C.; PS 1, Long Island City; Vancouver Art Gallery, 2007–2009).

- Claiming Space: Some American Feminist Originators (The Katzen: American University Museum, Washington, D.C., 2007).

---

mainstream thought; or, the careers—especially mid-careers—of women artists are stalled; at the same time feminists are taking charge in major cultural venues; but then younger women roll their eyes at the mention of the "F" word; at the same time, younger artists are flocking to these and other shows presenting historical and contemporary feminist work. Feminist art is either "so over," or it is gathering momentum.

Overlaying this commentary is a mostly cranky press inclined to trivialize and belittle with snide one-liners. The Global Feminisms show was a particular target: "Sisterhood Is Dispiriting: Power to the Curators at Brooklyn's New Feminist Enclave"; and "They Are Artists Who Are Women: Hear Them Roar."[2] But as a more sympathetic critic observed, "[Although] tagged 'ADHD' by one old school art critic, I personally find the mix [of video, photography, sculpture, and painting] fitting and illuminating. How could an exhibition dedicated to such weighty themes and confronting such daunting competiton for the attention of audiences (we are living in the age of info overload after all) be anything but chaotic?! Expect self-mutilation, violent sexuality and disquieting body images. Expect to be shocked. Expect to feel, to gasp, to think."[3]

The WACK! and Global Feminisms exhibitions were very large, very ambitious, and very different. Although they were conceived independently of each other, that they circulated at the same time invites our considering them in relationship to one another and from there assessing where they are situated in this cultural moment.

The curators of the big sprawling Global Feminisms focused on transnational feminist artists born since 1960, and they selected work created since 1990. In several ways Maura Reilly and Linda Nochlin sought alternative structures for selecting and organizing the show in order to escape familiar hierarchies of center/ periphery or linear chronology, opting instead for dissonant and dialogic relationships between artists. They aimed to provoke viewers "into

asking themselves ... hard questions about their usual assumptions about contemporary art" and positioned themselves as "mediators of cultural exchange" rather than attempting an integrated perspective. The idea was to escape *a priori* ideas about what feminist art might be or look like, say, in Jakarta, Guatemala City, or Kinshasa.[4] To accomplish this, they began their research and selection in countries outside Western Europe and North America and turned to a multinational and multidisciplinary team of specialists to create de novo what global feminisms might be communicating.

The exhibition and the catalog were organized very differently, producing quite different experiences. The exhibition was divided into four themes: Life Cycles, Identities, Politics, and Emotions.[5] Creating surprising, congruent, or dissonant relationships between individual works was the obvious intention. This worked by fits and starts. If two or several neighboring works could speak to each other in such a way as to offer new contexts and meanings that might not be produced otherwise, yes, this thematic grouping was helpful. In many instances, however, I was hard pressed to perceive any such relationship, either to other works or to the theme. In these cases, the whole thematic/ relational scaffolding melted down, and at times I felt adrift, at which point I even questioned the usefulness of such broad and ultimately vague categories. I give Reilly and Nochlin a lot of credit, however, for breaking out of the safe harbor of the curatorial metanarrative and reaching for new ways to think about difference across the spectrum of feminist sensibility. The ideal viewer of this exhibition (which I was not) would be someone able to make multiple visits to the show and from those experiences piece together their own narrative, their own knowledges, in good postmodernist fashion.

What, then, did this exhibition, inaugurating the Sackler Center, convey to this one-time visitor? Perhaps I forgot to mention that the centerpiece in these new galleries was Chicago's newly installed *Dinner Party*. And that was what initially

Related Exhibitions

1977	Ann Sutherland Harris and Linda Nochlin, Women Artists: 1550–1950 (Los Angeles County Museum of Art; University of Texas at Austin; Carnegie Institute, Pittsburgh; and the Brooklyn Museum of Art).
1989	Magiciens de la terre (Centre Georges Pompidou, Paris).
1990	The Decade Show: Frameworks of Identity in the 1980s (Museum of Contemporary Hispanic Art; New Museum of Contemporary Art; Studio Museum in Harlem, New York).
1993	Biennial Exhibition (Whitney Museum of American Art, New York)
1994–96	Inside the Visible: An Elliptical Traverse of the Twentieth Century in, of, and from the Feminine (Beguinage of St. Elizabeth, Kortrijk, Belgium; Institute of Contemporary Art, Boston; and National Museum of Women in the Arts, Washington, D.C.).
1995–96	Division of Labor: Women's Work in Contemporary Art (Bronx Museum of the Arts; Museum of Contemporary Art, Los Angeles).
1995	Sexual Politics: Judy Chicago's Dinner Party in Feminist Art History (Armand Hammer Museum, Los Angeles).
2002	Personal and Political: The Women's Art Movement, 1969–1975 (Guild Hall Museum, East Hampton, N.Y.).
2002	Gloria: Another Look at Feminist Art of the 1970s (White Columns, New York).
2002	Regarding Gloria: An Exhibition of Emerging Artists that Examines the Influence of the Feminist Legacy on a New Generation (White Columns, New York).
2008	Small Things End, Great Things Endure (New Langon Arts, San Francisco).

drew me and many other visitors to the center in the first place. It would be almost impossible to see and think about either of these exhibitions separately from the other, particularly at this inaugural moment, but this apparently was the curators' intention. When asked to comment on the relationship, Maura Reilly (also the director of the Sackler Center) stated that "although the show was placed around the *Dinner Party*, it had no formal relation to it other than that it was in the same space."[6]

Curatorial intentions aside, visitors perforce created their own as they navigated these exhibitions. The most apparent relationships were oppositional and mutually clarifying. The *Dinner Party*: enclosed in its own pristine, carefully controlled theatrical space; giving a sense of being closed off from the world outside; hushed, contemplative, reverential ambience; a linear progression around the triangular table from prehistoric goddess to artist Georgia O'Keeffe (still living at the time of its making); a sense of crystalline completeness. Emerging from this chapel, the white-box, brightly lit spaces of Global Feminisms was cacophonous—orally and visually—and messy, prompting us to wander, loop back, criss-cross; many of the most memorable pieces dealt graphically with mutilation, pain, and psychic disconnection; yet the strong pulsation of the show did lend a coherence so carefully avoided in its conceptual design. The tough subjects notwithstanding, I came away energized and newly confident that these feminist artists knew how to make themselves seen and heard and that this exhibition gave them an expanded space in which to speak their many languages.

The catalog—which is what endures, after all—is more academically organized. Here the artists are grouped regionally, rather than thematically, with essays by scholars and writers with on-the-ground familiarity with the local cultural contexts. In her extended introductory essay, "Toward Transnational Feminisms," Reilly does a great service by clarifying the goals and intentions of Global Feminisms and by situating it within emergent transnational discourses of the past twenty years and feminist art history of the last thirty years.

The ur-event we always return to is Nochlin and Ann Sutherland Harris's groundbreaking exhibition and catalogue, Women Artists: 1550–1950, which opened in Los Angeles in 1977, right at the moment the *Dinner Party* was taking shape in nearby Santa Monica. They are born of the same historical moment in seeking to reinsert women into a history as seen from a Western perspective, with its linear progression and periodization. At the time, we already knew that the recovery strategy of "insert women and stir" was inadequate but nonetheless foundational. More than that, it was an ironic coincidence that as women began to emerge into history and

---

The Dinner Party

The reception of Judy Chicago's *Dinner Party* is a story with many installments stretching over the thirty years it has been circulating (its inaugural exhibition took place at the San Francisco Museum of Modern Art in March 1979). Few feminists, few *people* are neutral on its significance or value, as it inspires tirades and hissy fits, or exultant epiphanies. This is not the place to rehearse this contentious story, but rather to pose some questions about how it will circulate and be received in the future. Whatever attitude we bring to a reading of the *Dinner Party*, it is a significant chapter in the story of feminist art, and its very grandeur, monumental scale, and apparent self-assurance have often invited a resistant reading—"essentialist!" "kitch!" "megalomania!" are some of the nicer epithets. Now that the *Dinner Party* is owned and permanently displayed in a public museum, no longer tethered to the nonprofit art and education organization Through the Flower (founded by Chicago in 1972) that owned and managed it since its creation, we will be watching to see how this will shape the discourse in, of, and around the *Dinner Party*.

Section 4: Feminist Art as an Instrument of Social Change | 105

were no longer "anonymous," other voices now proclaimed the "death of the author."

A few years later, a big hullabaloo erupted around the Museum of Modern Art's (MoMA) rigorously macho International Survey of Recent Painting and Sculpture (1984), the big show that inaugurated the reopening of their expanded galleries. Out of a total of 169 artists selected for the show, only 13 were women. When the curator, Kynaston McShine, was questioned on this, he responded, "any artist who wasn't in the show should rethink his [sic] career."[7] The newly formed Guerrilla Girls weighed in with this message: "I'm a Guerrilla Girl and I'm not at all incensed that the Museum of Modern Art showed only 13 women of the 169 artists in their International Survey of Painting and Sculpture show.... I know these figures occurred only by chance, there was no sexism, conscious or unconscious, at work."[8] A few years later there was an even broader spectrum of criticism of the MoMA's neocolonialist "Primitivism" in Twentieth-Century Art: Affinity of the Tribal and the Modern (1988).

The fallout from both these exhibitions helped to consolidate the new thinking—by negative example—around the interwoven discourses of gender, race, and class. The fruits of this public conversation emerged in the exhibitions Magiciens de la terre (1989), The Decade Show: Frameworks of Identity in the 1980s (1990), and the 1993 Whitney Biennial. Magiciens presented contemporary work and tribal art in a more egalitarian relationship than had MoMA's "Primitivism" show. The Decade Show further dismantled modernist hierarchies as it focused on the identity politics announced in its subtitle. And the Whitney Biennial of 1993 became the cri du coeur for many emergent postmodernist voices, coming as it did in the midst of the so-called culture wars. Even as these shows were being targeted by an exasperated press yearning for more order, more visual pleasure, less politics, and more "art," there was wide acknowledgment that something big was afoot that transcended any particular movement.

The feminism in Global Feminisms would not have come about without these earlier exhibitions; and just as surely, these earlier shows are thoroughly indebted to an expanded feminist discourse. This mutuality undergirds one of the most important arguments of this show: that the strategy of relational analysis "allows us to re-read political, activist, religious, anti-colonialist, environmental, and other work as a kind of 'subterranean, unrecognized form of feminism.'"[9]

The experience of being in the space of WACK! was not unlike Global Feminisms: emotional, rambunctious, sobering, hilarious, life-affirming.[10] Their almost simultaneous openings in March 2007 in prestigious museums on opposite coasts coincidentally marked the thirtieth anniversary of Nochlin and Harris's Women Artists show and the completion of the Dinner Party. As twinned as they appear to be, however, the conversations they engender and respond to carry us down different pathways.

As its subtitle hints, WACK! is a retrospective show, specifically showcasing Euro-American art of the 1970s. Cornelia Butler, the show's curator, writes:

My ambition for "WACK!" is to make the case that feminism's impact on art of the 1970s constitutes the most influential international "movement" of any during the postwar period—in spite of or perhaps because of the fact that it seldom cohered, formally or critically, into a movement the way Abstract Expressionism, Minimalism, or even Fluxus did. For that reason, I want to invoke bell hooks's proposal to resignify the term "feminist movement," to deliver it from its nomenclatorial fixity and reconnect it to the verb "to move"—with all the restless possibility that word connotes.[11]

For a veteran of Second Wave feminism like myself, the show had a comfortable familiarity about it, despite its edginess. I could readily see my own narratives confirmed in the selection and organization of the show, even as I was introduced to new artists and unfamiliar work. Near the entrance was an historical timeline of the period (unfortunately not included in the catalog) that invited multiple connections to the thematically grouped work in the exhibition.[12] I had the privilege of playing cicerone to two different groups—one, women's studies graduate students from the University of Maryland; the other, Veteran Feminists of America-Second Wave feminists like myself. All of them reflected back to me in a multitude of ways that what we accomplished in that decade or so may be history, but it's not over and done with. As with the music of that period, this art can reconnect us to the promptings of our hearts.

Claiming Space: Some American Feminist Originators-a smaller exhibition at American University—ran concurrently with the Washington, D.C., showing of WACK! and while participating in this ongoing historical project, chose a different strategy. If we can liken its bigger sisters—Global Feminisms and WACK!—to a sprawling mansion, each room with its own theatrics and with hidden nooks and a few trap doors, Claiming Space would be an exquisitely crafted jewel box, with each element chosen to create a pleasing and visually integrated narrative. Although curators Norma Broude and Mary Garrard did not pull back from the ugly and painful subjects of rape, social upheaval, or racism endemic to 1970s feminism, their objective also was to present visually stunning and monumental works.[13]

The curators invite us to think about the "space" they are claiming for feminism in several layered ways: first, a place at the table, then in the histories and in the ongoing discourse. The heroic scale of many of the objects in this show is yet another way of claiming space. The exhibition opens with three monumental works that announce some of the great themes of this show: Faith Ringgold's *Die* (1963–1967), Miriam Schapiro's *Big Ox* (1968), and a group of drawings, photographs, and a test plate for Judy Chicago's *Dinner Party* (1979). With her lament

for the violence against both blacks and whites, women and men of the civil rights era, Ringgold reminds us that feminism was born out of this struggle. Schapiro's Ox series is equal parts minimalism and the fleshy body-centric imagery writ large that is such a significant marker of feminist art of this period. And then there is an unexpectedly intimate view of some of the processes Chicago employed in creating the *Dinner Party*: collages, drawings, and a porcelain test plate for the Virginia Woolf place setting. The central core imagery announced in Schapiro's *Big Ox* became the generating iconography of Chicago's work. Seeing them together in this way makes clear their formal and conceptual congruence—one that extends beyond differences of intention, message or style.

Claimin Space makes a compelling argument that feminist artists working in the late 1960s into the early 1980s had an enormous role in defining and expanding out what constitues feminist culture and that any history of the period—social, political, cultural, or art historical—is woefully incomplete if these artists are not fully integrated into those stories. The history of this period and the art of the 1990s simply doesn't make sense otherwise.

Notes

1. The recently established Feminist Art Project, www.feministartproject.rutgers.edu, describing itself as "a collaborative national initiative celebrating the Feminist Art Movement," is an invaluable clearinghouse for feminist exhibitions and art events worldwide.

2. Lee Rosenbaum, "CultureGrrl." in Arts Journal, 23 Mar. 2007 (www.artsjournal.com/culturegrrl/2007/03/sisterhood is dispiritingpowe.html); and Roberta Smith, New York Times, 23 Mar. 2007 (www.nytimes.com/2007/03/23/arts/design/23glob.html?_r = I &oref=slogin).

3. Robin Hauck, in Misstropolis (www.misstropolis.com/index.php/arts/article/globalfeminisms-the-davis-is-back-with-a-bang/).

4. Maura Reilly, Curator's Preface, Global Feminisms: New Directions in Contemporary Art (New York: Brooklyn Museum of Art, 2007), catalog, 11, 12.

5. At its other venue, the Davis Center at Wellesley College, the show was organized around these themes: cultural encounters; power, violence and protest; self as subject/self as object; motherhood; and sexuality and the body (www.misstropolis.com/index.php/arts/article/global-feminisms-the-davis-is-back-with-a-bang/).

6. Lara Taubman, from a roundtable with Deborah Garwood and Sandra Sider, discussing Global Feminisms (www.artcritical.com/sider/SSRoundtable.htm. 4).

7. Quoted in Reilly, Global Feminisms, 23.

8. Josephine Withers, "The Guerrilla Girls," Feminist Studies 14 (Summer 1988): 286.

9. Ella Shohat, quoted in Reilly, Global Feminisms, 38.

10. I visited WACK! several times at the National Museum of Women in the Arts, Washington, D.C. Even the classical surroundings were not enough to tame the WACK! artists.

11. Cornelia Butler, "Art and Feminism: An Ideology of Shifting Criteria," WACK! Art and the Feminist Revolution (Los Angeles: Museum of Contemporary Art, 2007), 15.

12. WACK! themes include, Gender Performance, Gendered Space, Knowledge as Power, Collective Impulse, Social Sculpture, Silence and Noise, Speaking in Public, Making Art History, Taped and Measured, Autophotography. Female Sensibility, Pattern and Assemblage, Body Trauma, Goddess, Family Stories, and Labor.

13. See Josephine Withers, "Exhibition Review of Norma Broude and Mary D. Garrard, Claiming Space: Some American Feminist Originators," www.caareviews.org, posted 19 Mar. 2008.

14. Norma Broude and Mary Garrard used this in the title of their anthology, Feminism and Art History: Questionin8 the litany (New York: Harper & Row, 1982). A sequel was titled The Expandins Discourse: Feminism and Art History (New York: HarperCollins, 1992).

15. Catherine de Zegher, Inside the Visible: An Elliptical Traverse of the Twentieth Century in, of. and from the Feminine (Kortrijk, Belgium: The Beguinage of St. Elizabeth, 1994), 20.

16. See, for example, the special issue on feminist activist art, National Women's Studies Association Journal 19 (Spring 2007). Reilly lists a short but useful bibliography in Global Feminisms, n. 135.

17. Shoshana Felman, What Does a Woman Want1 Readins and Sexual Difference (Baltimore: Johns Hopkins University Press, 1993), 14, as quoted by Griselda Pollock, "Inscriptions in the Feminine," Inside the Visible, 81.

* * *

Discussion Questions

1. What is the importance of *The Dinner Party*?

2. Why do you think there was a resurgence of 1970s feminist art being displayed in the early twenty-first century? What relevance does it have with today's feminism?

3. Why have women artists struggled to be recognized as equal to male artists? Does this lack of recognition exist today? In what context? For example: Are there more male art openings and celebrated artists? Do male works of art still predominately fill museums and galleries?

What You Can Do

- Familiarize yourself with local female artists and support their openings and gallery showings

- Ask local museums and galleries to exhibit more female artists

- Stage your own "opening" in your home or other accessible place, and invite your female artist friends and women in their networks to display their art

CHAPTER 10

I am We

BLACK WOMEN ACTIVISTS WRITING

By Margo V. Perkins

As African American women intimately involved in the Black Power Movement in the United States during the late 1960s and early 1970s, Angela Davis, Assata Shakur, and Elaine Brown all shared a commitment to radical leftist politics and the building of a society free of race and class oppression. Disinclined to seek concessions within the existing socioeconomic structure, each participated in forms of revolutionary activism that sought to expose and aggressively challenge the structural underpinnings of race and class oppression in the United States. To date, they are the only women activists of the Black Power Movement to produce book-length autobiographies chronicling their experiences during this period. Because the nature of their activism as well as the character of their respective narratives is quite different, their stories taken collectively offer important insight into the range and quality of Black women's experiences in 1960s and 1970s revolutionary nationalist struggle.

Compared to Shakur and Brown, Angela Davis's exposure to leftist politics occurred early in life, first through her family and later as part of her formal education. The daughter of college-educated and politically active parents, Davis was granted a scholarship that enabled her to leave her birth town of Birmingham, Alabama, to attend Elizabeth Irwin, a private socialist high school in New York. There, she recalls her first encounter with the *Communist Manifesto,* as well as her participation in the

activist Marxist-Leninist youth organization Advance. As a member of Advance, Davis took part in numerous peace and civil rights demonstrations. Following graduation from Elizabeth Irwin, Davis attended Brandeis University, where she received her undergraduate degree in French, and also became acquainted with the eminent philosopher Herbert Marcuse, who was later to have a profound influence on her political career. Davis's tenure at Brandeis included a year abroad at the Sorbonne in Paris, followed upon her graduation by a fellowship to study philosophy at Goethe University in Frankfurt. While in Germany, Davis participated in several rallies and demonstrations, most protesting U.S. involvement in the war in Vietnam. Lured back across the Atlantic by the dramatic events unfolding in the United States (associated with the shift in the Black liberation struggle from civil rights to Black Power), Davis determined to complete her doctorate in philosophy at the University of California, San Diego, where she could take active part in the struggle while continuing to pursue her studies.

Back in the States, Davis became involved with both the Student Nonviolent Coordinating Committee (SNCC) and John Floyd's Black Panther Political Party (BPPP). (Floyd's BPPP was not affiliated with Newton and Seale's Black Panther Party, originally known as the Black Panther Party for Self-Defense.) Although Davis's work on the west coast included interaction with Newton's Black Panther Party (BPP)

Margo V. Perkins, "I am We: Black Women Activists Writing Autobiography," *Autobiography as Activism: Three Black Women of the Sixties*, pp. 1-20. Copyright © 2012 by University Press of Mississippi. Reprinted with permission.

as well, she decided in the end not to join that organization. Dissatisfied with the rampant sexism in the BPP and its tendency toward ad hoc political (re-)action, Davis states that she chose instead in 1968 to affiliate formally with the Che-Lumumba Club of the Communist Party USA. The Che-Lumumba Club was organized by and for Black members of the Party specifically to address the interests and needs of the Black liberation struggle. When Davis later became a professor at the University of California at Los Angeles (UCLA), her avowed membership in the Communist Party made her a target of the red-baiting campaign carried out by the Board of Regents under then-governor Ronald Reagan. In a case that drew widespread attention, Davis was eventually fired from her job. The chain of events that followed would catapult her onto the international scene. In August 1970, Davis became a wanted fugitive in the aftermath of Jon Jackson's failed Marin County Courtroom siege. Acquainted with Jackson and his family through her work on behalf of the Soledad Brothers Defense Committee, Davis was captured and formally charged by the FBI in October 1970 with murder, kidnapping, and conspiracy, as an accessory to Jackson's crime. For the next twenty-two months, Davis and her legal team, along with supporters in both the United States and abroad, worked diligently to secure her freedom. Finally, on June 4, 1972, Davis was acquitted of all charges. Davis's narrative, titled *Angela Davis: An Autobiography*, published by Random House in 1974, was written largely while she was awaiting trial on charges associated with the Marin County incident. Appearing shortly after her acquittal, Davis's text as resistance literature is tied to her impending struggle. In the preface to her narrative, she asserts, for example, that she deliberately set out to write a "political autobiography" (xvi) that would (1) raise the consciousness of readers by helping them better understand the particular conditions that necessitated resistance struggle by African Americans and other oppressed groups, and (2) encourage others to join the struggle.

Assata Shakur's introduction to political activism was quite different from Davis's. Born JoAnne Byron and reared by her mother and stepfather, maternal grandparents, and maternal aunt, Shakur grew up in both Jamaica, New York, and Wilmington, North Carolina. Although a spirited nonconformist even as a child, Shakur indicates that it was not until her association with a group of African students on Columbia University's campus that she began to acquire political literacy. The students, who were highly conversant in international politics, schooled Shakur in U.S. foreign policy and the issues underlying the war in Vietnam. As her political consciousness expanded, Shakur increasingly sought ways to become involved in resistance struggle. As a student at the City College of New York, she enthusiastically immersed herself in campus and community activism. For a brief period she affiliated with the Harlem branch of the Black Panther Party, before becoming disillusioned with the group for its authoritarian leadership, as well as for many of the same issues Davis identified. Increasingly subjected to police harassment and surveillance for her activities, Shakur went underground to continue her activist work with the Black Liberation Army (BLA), an offshoot of the BPP. The BLA was organized by supporters of Eldridge Cleaver in the aftermath of the Newton-Cleaver split in the Party. While operating underground, Shakur first garnered national attention on May 2, 1973) when she and two other BLA activists, Zayd Shakur and Sundiata Acoli, were violently apprehended by state troopers as they traveled on the New Jersey Turnpike. One state trooper, Werner Foerster, and Zayd Shakur were killed in the incident; Shakur herself was seriously wounded. Over the next several months in police custody, Shakur was indicted on numerous charges, including armed robbery, murder, attempted murder, and kidnapping. In all instances except one, she was eventually acquitted or had the charges against her dismissed. On March 25, 1977, however, she was convicted of Foerster's death. Shakur served six years in prison, from the time of her apprehension in 1973 to her successful escape in 1979 from the Clinton Correctional Facility for Women in New Jersey. Granted political asylum in Cuba, Shakur continues to reside there today. Although she is technically free, her status in exile is precarious since she remains on the FBPs list of wanted fugitives. Consequently, while Shakur's autobiography, titled *Assata,* was published by Lawrence Hill & Co. in 1987 (eight years after her escape from prison and flight to Cuba), her text, like Davis's, remains bound to impending struggle. The publicity that accompanied her conference with Pope John Paul II during his historic visit to Cuba in January 1998, for instance, resulted in a renewed push by New Jersey Governor Christine Todd Whitman and other local politicians for Shakur's extradition.

Compared to Davis and Shakur, Elaine Brown came to political activism late in life. Although the daughter of a politically active mother (Dorothy Clark was involved in union organizing), Brown confesses that she had little interest in or insight into the racial struggles taking place around the country. This changed for Brown primarily as a result of her pivotal relationship with Jay Kennedy, a wealthy White writer she met after moving from her hometown of Philadelphia to Los Angeles in April 1965 at the age of twenty-two. She and Kennedy, thirty-three years her senior, were introduced at the Pink Pussycat, an upscale club where Brown was employed as a cocktail waitress. Brown credits Kennedy with profoundly influencing her political evolution. By 1967, Brown's commitment to rigorous self-education through reading and studying had led to her immersion in Los Angeles's Black activist scene. Although not herself a student, Brown joined the Black Student Alliance organized by sociology professor Harry Truly, at the Los Angeles campus of California State University. Brown became the Alliance's first representative to the Black Congress, an umbrella organization of groups with similar political agendas. Her work with the Congress exposed her to a wide circle of leftist activists

both formally and loosely associated with the Congress. In April 1968, at the age of twenty-five, Brown formally joined the Southern California chapter of the Black Panther Party. By 1969 she was serving as Deputy Minister of Information of the Los Angeles chapter. She was promoted to Minister of Information of the Party in 1971 (the first female appointment to the Central Committee), formally replacing Eldridge Cleaver (Taste *of Power,* 304). Unlike Shakur and Davis, whose respective associations with the Party were fleeting, Brown remained an active member until the organization's eventual demise in the late 1970s. Although many individuals (activists and scholars) date the Party's effective demise even before Brown assumed leadership of the organization, a small and shrinking cadre of the Party did continue well into the late 1970s. Pulled into the organization's innermost circle through her close association with its founder, Huey Newton, Brown became the first woman to lead the Party after Newton's flight to Cuba in 1974.

Aside from her work to bolster such Panther community initiatives as the Oakland Community Learning Center, Brown is also credited with changing the direction of the Party in its later years to include active participation in electoral politics. Brown herself ran twice, though unsuccessfully, for the Oakland City Council. The Party's backing of mayoral candidate Lionel Wilson and diligent work to register voters helped ensure Wilson's 1977 victory as the first African American mayor of Oakland. Wielding the Party's influence, Brown additionally was instrumental in ensuring that the proposed construction of the controversial Grove-Shafter highway extension included provisions for jobs to benefit the predominately Black surrounding community. Finally, by her own account, Brown also used her power as head of the Party to move other women into more influential and visible roles within the historically male-dominated organization. Brown's autobiography, *A Taste of Power: A Black Woman s Story,* published by Pantheon in 1992, was written in the years following her 1977 departure from the Party. The time separating the autobiography from the period of her most intense activism means that Brown's text is less connected to impending struggle than either Davis's or Shakur's. While Brown's narrative treats some of the same political issues as Davis's and Shakur's narratives do, she appears to enter into the autobiographical project with a substantially different sense of purpose. Writing in a different era as well as from the vantage point of greater retrospective distance, her focus on gender and power dynamics during the era constitutes a different kind of political witnessing than that found in the other women's narratives.

While the three writers' shared commitment to revolutionary ideals and struggle creates numerous commonalities between their texts, some attention is due the important differences between the women and their works. This includes attention to the different contexts in which their respective narratives emerge, the way each writer approaches/negotiates the politics of the autobiographical form, and the different motives that impel each woman to tell her story. One noteworthy difference is the degree of immediacy characterizing each of the works. The heteroglossia of Davis's and Shakur's narratives, for instance, highlight the way in which both narratives are connected to impending struggle. While Brown's autobiography is dedicated to her daughter, and to those who assisted in the manuscript's preparation, for example, the dedication that appears at the beginning of Davis's autobiography and the poem that opens Shakur's text both affirm resistance struggle in a way that selfconsciously connects their narratives to each other as well as to those of other activists across historical periods. Davis dedicates her autobiography to her family, her comrades, and those who will continue fighting "until racism and class injustice are forever banished from our history." Shakur has no formal dedication, but begins her narrative with a six-stanza poem titled "Affirmation." The first part of the poem presents stark images of death and repression,

which Shakur subsequently contrasts with her own spirited determination to embrace life in the face of death. Noting that barriers to freedom are meant to be broken down, Shakur declares:

> I believe in living.
> I believe in birth.
> I believe in the sweat of love
> and in the fire of truth.
> And I believe that a lost ship,
> steered by tired, seasick sailors,
> can still be guided home
> to port.

Loosely modeled in form after the Catholic "Apostle's Creed," the poem's content reveals Shakur's reverence for life, her faith in humanity, and her belief in the redemptive value of resistance struggle.

Shakur's and Davis's autobiographies are generally consistent with values and conventions embraced by numerous other activist autobiographers in the United States and abroad. The expectations that have come to govern activists writing their life stories are manifold. These expectations, which collectively shape a genre of writing I will call *political autobiography* (after Davis's coining of the term), are implicitly revealed in the work of other activists as well as critics of resistance literature. They include the following: (1) that the autobiographer will emphasize the story of the struggle over her own personal ordeals; (2) that she will use her own story both to document a history of the struggle and to further its political agenda; (3) that she will provide a voice for the voiceless; (4) that she will honor strategic silences in order to protect the integrity of the struggle as well as the welfare of other activists; (5) that she will expose oppressive conditions and the repressive tactics of the state; and (6) that she will use the autobiography as a form of political intervention, to educate as broad an audience as possible to the situation and issues at stake.

Consistent with these expectations, many activists who write their autobiographies tend to evince a relational understanding of self. This is marked by both a redefining of the self through the story of the Movement, and a notable uneasiness with the project of autobiography because of the genre's historical emphasis, within the Western literary tradition, on heroic individualism. Repeatedly, human rights activists cross-culturally insist that their individual plight not be read in isolation from the communities they represent. The narratives of Winnie Mandela of South Africa, Rigoberta Menchú of Guatemala, and Domitila Barrios of Bolivia are exemplary. Referring to her struggle against South African apartheid, Winnie Mandela remarks, in *Part of My Soul Went With Him*: "I have ceased a long time ago to exist as an individual. The ideals, the political goals I stand for, those are the ideals and goals of the people in this country" (Mandela, 26). Rigoberta Menchú's narrative similarly opens with emphasis on the extent to which her own experiences are paradigmatic of others'. She insists: "I'd like to stress that it's not only my life, it's also the testimony of my people…. The important thing is that what has happened to me has happened to many other people too: My story is the story of all poor Guatemalans" (Menchú, 1). Perhaps Domitila Barrios captures the ethos of their shared project best when she speaks of her own autobiography as the "personal experience of my people" (Barrios, 15).

Within the United States, political prisoner George Jackson, in "Recent Letters and An Autobiography" (a twenty-page narrative preceding the collection of letters that make up *Soledad Brother*), also noted that he found difficulty in complying with the request to furnish a brief autobiography. He explains: "I don't recognize uniqueness, not as it's applied to individualism, because it is too tightly tied into decadent capitalist culture" (Jackson, *Soledad,* 10). He goes on to acknowledge, however, that he knows no other way to account for his difference from other Black people around him. Rhetorically, he ponders: "But then how can I explain the runaway slave in terms that do not imply uniqueness?"

In contrast to Angela Davis's vigorous attempts in the preface to her autobiography to downplay her uniqueness, Jackson seems more willing to openly acknowledge that he is both typical (in the sense that he shares the plight of other Black people under racist oppression) and atypical (in the sense that his resistance to oppression is both active and subversive). The uneasiness political autobiographers tend to experience with the personal "I" may even be symbolized in the lowercase "i" Assata Shakur uses throughout her narrative. Because the personal pronouns "she" and "he" are conventionally rendered in lowercase, Shakur's use of a small "i" suggests an understanding of self as neither more nor less important than any other.

Davis approaches the autobiographical project with a humility that comes close to apology. Her disclaimers are elaborate, the first appearing with the original publication in 1974 and the second appended, as she says, "nearly fifteen years" later (Davis, *Autobiography*, vii). In the original preface, Davis writes: "I felt that to write about my life, what I did, what I thought and what happened to me would require a posture of difference, an assumption that I was unlike other women—other Black women—and therefore needed to explain myself" (xv). Davis is most concerned that she not be viewed in isolation from the mass struggle with which she identifies, since she perceives that it is, in fact, the struggle that gives her speech legitimacy. In the introduction that appears with the book's second printing, Davis is less timid, though still inclined to qualify her decision to write. She explains: "I did not measure the events of my own life according to their possible personal importance. Rather I attempted to utilize the autobiographical genre to evaluate my life in accordance with what I considered to be the political significance of my experiences" (viii). With the advantage in the second preface of increased distance she is, however, confident that the work constitutes "an important piece of historical description and analysis of the late 1960s and early 1970s" (vii). Davis also uses the introduction to the second printing to mention her continued activist work up to the present (i.e., 1988), thus reestablishing her continued authority to write.

Like the uneasiness with or subjugation of the personal "I," other conventions and practices common to activists' texts tend to disrupt the kinds of values traditionally encoded in Western autobiographical practice. Of course, in recent years, the expectations for autobiography have undergone considerable changes owing in part to the contributions of feminist and poststructuralist theory and to scholarly attention to texts produced by writers outside the dominant culture. This notwithstanding, the conventional understanding of autobiography has been that it is the narrative ordering of an individual's life that illuminates, in the process, his or her uniqueness. It is, after all, this uniqueness that ostensibly entitles the prospective autobiographer to write in the first place. Autobiography by writers situated within (or influenced by) Western imperialist culture historically has taken as its impetus and focus the way in which the individual's life is distinguished from the lives of those around him. The assumption, then, is that the ideal autobiographical subject is that individual whose life achievements merit special recognition. The tendency of contemporary critics to cite—often for the purpose of problematizing—Georges Gusdorf's claims suggests that it was his writing in the 1950s about autobiography as a genre that truly exposed the ethos implicit in the Western autobiographical project. In his seminal essay, "Conditions and Limits of Autobiography," Gusdorf argued that "autobiography is not to be found outside of our cultural area: one would say that it expresses a concern peculiar to Western man, a concern that has been of good use in his systematic conquest of the universe" (Gusdorf, 29). He proposed that it is primarily the concern for preservation of self (the individual as he stands in relief to his environment) that motivates autobiography (29). In establishing a context (a series of prerequisites he termed "metaphysical preconditions"[1]) for

the emergence of autobiography as a peculiarly Western (read White, middle-class, heterosexual, male) form, Gusdorf failed to consider the possibility that members of non-hegemonic communities might undertake the telling of their own life stories for different purposes. He further assumed that there is only one understanding of "self" (i.e., the individual as apart from his/her community) from which autobiography might be generated. Gusdorf s assumptions implicitly link autobiography to an imperialist project and also leave no space for cultural difference or ways of knowing outside of those he privileges. If Gusdorf's claims can be read as capturing the ethos of the Western autobiographical tradition, then Davis, Brown, and Shakur, like other writers of political autobiography, write—to varying degrees—against this tradition. For them, autobiography is a vehicle used less to explore and glorify their individual uniqueness than to examine those experiences that connect them to their communities.

Shakur is especially emphatic in affirming the importance of connection to community. In addition to using her autobiography to educate, to expose, to correct, and to document, she also takes the opportunity to acknowledge a community of support. Speaking in the aftermath of her ordeal, she explains: "There were many, many people who i never got to meet, even though they worked so hard on my behalf. And even though i never got a chance to thank all the Black people, white people, Third World people, all the students, feminists, revolutionaries, activists, etc., who worked on the case, i thank you now" (Assata, 246). Shakur's text repeatedly alludes to her sense of solidarity with others. She asserts, for instance, that "there was never a time, no matter what horrible thing i was undergoing, when i felt completely alone" (223). Shakur also affirms connection to community through her use of the roll call, a convention of the oral tradition that recalls the names of other freedom fighters who have gone before and celebrates their place in a continuum of struggle. Roll calls of persecuted and/or slain activists have the effect not only of deflecting attention away from the uniqueness of the individual, but also of giving voice to the stories of those who have been silenced (through detention, death, or denied access to public media). There are at least three such roll calls in *Assata*. In "To My People, July 4, 1973," an audiotape she recorded to be smuggled out of the prison by her lawyer, Shakur charges: "They call us [the Black Liberation Army and its supporters] murderers, but we did not murder Martin Luther King Jr., Emmett Till, Medgar Evers, Malcolm X, George Jackson, Nat Turner, James Chaney.... We did not murder, by shooting in the back, sixteen-year-old Clifford Glover" (50). "To My People" concludes with a dedication "in the spirit of Ronald Carter, William Christmas, Mark Clark, Mark Essex, Frank 'Heavy' Fields, Woodie Changa Olugbala Green, Fred Hampton, LiP Bobby Hutton, George Jackson, Jonathan Jackson, James McClain, Harold Russell, Zayd Malik Shakur, [and] Anthony Kumu Olugbala White" (52). Shakur offers no detail to go with the names. Barbara Harlow aptly notes as one of the characteristics of resistance literature the demand such narratives "make on the reader in their historical referencing and the burden of historical knowledge such referencing enjoins" (Harlow, *Resistance*, 80). Shakur's roll call is foremost a gesture of giving names to the nameless (i.e., of insisting upon their humanity) and of resisting America's propensity for historical erasure or forced forgetting. Her memory of them is a reminder not to betray their sacrifice as well as a source of inspiration for her own activities. Shakur's catalog signifies both resistance and the state's continued violence against those engaged in human rights struggle. The names are entered into the record like court evidence, to be used against the power structure when the time arrives. Writing autobiography, for Shakur, is a way of collecting and consolidating this information, which would otherwise be widely dispersed (in newspaper accounts, court documents, political literature and propaganda, and personal correspondence) and effectively lost. Even in listing names without the corresponding

histories or circumstances, Shakur preserves vital information. Her roll call, like a library catalog, gives readers and researchers a place to start. The names of known and little-known (i.e., outside certain circles) activists are similarly sprinkled throughout the pages of Davis's and Brown's narratives.

Brown's *A Taste of Power* provides a perfect complement to the works by Shakur and Davis because its ethos and scope are notably different. This is in part the result of a nearly twenty-year hiatus between Brown's last association with the Black Panther Party and the manuscript's publication. Certainly, the publication of *A Taste* eighteen years after Davis's text means that the work emerges onto a very different sociopolitical landscape. Perhaps the most substantial differences between Brown's narrative and the narratives by Davis and Shakur, though, are attributable to Brown's own activist sensibility. While Brown's narrative treats some of the same political issues as Davis's and Shakur's, she appears to enter into the autobiographical project with a very different sense of purpose. In many ways, Brown seems less concerned with writing a "political autobiography" (as Davis defines her project) than with reconciling the meaning of her own past involvement in political struggle. This is reflected both in her narrative's avowedly personal slant (her foregrounding—as opposed to subjugation—of the individual "I") and her transgressing of the kinds of strategic silences observed in other activists' texts.

The subjugation or displacement of the individual "I" found in Shakur's and Davis's autobiographies is absent in Brown's more recent reflections on her life during the same period. Brown's negotiation of this convention appears to be complicated by the factors that motivate her decision to write. That is, she is concerned less with downplaying the self as unique than with recuperating a sense of self/identity *apart from* the Movement, and the Black Panther Party, even as her activities and experiences therein constitute the focus of her narrative. This quality, along with the fact that Brown's text is, as Barbara Harlow puts it, "less embed[ded] in the historical and material conditions of [its] production" (Harlow, Resistance, 98), tends to distinguish Brown's text from Shakur's and Davis's as a different kind of political writing. This difference notwithstanding, A Taste raises significant theoretical and pedagogical issues that make its discussion alongside the narratives by Davis and Shakur appropriate and important. Furthermore, because Brown's text frequently transgresses the expectations associated with autobiographical writing by political activists, A Taste is also valuable for the way it effectively illuminates a significant limitation of political narratives like Davis's and Shakur's: the lack of insight afforded into the interior or emotional life of the writer.

Within the genre of political autobiography, there is little room for activists' exposure of their interior lives, since focus on aspects of the struggle always takes precedence. Readers are given little detail about the more personal, intrapsychic dimensions of involvement in radical political struggle. In transgressing some of the conventions of political autobiography, A Taste is unique in offering such insight. Even as A Taste is about Brown's activities as a revolutionary, it is also about her ambivalence regarding those activities. In this way, she presents perhaps a less romanticized version of what it means to be engaged in radical political work. Unlike either Davis or Shakur, Brown relays retrospectively several moments of uncertainty in her continuing activism, citing the stress, fear, and anxiety of operating under intense police surveillance and repression, of existing outside social norms and expectations, and of enduring reactionary gender expectations within the Black Panther Party itself as factors prompting her to question her continued commitment. Clearly the latter issue constitutes at least one reason why both Davis and Shakur eventually distanced themselves from the Party to continue their activist work. For them, however, continued activism was never a question; the only uncertainty they acknowledge concerned the

form their future activism would take. Shakur asserts, for example: "The more active i became the more i liked it. It was like medicine, making me well, making me whole" (Assata, 189). In sharp contrast to Shakur's testimony, Brown characterizes her own experiences as marked by stress and psychic fragmentation. During her early years with the Party, she even resorted to Thorazine (an antipsychotic prescribed by a psychiatric social worker) as a means of escaping both the pressures and anxieties associated with her activist work, and her concomitant feelings of nonexistence, alienation, and displacement. Her eventual addiction prompted her to take an extended absence from the Party. There are thus several moments in the text where Brown admits to uncertainty about the life she has chosen, a move that, in many ways, deromanticizes what it means to be a revolutionary.

Given the extent to which Movement activists suffered massive repression at the hands of the state, it is curious that the reality of death and loss is not explored more extensively in their texts. Perhaps the reason is that any admission of emotional pain and devastation of that magnitude grants one's enemies too much satisfaction, since the most fundamental goal of oppression is to break the human spirit. In a recent dialogue with fellow activist Kathleen Cleaver, Davis recalls in reflecting on the period: "One of the things that we didn't do then was mourn. Our strength was often defined by our ability not to allow the death of someone we loved to set us back" (Cleaver and Davis, 160). For activists to explore this pain in the context of their autobiographies, then, would invite a kind of voyeurism that all of the writers seem to eschew as far as their own individual suffering is concerned. Referring to the loss represented by George Jackson's death, Davis writes: "the deeply personal pain I felt would have strangled me had I not turned it into a proper and properly placed rage. I could not dwell on my own loss" (Autobiography, 319). She goes on to describe the way in which she determined to use Jackson's death to renew her own commitment to continued struggle. Supplying detail elided from Davis's narrative, Bettina Aptheker (Davis's friend and attorney) notes that Davis, in prison at the time, was unable to sleep in the days following news of Jackson's death. Aptheker adds that Davis's resolve was, nevertheless, unshaken. She elaborates: "Overwhelmed with grief, her face ashen in shock, her eyes wet with unending tears, comprehending the magnitude of the loss with infinitely greater intensity than any of us, she could still write" (Aptheker, 42). Davis was, at the time, composing a public statement describing what Jackson had meant to the Movement.

Davis's determination to use Jackson's death to motivate her continued struggle is a sentiment echoed by Shakur in her poem, "Story." Both "Story," which closes chapter 1 of Assata, and Shakur's poem for Rema Olugbala, in chapter 11, capture well the way the pain of personal loss is transformed in political autobiography into something collectively empowering. Shakur's placement of "Story" (which follows her narration of her apprehension on the New Jersey Turnpike) suggests that Zayd Shakur is her intended addressee; however, the dynamic captured in the verse might well be applied to countless others killed in struggle. Her poem is the story of Zayd but also the story of the Movement. Succinctly, she writes: "You died. / I cried. / And kept on getting up. / A little slower. / And a lot more deadly" (Assata, 17). Revealing a determined forward progression, the short end-stopped lines suggest emotional restraint or containment. That all the lines in the poem are end-stopped, furthermore, seems to symbolize discrete and processional stages in contending with loss. The impact of loss here is acknowledged in two ways. The first is the speaker's grief ("I cried") and the concomitant drain of psychic and physical energy that accompanies violent repression (i.e., she comes back, but "A little slower"). The third and fifth lines of the poem, however, acknowledge the impact of loss in a different way: they announce the speaker's renewed determination not only to continue fighting, but to raise the ante in the process. It makes sense

that with each loss there is less to lose; and those with the least to lose are always potentially the most dangerous in any society. As Martin Oppenheimer notes in The *Urban Guerrilla*, increased repression directed toward those who already suffer the most extreme systemic oppression tends to augment group resistance. Indeed, the Panthers' desire to embrace the Black urban underclass (the lumpen proletariat) was based on precisely this awareness. This desire, however, was consigned mostly to theory. As cultural critic Amiri Baraka notes, the Party consisted predominantly of *working-class* Blacks. Despite the Party's "romanticization" of the Lumpen, he argues (citing information published in the Kerner Commission Report on Civil Disorders) that the rebellions that characterized the late 1960s "by and large were led by working class blacks, not the lumpen, as has been falsely projected" (Baraka, 28).

In her poem for Rema Olugbala (untitled), Shakur illustrates the sense in which the spirit of the Movement transcends individuals. Olugbala was scheduled to be tried along with Shakur and Ronald Myers for an alleged bank robbery committed in Queens, New York, on August 23, 1971 (160). (Shakur and Myers were later acquitted.) Although Olugbala died in a failed prison escape, his spirit of resistance is immortalized not only in Shakur's poem but most importantly, in all of the Olugbalas (i.e., angry "youngbloods") to come who undoubtedly will pick up where he has left off. Shakur writes:

They think they killed you.
But i saw you yesterday.
All them youngbloods
musta gave you a transfusion.
All that strong blood.
All that rich blood.
All that angry blood
flowing through your veins
toward tomorrow. (164)

For Shakur, incarcerated at the time she learned of Olugbala's death, writing the poem is a means of rechannelling as well as overcoming her own potentially debilitating feelings of rage and sorrow.

While Davis's and Shakur's texts show how activists use the experience of loss to renew their commitment to revolutionary struggle, Brown's narrative goes beyond this to also probe the *psychological* impact on activists of repeated personal loss. In *A Taste*, Brown paints a portrait of Erica Huggins following her husband John's assassination that offers a poignant illustration of the impact of loss. Although Brown's illustration here is of another's grief rather than her own, the portrait attests to activists' emotional vulnerability in ways not readily exposed by the other women autobiographers. Brown notes that in the immediate aftermath of John's death, Huggins appeared very strong. The determination to cling to righteous anger (like that evident in Shakur's poems) in the face of repeated loss is, after all, a necessary survival strategy making possible individual perseverance and also the advancement of the collective struggle. However, Brown eventually begins to notice changes in Huggins, which she describes as Ericka's apparent "loss of passion," following her release from prison. In the hours following her husband's death, Ericka Huggins was arrested along with Bobby Seale on charges of attempted retaliatory homicide. Whether as a result of John's assassination or of the seventeen months afterward that Huggins spent in solitary confinement before she was acquitted, Brown contends: "her emotional fire was surely gone ... and I found myself more and more frustrated by that. It seemed to take something away from all of us, especially me" (*A Taste*, 408). Although Brown does not explain what she means in referring to herself as "especially" affected by Huggins's alleged change, it is possible that she is referring back to the way in which the

Party fulfilled her longing for a sense of meaning, purpose, and identity, and by extension to the need for her faith in its righteousness to remain intact. Brown remarks: "The truth was her unburdened sorrow had begun to heighten

my sense of doom" (434). It is as if connecting with Huggins's loss—and possibly, her sense of despair—too closely (like Brown's fear later of identifying too closely with the victims of Huey Newton's violent purges of Party activists) could force Brown into an uncomfortable confrontation with everything to which she had up to that point devoted her life. If so, such identification might have threatened to plunge her into the kind of meaninglessness that she spends much of the narrative longing to escape. While Brown claims that she and Huggins were close comrades for nearly ten years, she neglects to speculate on the causes of Huggins's apparent change. Huggins seems the mirror into which Brown is unprepared to look. The glimpse Brown allows of Huggins's alleged change during her incarceration hints at the trauma and impact of loss for activists, the pain that must be kept to the margin.

In addition to the silences in Davis's and Shakur's autobiographies surrounding their personal, interior lives (in contrast to Brown's revelations about the same), their texts also withhold other kinds of information, especially that which might undermine the image of the Movement or imperil the welfare of other activists. Such silences function strategically in each woman's overall political objective. Both Davis and Shakur decline on several occasions, for instance, to mention names of people who supported or assisted them along the way, since such information could easily facilitate retaliation. Davis resists divulging the names of the guards working at the Women's House of Detention who were supportive of her while she was there. As she acknowledges, printing their names in her text at the time could have resulted in their losing their jobs (*Autobiography*, 43). Similarly, Shakur says of the individuals who supported her: "I would mention their names, but the way things are today, i'd only be sending the FBI or CIA to their doors" (*Assata*, 189). Her comment anticipates her readers' curiosity, particularly with regard to the details of her escape from prison, but also presumes her readers' understanding.

Astutely, she accounts for the reality of both hostile and sympathetic audiences. Most importantly, her silence in such instances, like Davis's, is intended to protect the interests and integrity of the Movement in a way that also leaves space for other activists to benefit from the kinds of opportunities made available to her.

In contrast to Brown's narrative, which occasionally includes details of specific missions (such as her rendezvous with John Huggins to carry out an act of guerilla warfare—*A Taste*, 154), Shakur avoids recounting her own involvement in clandestine activities. Instead, her narrative, like Davis's, is concerned largely with defending herself against bogus charges for crimes she did not commit. Whether there were other crimes she *did* commit in the course of her activist work remains notably vague, and—since political autobiography is in major part concerned with redefining criminality (by challenging a status quo that overwhelmingly favors the interests of a capitalist elite at the expense of all others)— even inconsequential. Although Shakur refers repeatedly to her participation in various community and campus political protests and demonstrations in New York City (*Assata*, 204), her involvement in the antiwar movement, her association with the Harlem branch of the Black Panther Party, and later her underground involvement with the Black Liberation Army, surprisingly the most subtle silence in Shakur's text is that surrounding details of her actual activities as a revolutionary. It is a subtle silence because her status and identity as a revolutionary is already overdetermined by the fact of the narrative itself. It is, after all, the basis of the authority from which she speaks, and the condition we, as readers, are led to take for granted. At one point, Shakur indicates that she was prepared to join the Panthers but postponed her affiliation for reasons that remain ambiguous in her account. Enigmatically, she explains: "i had some other things i wanted to do and i needed a low profile in order to do them" (204). What these "other things" are is never revealed. Later, on learning about a series of killings of policemen, she

indicates that she was shocked by the news and yet awed that "somebody was finally doing what the rest of us merely had fantasies about" (236). Shortly after this news, however, she learns from an article in the paper that she herself is wanted "for questioning" in association with the killings. Shakur is thus forced underground into hiding in the same way that Davis was after the Marin County courtroom siege.

If the silences around Shakur's *particular* activities can be described as subtle, then the silences surrounding details of her prison escape are commensurately glaring. Although Shakur's release is foreshadowed by a vision her grandmother relays, an ellipsis stands in for details of the actual escape. Shakur offers only a veiled reference to her own agency by explaining that once her grandmother prophesied things, it was the responsibility of those concerned to make the dream come true (260). The most potentially climactic moment in *Assata* (Shakur builds narrative tension by alluding to her own increasing restlessness and anxiety behind bars) is thus rendered anticlimactic by analepsis (261). In place of the details of her escape (e.g., when, under what conditions, and by what means), we are instead offered her first impressions of freedom as she seeks exile in Cuba (266). Only by recourse to secondary materials is some of the enigma dispelled. In "Self-Portrait of a Black Liberationist: An Appraisal of Assata Shakur's Autobiography," M. Annette Jaimes, for instance, indicates that Shakur was smuggled from the maximum-security building of New Jersey's Clinton Prison for Women on November 2, 1979, by members of the Revolutionary Armed Task Force, a wing of the Black Liberation Army (Churchill and Vander Wall, *Cages*, 242). Another source offering a little more detail describes how she was rescued after "three male visitors drew handguns, kidnapped two guards and seized a prison minibus in order to drive out of the grounds to two getaway cars." The source notes that the guards were left "handcuffed but unharmed," and also that the men involved were assisted by another woman (Kihss). Clearly, both silences (the first surrounding Shakur's specific activities as a revolutionary, and the second her startling escape from prison) are strategic, since the implications of her disclosures necessarily extend beyond her text. Such silences emphasize the inseparability of political autobiography from its social and political context.

Such strategic silences in Shakur's and Davis's narratives are a reflection of the kind of text each envisioned herself writing (i.e., one that would be an extension of her continuing struggle) as well as the sociopolitical context in which each text emerged. Brown, writing in a different era, is less concerned (and has more freedom to be so) with upholding Party propaganda or promoting positive images of the Movement than with illuminating the points at which both sometimes went wrong. In an interview with Renée Graham for the Boston Globe, Brown insists: "I didn't want to write a chronicle of the Black Panther Party. I wanted to write a chronicle of a black woman's life" (Graham, 32). Angela Davis, in a generally favorable review of *A Taste,* concedes that the book is less a history of the Party than an exposé of one woman's experience in that party—her "relations with the Party's men, ideas, disciplines and projects" (Davis, "The Making," 4). The story of the Party's relation to the larger culture is thus subjugated in *A Taste* to the story of Party members' relationships to each other, and, if one accepts fellow Black Panther Kathleen Cleaver's criticism in "Sister Act: Symbol and Substance in Black Women's Leadership," to the story of Brown's involvement with Huey Newton in particular (Cleaver, 96). Because *A Taste* addresses such issues as internecine violence, sexism, and misogyny within the Movement, Davis proposed that the book "would have been inconceivable in the seventies—or even the eighties. In radical circles, it would have been considered tantamount to treason, and among conservatives it would have been welcomed as the exposé of a fraudulent movement" (Davis, "The Making," 4). Brown's focus on the internal politics and affairs of the Black Panther Party

and on her own experiences negotiating within the Party's ruling elite subsumes concern over the political terrain outside the organization, and consequently marks her text as engaged in a different kind of political work. While Brown's transgressing of certain personal and strategic silences sets her text apart from Davis's and Shakur's, this move also makes worthwhile our reading her text alongside theirs. That is, Brown supplies information that, in many ways, complements Davis's and Shakur's accounts, and that, in the process, gives us greater insight into the forms and substance of Black female radicalism during the period. The noteworthy differences between their texts notwithstanding, what Brown's, Shakur's, and Davis's autobiographies share in common connects their works and lives to a formidable tradition of African American resistance writing and struggle.

NOTE

1. Gusdorf writes: "Autobiography becomes possible only under certain metaphysical preconditions. To begin with, at the cost of a cultural revolution humanity must have emerged from the mythic framework of traditional teachings and must have entered into the perilous domain of history. The man who takes the trouble to tell of himself knows that the present differs from the past and that it will not be repeated in the future; he has become more aware of differences than of similarities; given the constant change, given the uncertainty of events and of men, he believes it a useful and valuable thing to fix his own image so that he can be certain it will not disappear like all things in this world. History then would be the memory of a humanity heading toward unforeseeable goals, struggling against the breakdown of forms and of beings. Each man matters to the world, each life and each death; the witnessing of each about himself enriches the common cultural heritage" (30).

• • •

Discussion Questions

1. What makes the writings by women of color less recognized then those of men of color during the second-wave period?

2. Why are writings by women of color so powerful?

3. Besides feminism, what other issues are covered in the writings?

4. Women writers struggled for recognition outside of the feminist courses and feminist magazines. Women of color were exceptionally unrecognized. Why do you think feminist magazines and journals did not pursue more authors of color?

What You Can Do

• Support women of color writers by reading and promoting their works along with other feminist works

• Take a course on women of color and literature at your university

• Find local women of color writers, and attend their readings and promotions

• Be aware of the lack of women of color writers in all areas of literature, and work to change it

• Ask your instructors to include works by women of color

• Find faculty who can help you incorporate the works into a broader curriculum at your university

• Organize an event at your university celebrating women of color writers

• Start a book club with the intent of bringing recognition to women of color

• Remember, many works by Indigenous women and Latina women go unrecognized in mainstream book reviews, so include titles and works from these women in your advocacy

SECTION 5

Third-Wave Movements

Third-wave feminist movements began in the 1990s and focused more on individual identity than politics and legal achievements. This movement brought bands, journalism, magazines, and new organizations that concentrated on diversity and intersectionality. Some popular movements included the Riot Grrrls, Guerrilla Girls, Third Wave Fund (now the Third Wave Foundation), and activists like Rebecca Walker, Jennifer Baumgardner, and Amy Richards. Other facets of the movement included reproductive justice, sexual harassment, equal pay, and the expansion of Title IX.

CHAPTER 11

Remapping the Resonances of Riot Grrrl

FEMINISMS, POSTFEMINISMS, AND "PROCESSES" OF PUNK

By Anna Feigenbaum

Through women-oriented shows, conventions, and the circulation of zines, the 1990s Riot Grrrl movement foregrounded visions of punk feminism.[1] Locating what they deemed "mainstream" society's conflicting demands and values, Riot Grrrls spat critiques of patriarchy and spoke of the contradictions women face. Mimi Nguyen, the editor of the zine and producer of the Web site Worse Than Queer, and contributing columnist for *Punk Planet*, argues that "beyond a distinctive musical styling, Riot Grrrl was "an informal pedagogical project," a kind of punk rock "teaching machine … that existed in and sometimes replaced the classroom as the most meaningful context for the transmission and production of knowledge among its body of participants."[2]

Spreading through various media, from independent zines to local arts reviews, glossy magazines, and national newspapers, Riot Grrrl became visible as an infusion of punk and feminism. But as mainstream media got hold of Riot Grrrl the grrrls lost control of their words and actions. The grassroots movement became a spectacle, and the focus quickly shifted from reports on the feminist content and production values espoused by Riot Grrrls to features on their punk fashion sensibilities. Many journalists dismissed the Riot Grrrls as juvenile and their music as angsty noise.[3] A media blackout was called by some members and Riot Grrrl chapters in 1992, but this only sparked further commentary and profiles.

While the popularization of Riot Grrrl helped spread the word and at first led to the start of new Riot Grrrl chapters and legions of fan mail for early zinesters and bands such as Bikini Kill, eventually the movement dispersed. Reported dead circa 1995, Riot Grrrl suffered the fate of what Jennifer Pozner has termed the "false feminist death syndrome," in a media environment that attempts "to discredit and erase young feminists from the political landscape."[4] As report after report located the failure of Riot Grrrl within the movement itself, the relationship between independent and corporate production remained absent from the debate. And, perhaps unsurprisingly, the media failed to address its own accountability for Riot Grrrl's purported death.

Today the term *Riot Grrrl* still circulates, mapping a variety of women writers, poets, musicians, Web designers, hackers, and even pornographers.[5] The term continues to be used to designate everything from emergent consumer demographics to grassroots feminist activists. In this essay, I analyze some of the various ways in which the Riot Grrrl movement has influenced, informed, and inspired—both positively and negatively—feminist and post-feminist sites of creative production. Superimposing a spatial mapping on a retracing of Riot Grrrl history, I discuss Riot Grrrl at times as a catalyst, a feeling, an experience, a memory, and a journalistic convention.

Throughout this essay, I analyze young feminists' articulations that are often absent from documentations of the Riot Grrrl movement. In navigating this remapping, I turn to zine and Web site writings in addition to other academic scholarship on Riot Grrrl histories because it is in these sites that one can locate a different set of articulations about the political meanings of Riot Grrrl. As a scholar, a young feminist activist, a Riot Grrrl fan, a consumer, and a producer of feminist punk culture, my writing is infused with and influenced by my personal and political investments and engagements in this culture. Thus, my analysis privileges sites and processes of production and distribution that resist corporatization and commodification, highlighting the perspectives performers take in their own analyses of the political economics of cultural production, distribution, and circulation. I privilege these sites and voices not to discredit the impact and influence of "popular" performers and producers on major labels but rather to draw attention to the importance of political economic issues in the analysis of postfeminist media.

In what follows, I look specifically at the cultural productions of four off-shoots of Riot Grrrl: protogrrrls, pop "punk" girls, antiracist grrrls, and Web gurls. I then move to address the recent anxiety around Kathleen Hanna, the Riot Grrrl founder, and her move to Universal Records with her band, Le Tigre. The controversy surrounding Le Tigre's decision to sign with a major record label is distinctively marked by contemporary political economic concerns and conditions and current debates within recent feminist writing about the conditions of cultural production. Raising questions about the relationships between corporate, punk, and feminist production processes throughout this analysis, I end with a look at ongoing Riot Grrrl cultures.

Protogrrrls

Women have been involved in punk bands and the transatlantic punk scene since its inception in the 1970s, but it is the 1990s Riot Grrrl movement that is most frequently credited with bringing punk and feminism together. The contributions of the 1970s punk icons Chrissie Hynde, Patti Smith, Siouxsie Sioux, Poly Styrene, and Joan Jett—to name only a few—left their mark on the scene, but as punk diffused some bands signed corporate deals, some vowed to remain "underground," and some went defunct, high on disillusion. This proliferation of punk resulted in the further marginalization of women in punk scenes. As "hard-core" acts took over local venues, punk spaces became increasingly hostile and at times dangerous for punk girls. As Jennifer Miro of the Nuns famously stated in late 1977, "There were a lot of women in the beginning. ... Then women didn't go to see punk bands anymore. ... It was so violent and so macho and that was repulsive. [We] just got squeezed out."[6]

Rather than serving as an origin or point of lineage, the label Riot Grrrl—and at times just grrrl—is now used to describe women who were directly, indirectly, and sometimes barely associated with the 1990s Riot Grrrl movement. Analyzing how the term maps associative connections between various feminist cultural producers, I argue that this marker constructs feminist histories and lineages. While at times these associations offer accounts of feminist alliances, creating positive connections between seemingly disparate feminists, they also group women together with little concern for their political, cultural, and personal conflicts.

For example, the avant garde feminist author Kathy Acker was labeled a "theoretical grrrl" in an homage after her 1997 death from cancer. The article claims that Acker was "a riot girl ahead of her time."[7] Likewise, the 1980s punk pop performer Joan Jett is often heralded as "the original riot grrrl,"[8] while the novelist and poet Marge Piercy deemed herself "an early grrrl" in the title of her 1999 book of poems expressing her admiration for contemporary Web-based gurl feminism and noting that she has since created her own Web site.[9] Yet Kim Gordon, the bassist of Sonic Youth, and Courtney Love are also often cited as protogrrrls, even though Gordon maintained a peripheral and mildly supportive position toward Riot Grrrl and feminism more generally, while Love has publicly voiced scathing critiques of Riot Grrrl and Kathleen Hanna in particular.

Journalists' mobilization and employment of the word *grrrl* (which officially entered the Oxford English Dictionary in 2001) creates, in this way, a retrospective genealogy. However, this mapping can function to contain, as well as celebrate, these "popular" women. Often employing the terminology of motherhood and sisterhood, the mark of Riot Grrrl carries with it matriarchal or familial connotations that are all too common in discourses about feminism. This is perhaps most visible in the case of Courtney Love. Tagged a "bad mother" for her heroin use and perceived maternal deficiencies, Love is also deemed a bad mother for abandoning her grrrls. This was exemplified in the media's portrayal of the 1995 "catfight" between Love and Kathleen Hanna at the Lollapalooza music festival. Media coverage of the altercation between Love and Hanna made an event out of these women's failure to fulfill their falsely constructed relational ties. As Astrid Henry writes, "Whether dutiful daughters or insolent ones, we all appear unable to leave feminism's 'family.'"[10]

While some young feminists do take up a language of rebellion, seeking to resist the "rules" or "victim model" purportedly espoused by second wavers, most of this familial language fails to accurately represent the disassociative and associative moves that young feminists make in their performances, writing, and activism.[11] For example, academic activists such as Emi Koyami and Kimberly Springer have gone to great lengths to rearticulate such divides. While Koyami insists on discussing the third wave of feminism as "outside of but not after the Second Wave,"[12] Springer has worked to renarrativize feminist histories, complicating the second-wave mother/third-wave daughter binary by focusing on the roles of women of color and postcolonial

theorists in the shaping of young feminists' thought.[13]

The employment of a "familial" vocabulary, as these young writers and others have pointed out, traps women within a restrictive set of predefined female relationships, precluding a more complex discussion about women's various friendships and conflicts. At the same time, it also functions to obscure and depoliticize feminist history. When critics and journalists chart "rebellion" by mapping only the work of "famous" white feminists—be it Andrea Dworkin, Catharine MacKinnon, Gloria Steinem, Germaine Greer, Naomi Wolf, Katie Roiphe, Jennifer Baumgardner, or even Courtney Love—they leave too little room to debate and discuss other connections between feminists. The political, everyday work of feminists that falls below the media radar leaves in its path what Gloria Anzaldúa calls "los desconocimientos" or ignored knowledge.[14]

Kathleen Hanna has reflected on this, stating, "Even though I paid bullshit lip service to the feminism of the past, I don't think I knew my history like I do now."[15] Hanna's 1999 track "Hot Topic" with Le Tigre works to re-articulate a feminist genealogy in this light. The band shouts the names of influential feminists such as Yoko Ono, Ani DiFranco, the Butchies, Angela Davis, Dorothy Allison, Gertrude Stein, Nina Simone, and Joan Jett. Each name unfolds over the next while Hanna sings:

> You're getting old
> That's what they say
> But I don't give a damn
> I'm listening anyway . . .
> (chorus) Don't you stop
> I can't live if you stop.[16]

Le Tigre's ode draws these women together, intentionally meshing and juxtaposing feminist-identified writers and musicians from the last eighty years. Seen as an alternative articulation of feminist histories, "Hot Topic" acts as an archive that disrupts linear narratives while reimagining the potential and futurity of feminists' associative connections.

As mentioned above, some of the women Le Tigre lists, such as Joan Jett and Kathy Acker, have worked directly with the Riot Grrrl movement as well as with other feminist punk bands. Jett's collaborations with Hanna, Kat Bjelland (Babes in Toyland), and Donita Sparks (L7) have led to her iconicization by the third-wave feminist magazine *Bust*, which recast the aphorism "What Would Jesus Do?" as the basis for a parody clothing line, "What Would Joan Jett Do?" The relationship between Hanna and Acker also gives way to a narrative that bridges rather than divides feminist performers. Reportedly, Acker told Hanna fifteen years ago, "If you want to be heard … you should be in a band," after which Hanna went home and started Bikini Kill.[17]

Associative connections like these chart positive influences and partnerships, expanding our knowledge of women's popular histories. Rachel, the guitarist and singer of the (former) British band Pixie Meat, explains that Riot Grrrl "help[ed] me discover amazing bands practically ignored by … rock family trees."[18] However, unfortunately and all too often the *feminist* family trees we construct function similarly—rooted in false narratives and branching out only as far as the mainstream press can see.

Pop "Punk" Girls

Emerging "girl" groups and performers are also frequently marked as part of an ever expanding new Riot Grrrl order. Constructing everything from these maternal lineages to stylish singing sororities and "chirping chick" categories of women, rock critics and discourses of rock criticism often group artists in order to familiarize readers with them.[19] John Charles Goshert argues, "While the mass media label of punk may be applied indiscriminately … it is precisely because of punk's local production and consumption, as well as the geographic specificities in musical forms, style of dress, and political

practice … that it cannot be reduced simply to a musical or otherwise stylistic genre."[20]

Following from this, broadly terming women artists "punk" or new "grrrls" often indiscriminately groups them together. No matter what the production ethos or articulations of these artists (be they anticorporate, anti-misogyny, or anti–Britney Spears), they are left undifferentiated. As *NME* declared in its 2003 "Women in Rock" issue—which featured, among others, the "pop" punk performers Avril Lavigne and The Donnas—"All Hail the Heroines of the No Cock Revolution!"[21] Only the heroines aren't having a revolution, and the same critics who hail these young women also mobilize discursive conventions that confine, demean, and marginalize them.[22]

Moreover, as both the punk and feminist movements have historically been grassroots, locally organized endeavors, their emergence as "popular" may render them apolitical or already co-opted. Goshert writes that "it is precisely when punk becomes popular culture that it ceases to be punk," while Catherine Driscoll asks in *Girls*, "Can feminism be a mass-produced, globally distributed product, and can merchandized relations to girls be authentic?"[23]

This concern resonates in the criticism of artists such as Gwen Stefani, Avril Lavigne, the Donnas, and Pink, who are commonly discussed as "punks," "punky," or (my personal favorite) "pop punkettes." However, these women's aggressive performances at times demand that the content of their songs be considered. *Feminism*, a word one rarely reads in the mainstream press in regard to popular music, is explicitly addressed. So, while Pink belts "neofeminist anthems" demanding "power, choice and halter tops," Stefani sings "like a little riot grrrl lost," Avril Lavigne has a "charming punk attitude," and the Donnas are "punk-rock debutantes" who cite L7 and the Riot Grrrl bands Bikini Kill and Bratmobile (among others) as inspiration.[24]

The intersections of punk and postfeminism can be readily mapped onto any of these performers. However, while discourses around

Stefani, Pink, Lavigne, punk, and feminism are ripe for commentary, the trajectory of the Donnas' career appears ready-made for an analysis of post–Riot Grrrl, post-feminist punk. In 2001, the Donnas, an all-female "pop" punk act from Northern California, signed a deal with the multinational conglomerate Atlantic Records. A staple of their local, small venue circuit for over five years, the Donnas' corporate backing has taken them onto the mainstream airwaves, on tour with the traveling rock festival Lollapalooza, and to the pinnacle of all that is American pop—the gatekeeping MTV program *Total Request Live*.

Before signing with Atlantic, the Donnas were backed by Lookout! Records—a moderate-sized noncorporate label run out of Berkeley, California. Founded in 1987, Lookout! began and continues to function as a profit-sharing label that preserves artist control over records and marketing. Although Lookout! has maintained its position on the fringes of the multinational industry, it has also become a vehicle through which bands can rise to conglomerate fame. As the name Lookout! suggests, artists and repertory (A and R) men do just that, monitoring "underground" success and campus airwaves in search of untapped (fan-base-intact) talent.

It is perhaps no surprise that a major label would be on the lookout for the commercial possibilities, the niche market eagerly but unknowingly awaiting the shrill sound of the Donnas' kitsch rhymes and quippy social commentary over speedy rifts. Based on the success of previous performers, the marketing potential of four conventionally attractive, young white women is clear (although the heaviest is always positioned in the back). The Donnas soon became the poster girls for the Pantene Pro–voice (no need to write your own songs) singing competition—in addition to their radio commercial for Budweiser, a Levi's fashion spread, and music licensed for Sprite and Target advertisements.[25]

Kristen Schilt writes that "the appropriation and packaging of Riot Grrrl Politics" has contributed to the dispersal and depoliticization of the Riot Grrrl movement. She cites the success of such major-label women performers as prominent examples of the corporate packaged girl power that morphed out of Riot Grrrl's success.[26] Yet narratives of co-optation and commercialization often overlook too soon the legions of young girls who now have access to the Donnas' assertive, sex-positive music. The Donnas is one of the most popular all-girl rock bands whose members play their own instruments and write most of their own songs. Often compared to the Runaways and the Ramones (in part because each member of the group uses the stage name Donna), over the last few years the Donnas have received positive attention from the music press, establishing them as a "legitimate" pop act—critical praise that is rarely lavished on any band with an overwhelming majority of young female fans.[27]

Articulating a common response to claims of selling out, band member Donna R. (Allison) comments, "Women deserve to have a female rock band that is accessible for people. Not everybody lives in towns where they can find independent labels."[28] In 1999 and 2001, the Donnas toured with the original Riot Grrrl act, Bratmobile, only rather than opening the Donnas headlined the tours, causing critics to comment on the "irony" of this fan and role model reversal. Reviewing a 2001 concert at the Bowery Ballroom for NY-Rock.com, Jeanne Fury writes, "Watching Bratmobile open for the Donnas is kind of like watching your older, wiser sister open for you.… You know full well you'd be nowhere without big sister, but her time to shine has passed and now you're the one the masses want to see."[29] As Fury suggests, the Donnas frequently voice appreciation for their Riot Grrrl predecessors.[30] And, although they may be articulating "minimart feminism" with lyrics such as "Need your love 123 / Stop starin' at my D cup / Don't waste time just give it to me"[31] shouted over heavy guitar, the group does offer the attraction of "thrills, hard, fast rock music, drugs, and alcohol," which, as Holly Kruse argues, is rarely acknowledged as part of adolescent girls' identification with popular music.[32]

However, as critics such as Schilt note, these overtly sexualized articulations are far from the explicit critiques of "staring at one's D cup" made by Riot Grrrl bands such as Bikini Kill.[33] And, although Donna R. certainly has a point about the accessibility of independently produced and distributed music, "what the masses want to see" is largely determined by what the massive record labels make visible. Unlike the Donnas, Bratmobile continues to release LPs on independent labels such as Kill Rock Stars and Lookout! Records, which perhaps contributes, even more than their aging (at over thirty!) to this smaller fan base.

Articulating a common neoliberal position, in *She's a Rebel* Gillian Gaar argues, "The Donnas chose to sign with Atlantic; [Riot Grrrl band] Sleater-Kinney chose to stay with Kill Rock Stars. Neither choice was "better"—each group simply had an equally valid way of defining success on their own terms."[34] Comments such as Gaar's, which appear to be complacent with—or at least uncritical toward—the corporate conglomerate structure of the music industry, are quite common in anthologies and histories of women in rock music. Many texts of this type celebrate women's success while attempting to neatly sidestep issues of political economy. In doing so, they uphold statements such as Donna R.'s, and, although they often offer in-depth information on feminist music practices, their refusal (or perhaps reluctance) to address global market conditions speaks to the need for both "a friendly alliance" between feminist theory and political economy and an analysis that documents manifestations of punk's economic opposition to capitalism.

My analysis of the cultural location of bands such as the Donnas does not simply lend itself to, but demands a consideration of, the pathways of capital that inform and produce any feminist politics that is subsumed in their performance. In the remainder of this section, I offer a critique of "girl band feminism" waged from a vantage point

that moves beyond textual analysis in order to work through the political economic aspects of such major-label performers' engagements with feminist issues and specifically with the embrace of "female" pleasure. Gaar and Fury's comments, as well as the Donnas' disassociation from the anticapitalist ethos of former feminist punk acts, obfuscate feminist histories while promoting a collectivization of women in rock and a universalization of female expression.

While speaking about these "pop punkettes" through the familial connotations of Riot Grrrl can expand on and inform our memory of (post)feminist culture, I seek to locate political and economic differences in the production and distribution processes of these performers. Just as women of color are written out of many journalistic and academic histories of women's contributions to both punk and feminism, anthologies of "women in rock" also tend to chart only the popular successes of white acts and to define "female expression" in white, middle-class terms. This is largely due to the domination of the pop punk genre by white acts resulting from cultural and musical histories marked by pervasive exclusion and oppression of nonwhite feminists and punk performers.[35] As discussed in the section that follows, it is crucial to raise questions from a political economic perspective about the production and distribution structures of "the popular" that exclude and render invisible nonwhite acts and performers.

My remapping of Riot Grrrl thinks through the lens of feminist political economic analysis in order to create a new canon of feminist punk that privileges the tenuous relationships between performers and structures of race, class, and gender relations, making space for more informed critiques and ways of (re)telling women's "popular" histories. Furthermore, this remapping makes visible linkages that complicate mother-daughter binaries and the universalizing language of sisterhood, positioning girls (and grrrls) at the center of the debate without eschewing their many political, as well as performative, differences.

Antiracist Grrrls

The Riot Grrrl revolution formulated many of its positions from an investment in gender and sexual difference, leading many participants to feel alienated from the movement because of its failure to acknowledge how class and race construct the oppression of many women. For example, Kathleen Hanna's appeal for "girl love" in many ways could be interpreted as an extension of a second-wave feminist rhetoric that has been criticized for promoting a myth of "universal sisterhood" that treats gender oppression as the dominant oppression of *all* women.

Pseudonymous spaceblaster writes on her Web page, "There are no overt gestures of racism. no crosses are burned. no dolls of me are hung in effigy from trees outside clubs. but … i am not regarded as fully female, and this, i attribute to my race."[36] Articulating a similar response, Leah Lilith, the creator of the zines *Patti Smith* and *Sticks and Stones*, writes, "I was coming to realize that the reality of [Riot Grrrl] groups was far less than their reputation, and much of the time they did not understand or respect my colored girl, leather-dyke, femme, survivor self."[37]

Although Riot Grrrls sang about racist, misogynist "white boys" and sent these messages of girl love across racial divides, they were often not actually engaged in dialogue with the women of color they sought to include. Middle-class whiteness often subsumed all social difference without much interrogation, leaving out or glossing over the experiences of many young punk women of color. However, these critiques were often leveled from within the community, and many of the women critiquing the movement identified themselves with it or in proximity to it. As spaceblaster writes, "i completely support the ideals of the punk feminist movement…. i simply believe that there needs to be total honesty about the fact that … just because you call yourself a feminist does not absolve you of the responsibility of your racism."[38] Mimi Nguyen, in the zine collection *Evolution of a Race Riot*, articulates a similar position informed by an antiracist, feminist standpoint. She writes, "I truly believe that riot

grrrl was—and is—the best thing that ever happened to punk…. Unfortunately, riot grrrl often reproduced structures of racism, classism, and (less so) heterosexism in privileging a generalized 'we.'"

Briefly drawing attention to such covert racism in the Riot Grrrl movement, Stacy Thompson argues in *Punk Productions* that critiques of Riot Grrrl "mimicked historically earlier ones aimed at the Second Wave." However, he quickly claims that these failures of inclusion were a "shortcoming" common to punk scenes. Stressing the gender empowerment that Riot Grrrl provided young women, within the span of four sentences race not only disappears as a problem in Thompson's narrative but it is explicitly coded in efforts to purify the grrrls' historical contributions.[39]

While I support Thompson's desire to document the potential of anticapitalist punk productions, reading racism out of social movements' histories maintains systems of racial privilege while it eclipses the critical voices of people of color whose thoughts—and bodies—are often at the forefront of radical social change and transformation. By attempting to engage rather than

Mi Cuerpo Es Mio from the Los Angeles Riot Grrrl splinter group Spitboy

eschew criticisms of Riot Grrrl's implication in upholding structures of privilege and racialized oppression, a more dynamic and honest account of punk productions can be developed by reflecting on these failures in our current efforts to document and construct antiracist, feminist knowledges, communities, and movements. In order to map this crucial dimension of Riot Grrrl's politics, one can look at the e-zines and print zines that emerged throughout the 1990s and offered critical and self-reflexive assessments of race and racism in Riot Grrrl culture. These media allowed women identified with Riot Grrrl to construct their own critiques of the movement.

For example, Mimi Nguyen, among many other grrrls, including Leah Lilith and Sabrina Margarita Alcantara Tan, the editor of *Bamboo Girl*, outlines a sophisticated critique of how Riot Grrrl often perpetuated race and class privilege in its attempts to counter gender and sex oppression. Lilith and Tan acknowledge that Riot Grrrls' claims to be nonracist, nonhomophobic, and nonmisogynist differ from an engagement in an active, affirmative process of inclusion and self-reflection that insists on "making whiteness strange" and working with and through questions of social difference.

As critiques such as those of Lilith and Tan were circulated within Riot Grrrl communities, many grrrls—of all races—began to think more critically and self-reflexively about social difference. Although these Web sites and zines were fostered as a reaction to Riot Grrrl's perpetuation of race-and class-based exclusions, as many of these women continue to write, the political tensions that first prompted their texts have carried them far beyond issues of racial identity. While there is still much work to be done in remapping the effects of racism in feminist punk, these issues occupy the minds and meetings of many (punk) feminists more and more frequently. As Leah Lilith explains, "I left Riot Grrrl.… But I will always remain grateful to grrrl-punk and zine culture for teaching me to speak the truth, love my freakishness and make

my own freedom."[40] It is in this way that Riot Grrrl can be said to resonate, as part of a process in which, as Adrienne, vocalist for the Riot Grrrl splinter group Spitboy, sings, "We try to figure this one out."[41]

Web Gurls

Turning to the Internet, Riot Grrrl is often also cited as a catalyst for Web-based gurl feminisms. The Internet site Webtalkguys.com links these two movements, stating, "RiotGrrls [are] taking on the male dominated world of rock and WebGrrls [are] taking on the internet."[42] Discussing the role that technology played in the Riot Grrrl movement, Ednie Garrison mobilizes the term *technologics*, arguing that it articulates an awareness of "the ways our cultural repertoire of discourses, objects, ideas and modes of resistance merge and regroup in a cultural milieu that is proliferatively technologically saturated and mediated."[43] To engage technology, as Garrison points out, is not simply to travel the terrain of cybergeography. But neither is it only to utilize a "tool kit" or "master technology" as Garrison suggests. For many grassroots Riot Grrrl organizations, bands, and other cultural producers, having a Web site both resulted from and generated a greater circulation and distribution of goods and ideas.

Rather than operating with technologics, I suggest that employing technologies involves shifting interactions between users and machines that are crucial for an investigation of the technological resonances of the Riot Grrrl movement. In this section, I look at how gurl producers are embedded in nonlinear pathways established by Riot Grrrl's rhizomatic structure, which, as Marion Leonard argues, "matches the idea of an underground culture multiplying via lines of connection which are not controlled from a primary location." This, she writes, "splits apart any concept of [Riot Grrrl] as a unified progression."[44]

In what follows, I also address how Web mediation is criticized for cutting down on the face-to-face communication that Riot Grrrl concerts and conventions offered, often further rendering—for better or worse—the "bedroom" as the site of girls' cultural production.[45] This has led critics to either reformulate Web-based activism as something that can take place from within the private sphere or claim that the potential for collective action automatically decreases in the face of Web proliferation. As the chorus for one of Le Tigre's tracks goes, "Get off the Internet, I'll meet you in the street, destroy the right wing."[46]

Both this position vis-à-vis Web-mediated feminist activism and Garrison's view that feminists have developed a mastery over technology fail to address the shifting interactions that take place when users engage "new" technologies. For example, in 1996 Rebecca Odes, the former bassist of a punk band and proclaimed riot grrrl,[47] along with Esther Drill and Heather McDonald, founded www.gurl.com, the largest Web site for teenage girls. In 1999, these three women edited a softcover book, *Deal with It! A Whole New Approach to Your Body, Brain, and Life as a Gurl*,[48] which offers frank advice on sexuality, development, sexually transmitted diseases, and reproduction. Its content, made up in part of girls' comments from the Web site's pages, is informed by feminist theory. And, while it was published by a corporate subsidiary, Pocket Books, its layout is inspired by the do-it-yourself aesthetics associated with punk and Riot Grrrl zines. With lower-case lettering, line drawings, and a description of Adrienne Rich's "lesbian continuum," the nonconformity of *Deal with It!* was dealt with by concerned parents and politicians, who relegated the book to "self-help" sections and pulled it from public library shelves in Florida.

In print form, the book's content was susceptible to censorship and surveillance. But at the same time this Web-inspired print text became accessible to non-Internet users. Many young women familiar with the Web site eagerly awaited the book's arrival, ordering numerous copies for adolescent girls and mothers. In fact, the press coverage that *Deal with It!* received after protests

(in the street) for and against its availability in stores and libraries spread the word about the text. This points to the rhizomatic—or nonlinear and multi-dimensional—circulation patterns of Riot Grrrl production, as well as to the constant dialogue that exists between technologies, institutions, and political positions that render information more and less accessible, sometimes seemingly at once.

Riot Grrrl Reconsidered

When I learned in 2004 that Le Tigre had signed a deal with Universal Records after the closure of their previous label, Mr. Lady Records, I was angry at Kathleen Hanna for going back on her words, words that functioned to demarcate what appeared to be a clear distinction between indie and corporate affinities. And so, after hearing this news, I went back through this article, retaining Hanna's aesthetic and discursive articulations of feminism while reconsidering her thoughts on the political economics of feminist punk production. One omitted excerpt from a previous draft of this essay comes from Hanna's *Punk Planet* interview, published in 2001: "We need to earn a living, but the ultimate goal is to change the entire system. But unless we build models—even small little lego ones in our houses—we're not going to figure out how that's going to come about."[49] How Hanna planned to change the system by making a corporate deal with Universal Records—part of Vivendi Universal's Universal Music Group (UMG)—was not only beyond my essay's analysis but beyond my comprehension. How was I going to figure this one out?[50]

In his introduction to *Punk Productions* Stacy Thompson asks, "Can the commodity form be taken up and used against capitalism?"[51] This question appears to me to be at the crux of the debate over the political potential of utilizing corporate venues and corporately produced media forms to promote feminist punk agendas. In fact, it is precisely this question that Le Tigre's members asked their fans and critics to reconsider in interviews and press releases surrounding the move to Universal. Le Tigre member Johanna Fate-man told Northeastern News, "There were no feminist voices at all in the mainstream [media] and we felt like it would be really great if we could have some kind of a presence to a larger audience."[52]

Claiming that the pop musical form ensures listeners' engagement with a song, Le Tigre's major label debut album, *This Island*, bops and rhymes—as well as screams—its punk and feminist investments. Le Tigre's 2003 participation in the Bands against Bush tour and tracks from their album such as "Seconds," a song about President Bush with a vehement chorus that repeats, "You make me sick sick sick sick," and "New Kicks," which contains sound bites from

Handbill from a 2003 Le Tigre show in Montreal with the opening acts Lesbians on Ecstasy and Les Georges Leningrad

Iraq war protests, are marks of the band's commitment to oppositional politics and positions. In its concert performances, Le Tigre's video for "Seconds" flashes pictures of Bush interspersed with the word *sick*. Hanna also frequently speaks of her intense disdain for the current president during intervals between songs.

These political articulations can certainly engage listeners, but if the alternatives Le Tigre's members propose are in the product and not the production of their music, what kind of feminist transformation is being imagined? As my analysis of Riot Grrrl has argued, I think it is important that we ask questions about the messages articulated in postfeminist media, as well as the political economics of feminist punk production. As Annalee Newitz writes in an article for AlterNet, "I know Le Tigre deserve a big cash injection, and lead singer Hanna has been a dedicated champion of underground culture for almost a decade and a half. I don't actually believe there's anything wrong with selling out if it will help liberate an artist from a crappy day job or give her access to better resources. And yet—isn't there another way?"[53]

Newitz articulates a distinction between corporate conglomerates and independent labels, but in doing so she problematizes proscriptive notions of "selling out" that create an authentic-inauthentic binary, particularly in considerations of punk and feminist cultures. Newitz's commentary leaves room for considering the contextual specificities of artists' decisions while maintaining the desire for a less corporatized, mainstream cultural industry. Newitz, like Hanna in 2001, wants models of alternative economic practices to begin in our living rooms. Such a desire does not render every articulation Le Tigre makes irrelevant, irrational, or inauthentic. Rather, the band's corporate backing forces those who consume and engage with its punk feminism to renegotiate the linkages between economic production and political articulations. The conclusions one comes to may differ as political investments and ideas about the functions of capitalism diverge among critics and fans. However, whatever conclusions—or even partial conclusions—one draws, it remains crucial that analyses address, rather than avoid, the complex and often ambiguous alliances between feminism and the political economy. As my remapping insists, documenting the movements of Riot Grrrl demands that we acknowledge the various economic, as well as aesthetic, forms that feminist punk assumes.

Riot Grrrl Resounding

While Le Tigre can no longer be heralded for its noncorporate feminist punk, young women committed to anticapitalist processes of production and distribution continue to find it increasingly difficult to build infrastructures that make their music and media accessible and their incomes sustainable without amending their political values. In the face of an ever-infringing, profit-motivated industry, the ability to think realistically and transformatively is continually in jeopardy. Yet grrrls across the globe are finding ways to connect and build communities without signing with corporate labels or selling shampoo.

Kill Rock Stars (Sleater-Kinney) and Lookout! Records (Bratmobile) continue to produce and release albums influenced by Riot Grrrl while even small, local labels such as Lucky Madison navigate the music business, releasing the work of Riot Grrrl bands such as the Roulettes. Riot Grrrl chapters still exist, with local activist efforts based in cities across North America and Europe, while Ladyfest, a series of performances and workshops organized by Bratmobile's Allison Wolfe in Olympia, Washington, in August 2000, continues to expand in cities throughout the world, including Monterrey, Mexico; Malmö, Sweden; Brighton, England; Melbourne; Bielefeld, Germany; Ottawa; and Denver. Ottawa's 2004 Ladyfest held sessions on topics ranging from punk rock aerobics to the politics of menstruation.[54] Ladyfest Europe discussion boards contain news and information on international Ladyfests and provide a space for young feminists to make connections, linking

participants and organizers, as well as offering a "start your own" Ladyfest guide.[55] This ongoing festival carries out Riot Grrrl's punk feminist tradition of do-it-yourself production and grassroots organization.

The Grrrl Zine Network, a Web site run by the Austrian feminist and zine writer Elke Zobl, is one of the most prominent examples of how grrrls have created a sustainable infrastructure that allows for the circulation of goods and ideas. Serving as both an active forum and an archive of feminists' work, this "network" provides links to zine distribution outlets (called distros), as well as articles by feminist academics and interviews Zobl has conducted with other zine writers and distributors. The Web site includes young feminists' work and writing from across Europe, North America, Australia, New Zealand, Southeast Asia, and parts of the Middle East, fostering transnational dialogues about contemporary feminist issues.

These sites point to the ways in which Riot Grrrl lingers and expands. Although the term has been appropriated by major media corporations and profit-driven marketing industries, it has not faded into oblivion or collapsed as an apolitical assignment of a once meaningful term. Rather, Riot Grrrl is unfinished and fluid, and its residual effects can be found in new manifestations of feminist and postfeminist punk. While the term can be mobilized to excuse or obfuscate exploitive and commercialized versions of (post)feminism and punk production, it also maps a politics in process that engages in constant and shifting interactions with institutional and capitalist structures and technologies that delimit and determine its content and accessibility. One grrrl based in the United Kingdom, Cassandra Smith, captured this idea when she wrote, "Riot grrrl was not so much a culturally specific phenomenon as [a] mindset or form of energy. As we all know energy is neither created nor destroyed, but rather passed on."[56]

Perhaps what is most important is precisely this "passing on" of energy. Riot Grrrl continues, resounding in the echoes of young feminists' knowledges, reverberating against the walls of concert halls, classrooms, and girls' bedrooms. The term *Riot Grrrl* charts a genealogical history of women's activism and engagement with punk forms of cultural production. Riot Grrrl is, in this sense, a cartography of punk feminisms' successes and failures, exclusions and inclusions, as they continue to resonate in print, online, and over the airwaves. As a remapping of Riot Grrrl suggests, the political is always a shifting site of potential, of the words not yet on our lips.

NOTES

1. A zine is a small magazine with very low production costs usually assembled by an individual or a small group of people.

2. Nguyen, "Punk Planet 40."

3. Schilt, "A Little Too Ironic." See also Press and Reynolds, *The Sex Revolts*.

4. Pozner, "The 'Big Lie,'" 35.

5. See, for example, Tomlin, "Sex, Dreads, and Rock 'n' Roll."

6. Quoted in Klatzker "riot grrrl."

7. Carr, "The Legacy of Kathy Acker, Theoretical Grrrl," 49.

8. Gill "The Original Riot Grrrl Keeps It Pure," 10.

9. Seaman, "Piercy, Marge," 959. The oldest grrrl I've found to date is nearly two thousand years old. The remains of a female gladiator discovered in London were named Gladiator Grrrl in Dalai, "Gladiator Grrrl."

10. Henry, "Feminism's Family Problem," 211.

11. Both Katie Roiphe and Naomi Wolf are frequently critiqued and discussed in terms of the mother-daughter (and consequently the feminist-postfeminist) divide, while newspaper headlines such as "Not Your Mother's Feminism" have also become commonplace, proliferating the disjunction between feminist "mothers" and "daughters."

12. Koyama, "On Third Wave Feminisms."

13. Springer, "Third Wave Black Feminism?" I use the term *women of color* throughout this essay with some reservations. While I think it remains, for now, a useful term for affirming the presence of women who are racialized, it cannot capture the intersections and complexities of oppression or undo the hegemony of whiteness. For a discussion of how this term often functions to reaffirm the invisibility of whiteness and efface differences of privilege and power among and between women of color, see Carver, "I Am Not a Person of Color."

14. Anzaldúa and Keating, *This Bridge We Call Home*.

15. Hanna, interview with D. Sinker, in Sinker, *We Owe You Nothing, Punk Planet*, 65.

16. Le Tigre, "Hot Topic," *Le Tigre* (Mr. Lady Records, 2001).

17. Carr, "The Legacy of Kathy Acker, Theoretical Grrrl," 19. Notably, Ann Cvetkovich's book, *An Archive of Feelings: Trauma, Sexuality, and Lesbian Public Cultures*, begins with a discussion of Le Tigre and Tribe 8, perhaps unwittingly ending with a Kathy Acker quote, "Keep on living," which is the chorus to one of Le Tigre's tracks. Cvetkovich moves on in the second chapter to discuss the writer Dorothy Allison's work. Her methodology throughout attests to the possibilities for reimagining nonlinear associations between feminist texts.

18. O'Brien, *She Bop II*, 161.

19. Feigenbaum, "Some Guy Designed This Room I'm Standing In."

20. Goshert, "'Punk' after the Pistols."

21. "Women in Rock," *NME*, 22 March 2003, cover.

22. Feigenbaum, "Some Guy Designed This Room I'm Standing In," 37–56.

23. Goshert, "'Punk' after the Pistols," 85; Driscoll, *Girls*, 272.

24. Chonin, "Diva Demands Power, Choice, Halter Tops," 30; "Play That Punky Music," *People*, 9 September 2002, 41; Dunn, "Punk-Rock Debutants," 35; Kat, "The Donnas," 58.

25. Martens, "The Donnas Keep Building with Move to Atlantic," 17; "Pro-Voice Party with the Donnas," www.pantene.com, 15 April 2003.

26. Schilt, "A Little Too Ironic," 5–16.

27. See Wald, "Just a Girl?"; and "I Want It That Way."

28. The comment was made on www.teenmusic.com, 20 March 2004.

29. Fury, "The Donnas and Bratmobile at the Bowery Ballroom."

30. In the occasional interview, the Donnas speak of going to a Bikini Kill concert and handing the band a tape, only to find it in shreds on the venue floor later that night. Calling the event "disappointing," Donna R. told the "indie" magazine *ROCKRGRL*, "If those people had just said something nice to us, it would have totally made our day. But nobody ever did" (ibid.). The Donnas also opened for Joan Jett in 2000.

31. The Donnas, "Take It Off," *Spend the Night* (Atlantic Records, 2002).

32. Kruse, "Abandoning the Absolute," 145.

33. Schilt, "A Little Too Ironic," 5–16.

34. Gaar, *She's a Rebel*, 484.

35. For an in-depth discussion of racism in the punk scene and the experiences of punks of color, see James Spooner's documentary *Afropunk* (2003).

36. "Race and Riot Girl," Spaceblaster.com, 22 February 2004.

37. Lilith, "Sticks and Stones May Break My Bones," 3.

38. These comments appeared on Spaceblaster.com.

39. Thompson, *Punk Productions*.

40. Lilith, "Sticks and Stones May Break My Bones," 4.

41. Spitboy, "Word Problem," *Mi Cuerpo Es Mio* (Allied Recordings, 1994).

42. www.webtalkguys.com. 22 February 2004.

43. Garrison, "U.S. Feminism-Grrrl-Style!"

44. Leonard, "Paper Planes," 111.

45. It is important to note that, although Internet access is on the rise, the ability and money required to run and finance a Web site are very different from the know-how, "leisure" time, and resources needed to produce a narrowly circulated paper zine. Even do-it-yourself zine culture is criticized for overlooking the "privilege" involved in access to photocopiers, free time, and materials. However, both of these forms of production have been utilized by a wide demographic of girls. See, for example, Green and Taormino, *A Girl's Guide to Taking over the World*.

46. Le Tigre, "Get off the Internet," *From the Desk of Mr. Lady* (Mr. Lady Records, 2001).

47. Lange, "Deal with It," 102.

48. Drill, McDonald, and Odes, *Deal with It!*

49. Hanna, interview, 67.

50. In 2003, Universal Music Group was the world's largest music company, operating in seventy-one countries with an estimated global market share of 23.5 percent. It lists Polydor, Decca, Verve, and Mercury Records among its sixteen principle labels. Its owner, Vivendi Universal, also owns 18.5 percent of NBC Universal, as well as large shares of the telecommunications industries of France and Morocco. Vivendi Universal's revenues for 2004 were 21,428 million euros ("Vivendi Universal," www.vivendi-universal.com, 27 June 2005).

51. Thompson, *Punk Productions*, 3.

52. Hankinson, "Le Tigre Talks Song Writing, Politics, and *Spin* Magazine."

53. Newitz, "Suck My Left One."

54. "Workshops!!" Ladyfest Ottawa, 2004, www.ladyfestottawa.com, 24 April 2005.

55. "Homepage," Ladyfest Europe, www.ladyfesteurope.org, 24 April 2005.

56. Smith, "Riot Grrrls."

■ ■ ■

Discussion Questions

1. What did the riot grrrl movement represent?

2. What made the movement so unique?

3. How did the media affect the movement?

What You Can Do

- Recognize movements similar to riot grrrl, and support the movement by attending concerts, openings, and other performances

- Be consistent in your support of other women, even if it is not a type of activism you completely grasp

- Underground movements avoid mainstream for a reason; be careful not to breach etiquette

CHAPTER 12

One Is Silver and the Other's Gold

By Jennifer Baumgardner

When I was a little girl, I played with Barbies religiously. They weren't my only pastime—I also loved the *Carol Burnett Show* in reruns, singing Barbra Streisand songs at the top of my lungs, and roller-skating. But the summer of 1979, Barbie reigned supreme. I played Barbies every day with my next-door neighbor Missy, a green-eyed ten-year-old (I was nine), who was the daughter of the pastor at United Methodist. I had Malibu Barbie (who had straight hair with bangs, a tan, and suggestive lighter lines of paint where her bikini had blocked out the sun) and another Barbie with knee-length wavy hair and an opulent pink evening gown (Vegas Barbie? Barbie Dream Girl?). Each day I would drag my Barbies, Barbie furnishings, Barbie car, and Barbie clothing over to Missy's. We established a narrative: The Barbies were in college and living in dorms and were always getting ready to go out on dates. They were, while possibly not gay, bi-curious—in the sense that I often positioned them to lie on top of each other naked. Missy had a Ken, and that came to no good end. Pretty soon Malibu Barbie was pregnant and needed an abortion. She got pregnant many times and always chose to have an abortion. After all, she was in college, bisexual, and popular, and abortion was legal.

I was raised steeped in a brew, however weak at times, of feminist values and culture. It was a function of era (the '70s) more than location (Fargo, North Dakota) or sensibility. During the Vietnam War protests and drug experiments of the 1960s, my parents were struggling young marrieds, scraping by while Dad finished med school, and then we spent five years on army bases while my dad did his military service. Still, my mother read Ms. My father wanted everything for his three daughters that sons would have gotten. We talked about abortion and gay rights at the dinner table—the whole family was for both. My childhood was invisibly, but perceptibly, enhanced by Title IX, access to birth control and abortion, and a *Free to Be ... You and Me* attitude. But these gifts from the women's liberation movement weren't clicks, as made famous by Jane O'Reilly's 1971 "The Housewife's Moment of Truth"—they didn't unlock a feminist consciousness but rather enabled me to live a pretty unencumbered life *without* having to be part of a movement.

By college, 1988 to 1992, I was a passionate, if conflicted, feminist. I danced suggestively at frat parties in miniskirts with my friends while yelling, "Don't look at me!" at any oglers. I read the big authors: Millett, Firestone, hooks, Dworkin, Anzaldua ... still nothing had occurred that could be called a "click." It was more like I was channeling clicks from another generation, nodding my head in agreement with "all men benefit from sexism" and "abortion on demand without apology!" I quoted from brilliant, outraged manifestos written by women who were raised in the 1950s, women for whom feminism landed like a meteor in their lives, initiating cataclysmic change in their carefully laid-out existences. I laughed ruefully about my preconsciousness nine-year-old self who played with Barbies, those pink, plastic, acceptable versions of womanhood.

By age twenty-one, the ideas of feminism thrilled me. The power the movement had put in so many women's hands was palpable to me. Its recent history was so glamorous and righteous; I was sad I hadn't been around for it. Jealous, even, of these revolutionized housewives and women who had been excluded from jobs, college, the military, leadership, and drinking at McSorley's Ale House. Why couldn't I be one of the women so angry about the high-dose pill (which caused blood clots and strokes and had been unethically tested on women in Puerto Rico with no attempt at informed consent) that I broke up the Senate Pill Hearings in 1970? By the time I was on the Pill, the hormones were at a mere fraction of the previous dose, safe for most intents and purposes.

But later, at the magazine where I worked after college, I got my click. It came not from desperately defying the housework my husband didn't help me do (I was unmarried and dating a girl), nor from learning that men in my office were paid more for the same work (I worked at Ms. magazine; there were no men). My click came from having an ally—a peer raised in much the same brew as I had been—who could reflect back to me what I was experiencing as a feminist raised *after* the Second Wave. If not for her, would I have continued recognizing feminism only if it looked and sounded like the Second Wave? Would I have continued to pile on to my own generation, agreeing with sentences like, "young women are so much less radical" and "so much less pro-choice" and "there are no young leaders"?

The ally was Amy, also born in 1970, though in a different kind of family than mine. She was raised by a young single mom, had never met her father, and had attended boarding school and Barnard—a somewhat common trajectory in New York City, but exotic to my Midwestern perceptions. I worked at Ms. magazine in the editorial offices, total peon job; Amy worked down the hall in Gloria Steinem's office.

At first, our interest in one another was social—two young colleagues, one new to the city, going out for a drink or to hear a band or dance at Nell's. But within a few months, we began talking shop: She would tell me about the younger activists she had met at the women's conference in Beijing or through her foundation, Third Wave, which at the time was basically Amy and a recipe file box with names of a few hundred donors and members. I would share my increasingly confident belief that women who were creating—not just critiquing—culture were the new generation of feminist leaders, the dearth of whom was so bemoaned at meetings we attended. Through Ms. (and my own initiative), I was meeting writers, musicians, and activists like Kathleen Hanna, Christina Kelly, Nomy Lamm, Ani DiFranco, Debbie Stoller, and Farai Chideya—women my age who were feminist and responding to their own era.

Those first heady conversations prompted an independent and accurate assessment of my own world and generation, its problems and potential solutions. Rather than my continuous repetition (and romanticizing) of feminist truths that came before me, I began to look in the mirror and see myself as important to feminism as the women who had come before me. I believe what I went through was entirely natural. When you are becoming radicalized, you gravitate to recognizably radical spaces. I felt I was a feminist but wasn't totally secure in what that might mean in my life. Therefore, I pretended to have Andrea Dworkin's life—or at least her perceptions, which were, of course, born of her personal and generational experiences.

At times, this new ability to see my own generation and myself as powerful and relevant felt like a betrayal of—or at least a conflict with—the Second Wave. I saw that social justice has a natural evolution to it. The '60s were a Big Bang. Abortion was illegal, contraception was illegal, black people were actively barred from rights of citizenship and living with dignity—or even living. To be gay or trans was to live in secret or face constant ridicule and prejudice. Women were hostages to a single stray sperm, allowed to be educated without a chance to apply this education in meaningful work. People protested their exclusion and oppression—they kicked open doors, they demanded to be let in.

But that way of being activist is less germane today, when exclusion is not the primary oppression. The activism of today is subtler, intersectional, individual, and sensitive. It requires listening as much as, if not more than, speaking out. It is the activism of inhabiting a space once the door has been kicked open, warming up the chilly atmosphere, creating the infra- structure for a healthy social environment.

I now lecture widely across the country. I've visited more than 250 schools, and at every school there is this anxiety that students today are too apathetic, that they are not angry enough about the wars, about abortion rights, about capitalism. When I was in college, I felt that anxiety and made the exact same indictment of my generation—not being angry enough—a direct comparison with the '60s. But I've come to realize that the job of each generation is to make sense of its own era—to understand what is needed now, when some past issues of oppression are not so in-your-face. To acknowledge that I am living a far more socially free and empowered life than my mother could have imagined at my age. I want to thank her and her generation for that groundwork, but more importantly I want to commit to inhabiting the rooms they helped to open up, and not continue banging loudly on a door that is unlocked.

Identifying that distinction between my generation's feminism and that of the Second Wave was a critical step in seeing what truly ties the eras, generations, waves (whatever you want to call it) of feminism together. It's this: It's a relationship with an ally that enables you to inhabit your feminism. The women of the 1960s and 1970s talked at kitchen tables, held CR meetings, formed countless groups, but the main thing they did was reflect back each other's experiences and call them, not just valid, but political.

One day in 1998, when Amy and I were in the middle of writing our first book together, we were struggling with our resistance to some earnest, feminist magazine targeted at girls. It might have been *New* Moon; it might have been *Teen Voices*. Something about it felt inauthentic to young girls today and imposed from another era—that whole aping of '70s feminism we felt encouraged to do early in our consciousness. Then we began to talk about Barbie. It took a while to jog my memory, but I recalled how much fun I had imagining adult life via that doll—and how much my Barbie was expressing the changes wrought by feminism, from sexual freedom to legal abortion. Meanwhile, Amy recalled that she would take photos of her Barbies, as if they were her older siblings, filling out her female-only family of two. "I liked Barbie," said Amy, decisively. "She was sort of a friend."

"Yes," I said and sent up to the gods of feminism a silent word of thanks for this ally with whom I reliably, and powerfully, clicked.

■ ■ ■

Discussion Questions

1. Why did Jennifer Baumgardner's "co-opting" of second-wave feminism in her early years distress her?

2. How does she describe the differences in second-wave issues and third-wave issues?

3. How did the differences cause guilt and concern in her interpretation of feminist activism?

4. What is the relevance of her memories of Barbie dolls and her feminist advocacy? How did the memories change over time?

What You Can Do

- Remember all feminist waves have different ways of creating activism, and as the issues evolve, so do the responses

- Never discredit your memories or earlier actions, even if you don't think they were "feminist"-oriented

- Feminist advocacy comes in all shapes and forms, so embrace yours for everything it's worth

CHAPTER 13

Heartbroken

WOMEN OF COLOR FEMINISM AND THE THIRD WAVE

By Rebecca Hurdis

This essay isn't just about an adopted, woman of color feminist; rather, it is a story about how I came to believe that I was worthy of all of these identities. It isn't just a story about feminism or solely about adoption. It is an exploration of where the mind stops and the heart follows. It is too easy to distract myself with ideas about "deconstruction" and "critical analysis," terms that lack the emotional depth to explain my experiences. The struggle is not to find one place where I can exist, but to find it within myself to exist in all of these places, uncompromisingly. To live a life of multiplicity is as difficult as it is to write about it.

All of my life I have been told the story of when my mother held me in her arms for the first time. It was late at night at the airport in Newark, New Jersey. My mother, father and two brothers, along with my grandparents and uncle, were all waiting in the terminal lounge for my plane to arrive from Seoul, Korea. There were other families also waiting for their new babies to be brought off the plane. My mother tells me that she watched in anticipation as all the escorts walked off of the plane with small bundles of Korean babies. Each time they walked toward her, they would pass by, giving the babies to other families. My family grew anxious and nervous as the flow of people exiting the plane grew sparse. My chaperone and I were the last to deplane. The woman walked toward my family and placed me in the arms of my mother. I was six months old. I clung to her, put my head on her shoulder, patted her back and called her "mother" in Korean. The year was 1975. The day was Mother's Day.

Growing up in a transracial adopted family, I was often confused by the images of the "normal, nuclear families." We didn't look like any other family I saw. I couldn't comprehend how I could love my family, feel accepted by them and believe that I belonged to them as much as my phenotypically white brothers. Yet every time I looked in the mirror, my reflection haunted me, because the face that stared back was not the same color as my family's. This awareness was reinforced by the sometimes brutal questions of others. I constantly had to explain that I really was my brother's sister. He was not my husband but truly my brother. I was not the foreign exchange student that just never left. Embarrassed by the attention, I tried to ignore the differences. I took the negativity and dissociation I felt and began to internalize the feelings. I fooled myself into thinking and acting the role of a "good little Asian saved from her fallen country and brought to the land of salvation." I began to believe the messages about being an Asian girl and about being adopted. This compliance was one of the only ways I learned to gain acceptance and validation as a child. I realized that my identity was being created *for* me not *by* me.

When I was ten years old, we moved from a progressive city in Maryland to a small town in Connecticut. Aside from the infamous New England fall foliage, the only color I saw was white. I suppose it wasn't such a radical change for the rest of my family, because they didn't need the difference and diversity I required for spiritual survival. I quickly realized the key to acceptance was to not be too ethnic, or ethnic at all. To be accepted, I had to grasp and identify with whiteness, completely denying my Asian self. I spent my teenage years running away from myself and rebelling from the stereotype of the "good, cute little Asian." The only images of Asian Americans that I saw came from the television. I accepted the misrepresentations as real and accurate because our town only had a few people of color to begin with. I always thought they were the exceptions to the stereotypes. We were the "fortunate ones" and we self-perpetuated the lies about ourselves and about our people.

I fooled myself into believing that life was so great. I was accepted and had all of the things that I thought made me just like everyone else, yet I couldn't understand why I still carried around a sadness. I was playing out the script that had been given to me, yet I kept feeling as though I was in the wrong play. When I would talk to my friends about it, they wouldn't and couldn't understand. I was told that I was making too big a deal out of being Asian and besides I *was* just like everyone else. They thought that I just worried too much. My friends went so far as to convince me by telling me that "I wasn't really Asian, I was white." But the truth couldn't be denied, just as the color of my skin couldn't either. They thought that because we were friends they were entitled or allowed to nickname me "Chinky." They tried to justify it by saying that it was only a joke. My boyfriends were ashamed that they had an Asian-American girlfriend. They assumed they had a right to physically, mentally and sexually abuse me because they thought they were doing me a favor by lowering their standards to be with a woman of color. I came across feminism as a first-year student at Ohio State University. I was extremely depressed at the time. Everything—my created identity, the world of whiteness that I knew, the denial of my race—that I had worked so hard at

repressing and ignoring throughout my life was finally surfacing and emerging. I no longer had the validation of whiteness to protect my false identity. The world that I had understood was changing, and I was confronted with defining myself without the associations of my family and friends. I was forced to step outside of my white world, shedding my blinders to find that I wasn't white and that I had never really been so. The only illusion was the one that I had created for myself, the one that had found acceptance. But I was beginning to realize the cost of this facade.

Yes, I had a large circle of white friends and boyfriends throughout high school. Despite their acceptance, however, I was simultaneously cast as the other. I was undeniably Asian. I was the subject and the object. I was the china doll and the dragoness. The contradictions and the abuse confused me. How could my friends and boyfriends love me, yet in a heated argument spit out "chink" at me? How could they respect me, yet sing the song that had been popularized from the movie *Full Metal Jacket*, "Me So Horny?"

My first women's studies course focused on the history of the women's movement, the social context and the contemporary issues facing feminism today. We looked at issues ranging from violence to sexual orientation to women-centered spirituality to representation in music and film to body image. I began to recognize my extensive history of sexual, mental and physical abuse with boyfriends, and I started to comprehend the cycle of abuse and forgiveness. I was able to begin to stop blaming myself and shift the responsibility back to those who had inflicted the abuse. Initially I had disconnected the abuse from racism, even though it was heavily intertwined and simultaneous. It was just too large for me to understand, and it was still too early for me to grapple with race. I still was thinking that I just needed to become the "right" kind of Asian American and then everything would make sense.

I know that for a lot of women of color, feminism is perceived as being a white woman's movement that has little space or acknowledgment for women of color. I understand how that is true, but back then this class became a catalyst for change and healing. It was a major turning point in my life, where I was able to break my silence and find empowerment within myself and for myself. Women's studies offered me a place where there was validation and reason. I was uncovering and understanding how my own internalization was tied to ideologies of racism and sexism. Although the analysis of racism was somewhat limited in these courses, it served as a lead for future interests. Women's studies and feminism was a steppingstone toward striving for a holistic understanding of myself.

Initially I identified my experiences as being part of a larger discourse and reality. I named the abuse and trauma of my past and could therefore heal from it. I proudly began calling myself a feminist. I viewed feminism broadly as the eradication of sexism, racism, ageism, ableism and heterosexism. It was a social and political commitment to a higher vision for society by resituating women from the margins into the center. I began recognizing and naming what I believed was sexism. The summer after my first women's studies course, I returned home and wrote a dramatic letter to the Congregational church of which I was a member. I earnestly asked them to remove my name from their list because "I did not want to support or be affiliated with a patriarchal institution such as a Christian church." I felt this act was a rite of passage, my initiation into the feminist movement.

But I left college feeling as though there was something missing to this feminism. Professors would talk about Black feminism or women of color feminism, but merely as another mark on their feminist timeline. Little time was dedicated to really examining the intersection of race and gender. Back home I went to my local new-age store (which also doubled as the feminist bookstore) and stumbled on *This Bridge Called My Back: Writings by Radical Women of Color* (edited by Cherríe Moraga and Gloria Anzaldúa). It was the first time I had found a book that had the words "women of color" as part of the title.

It was as if I had found the pot of gold at the end of the feminist rainbow. Even though I didn't find myself completely represented in the book, specifically because none of the contributors had been an adopted child, I did find my thoughts, anger and pain represented through the eloquent voices of other women of color. Their writings incorporated race and sexuality.

Reading this anthology, I realized I was entitled to feeling something other than apologetic. I could be angry. I could be aggressive. I could be the opposite of this little china doll that everyone expected me to be. Given my background, this book was life-changing. It represented one of the first moments where I could claim something that was mine; something different from my parents, my friends, my community; something other than whiteness. I remember sitting at the town beach on a hot and humid August day, flipping through the book, my mind exploding and expanding. As I sat there frantically reading, I recall looking up at the sun, closing my eyes and thanking the goddess that I had found this work. Through this discovery I had found that I was not alone. Not only was I feminist, but I was a woman of color feminist.

What makes my relationship to women of color feminism different from most other women of color is how and why I entered the conversation. I began looking at race through gender, where most have the reverse experience. This idea of entry point is crucial. I call myself a woman of color before I call myself an Asian American. It reflects how I have come to see myself and how I understand my own identity. The term "women of color" seems broadly inviting and inclusive while "Asian American" feels rigid and exclusive. Women of color feminism took me from being a victim to being a warrior. I am now in an ethnic studies graduate program trying to explore if women of color are within feminism's third wave, and if so, where. I began this project as an undergraduate but I had hit a wall. It was difficult locating voices that represented generation X or third wave women of color feminism. Not much had been written, as our voices were just beginning to emerge. I found women of color feminists in alternative places such as zines, anthologies, magazines and pop culture. I felt frustrated that our voices were deemed not "accredited" enough to be represented in the mainstream.

I held a certain expectation for Jennifer Baumgardner and Amy Richards's book, *Manifesta: Young Women, Feminism, and the Future*. This book markets itself as being *the* text for the third wave of feminism, and I had high hopes that it would address issues of race, gender and class sexuality. Instead, I found the specific history of white (privileged) women. This is a great book for the college white woman who has recently been inspired by feminism and wants to know about the past and how she should contribute for the future. Yet this history is complicated by the fact that the authors do not honestly acknowledge that this is their intention. Rather, they assert that this book is a history of all women, dropping the names of such women of color as Rebecca Walker and Audre Lorde.

I found it astounding that there is no extensive discussion of women of color feminism. This indicates that Baumgardner and Richards feel as though this is a separate issue, a different kind of feminism. It is as if their work is the master narrative of feminism, with women of color feminism as an appendage. I had hoped that they would have considered such books as *This Bridge Called My Back* and Audre Lorde's *Sister Outsider* as groundbreaking, as they are deemed by most generation X women of color. These books were life-changing to me not only because their critiques have historical value, but also because what these writers were saying in the 1980s was still relevant in the 1990s. *Manifesta* is successful in creating momentum for young white women's activism through the attempt to move feminism out of academia and back into a social and political movement. But the book's greatest contribution was that it raised a need for creating a lineage for women of color feminism. Is it possible to construct a feminist genealogy that maintains inclusivity? Does feminism still

exist for women of color or is it just a "white thing?" Are generation X women of color participating in feminism? These questions propelled me to further think about the connections as well as the separations between women of color and feminism. In the exploration of the third wave of women of color feminism, I talked to several women of color professors and students at the University of California at Berkeley. Their responses and our conversations together were incredibly helpful. These women challenged me to further think about my own conceptions surrounding feminism.

I had expected that as women of color, most of these students would also identify as women of color feminists. I believed the two terms to be synonymous. Instead, I found a rejection of the word "feminism." I hear many women of color refer to themselves as such, yet they make the distinction that they are not claiming a feminist identity. Although many of the women support and stand in alliance with women of color feminism, there is still a lapse in their chosen identity. Many report to have read the popular and pivotal texts within women of color feminism and have felt moved, but their "empowerment" only goes so far.

What is it about the word "feminism" that has encouraged women of color to stand apart from it? Feminism has been indoctrinated into the academy through the discipline of women's studies. It has moved out of the social and political spaces from where it emerged. Women's studies have collapsed the diversity that was part of the feminist movement into a discipline that has become a homogenous generality. For women in the third wave then, one needs to have the academic training of women's studies to be an " accredited feminist." Once race is added to the complexity, many women of color feel as though the compromise or negotiation is just too high a price to pay to be called a feminist. Women of color's participation in women's studies and feminism still causes splintering in our identities.

Many women believe that there is a certain required persona to be a feminist. In the ethnic studies course "Women of Color in the U.S." at Berkeley, for example, students expressed feeling that they didn't have enough knowledge or background to be able to call themselves feminists. The students' comments reflect how many women of color find difficulty in accessing feminism. Often the response is that "feminism is a white woman's thing." Whiteness in feminism comes to represent privilege, power and opportunity. It rarely positions women of color as being as legitimate as the identities of white women. Women's studies has been accurately accused of treating race as a secondary oppression through offering courses about race that are separate from the central curriculum, while ethnic studies feels more comfortable as a place to discuss race and gender. But even in ethnic studies, women's experiences and histories still remain on the margins. Like women's studies, they too have had problems integrating gender into the analysis of race.

Women of color often feel women's studies is a battlefield where they are forced to defend their communities and themselves. Women's studies, the academic endeavor of feminism, has a history of relegating women of color as second. When women of color raise issues of race in these classrooms, the response from other students is often defensive and loaded with repressed white guilt. For young women of color, there is a sentiment that we must find a central identity that precedes all others. We are asked to find one identity that will encapsulate our entirety. We are asked to choose between gender, class, race and sexuality and to announce who we are first and foremost. Yet where is the space for multiplicity?

Although I am a self-proclaimed woman of color feminist, I struggle with being an "authentic" woman of color feminist. Even though I realize it is self-defeating, I worry that other women of color will look at my feminism and judge it as being socialized whiteness and an effect of adoption. The roots of my feminism are connected to my adopted mother, although I am uncertain whether she would identify as a feminist. She was a woman who wouldn't let

us watch the *Flintstones* or the *Jetsons* because of their negative portrayal of women, yet she unquestionably had dinner on the table every night for her husband, sons and daughter. Most important, she raised me to believe I could be whoever I wanted to be and in that a strong woman. If feminism has been bestowed onto me from my adopted mother, then I choose not to look at it as another indicator of whiteness or of being whitewashed. Rather, I see it as a gift that has shown me not the limitations of mainstream feminism but the possibilities of women of color feminism. People sometimes question my attachment to feminism. Despite the criticisms, it has served as a compass that navigates me away from paralysis into limitless potential.

One of the reasons that my project is now at a standstill is that the conversation has changed. In the 1970s and 1980s women of color feminists seemed to be in solidarity with each other. Their essays showed the racism and classism within mainstream feminism, forcing mainstream feminism to be accountable. Today, however, women of color are focused on the differences that exist among us. When we try to openly and honestly acknowledge the differences between us, we become trapped in difference, which can result in indifference.

Women of color feminism has currently been reduced to a general abstraction that has flattened out difference and diversity, causing tension between women of color. Instead of collectively forming alliances against whiteness, women of color now challenge the opposing identities that exist under the umbrella term "women of color." It raises questions about entitlement and authenticity. It tries to suppress the heterogeneous composition of women of color feminism by trying to create a unifying term. Yet the differences of class, racialization and sexuality have arisen and persisted, challenging assumptions that all women of color are in solidarity with each other. We all come with backgrounds and histories that differ from one another and despite knowing this, we still maintain this ideal and creation of the authentic "women of color." The one that is the right class, the right race, the right sexuality. We must refuse being reduced to an abstraction. We must address the conflicts that have begun to fester paralysis instead of fostering change. But that also means that we need to revitalize women of color feminism so that those actions can begin to take place.

I see women of color feminism at this moment of indifference. I see the backstabbing. I hear the gossip. I feel the tension. We use our words like fists to beat each other down and beat each other silent. It is not pretty and certainly not productive. When do we recognize that the moment has come to move forward? I wish I had some solution of a way to "use our difference to achieve diversity instead of division." But we know that clichés are just clichés. They don't provide us with the fairy-tale endings. They don't make us feel better or more hopeful. More often than not, I think clichés just annoy us and leave us sarcastic.

It is crucial to explore and expose the problems of women of color feminism, but we also need to be weary of what we are willing to sacrifice. I think a new, third space is being created in women of color feminism. Those of us who are not easily recognized and acknowledged as women of color are coming to feminism as a place to discuss the implications of invisibility.

We are pushing, expanding and exploding ideologies of multiplicity and intersectionality. We come as transracial adoptees, women of mixed race, bisexuals, refugees and hundreds of other combinations. For us, women of color feminism continues to be a living theory and a way to survive.

■ ■ ■

Discussion Questions

1. How did the author's first women's study class help her understand racism and identity?

2. The intersectionality of race and feminism was lacking in third-wave discussions and works. How did this affect the author's view of feminism?

3. The author observes how women of color embrace feminist theory, but often do not identify as a woman of color feminist. Why? What does the author hope to see in the future for women of color feminists?

What You Can Do

- Recognize women of color need a voice in feminist change
- Understand intersectional feminism and why it is important
- Be inclusive
- Take note of feminist works that do little to acknowledge race, disability, GLTBQ, and other identities, and seek more inclusive material
- Be an advocate for all feminists

The Fourth Wave and The Future of Feminism

Feminist activism has witnessed a surge in the last year. According to womensmarch.com, the Women's March on January 21, 2017, is considered the largest single-day protest in US history. Momentum has built up to encourage women to run for political positions, become more locally active, and begin to demand change by calling out men in power for sexual misconduct by using social media. Around the world, feminist activism has changed laws, as women demand action for unjust treatment. The feminist movement continues to grow and focus on the future of equality. Please read the following article and watch the short videos on the future of feminism.

CHAPTER 14

The Women's March and the Show of Resistance

By Joanna Wall

On January 21, 2017, over five million people came together to march in what was known as the Women's March.[1] This global movement was a show of resistance against the various powers and policies infringing on women's rights. Marches across the world were intersectional in both issues and personal identity. Children, people of color, GLBTQ folks, and men from all walks of life joined together with women to begin the movement for change. The show of support brought a new momentum to women and our pursuit for social change.

The Rise of Discontent

As a third-wave feminist, I basked in the success of the second wave. I could easily get birth control and felt secure with my access to abortion should I ever need it. Title IX further championed my educational goals and gave me a seat at the university table. Women seemed to be progressing at a pace fast enough to shatter the glass ceiling. There was much hope and comfort in what the second wave had accomplished. But then, in 1991, the Anita Hill–Clarence Thomas hearings occurred. I watched in shocked silence as an all-male judiciary committee asked Ms. Hill if she was a scorned woman. Political pundits accused her of lying; the country overwhelmingly believed Thomas and accused Hill of exaggerating; and perhaps most eye opening to my third wave ideals, the Senate confirmed Thomas. Though it was the narrowest margin in recent history (52–48), Thomas was still confirmed with the help of one of two women serving in the Senate.[2] To add insult to injury, several Democrats crossed party lines to vote for Thomas, including David Boren—the Democratic Senator from Oklahoma where Hill was at the time a law professor at the University of Oklahoma.[3] Boren would become the president of the University of Oklahoma just three short years later, while Hill was still a tenured professor in the school of law. How could this have happened? What happened to the second-wave momentum? How was it possible to be looking at a sea of white male faces without one woman in sight? Had we really not elected more women over the last decade? But this was just the beginning. Like a domino effect, more affronts aimed at women began to occur. *Planned Parenthood of Southeast Pennsylvania v. Casey* was decided in 1992, adding several burdens to the process of obtaining an abortion.[4] The wage gap continued to exist, the glass ceiling was still solidly in place, and racism, violence, and sexual assault still slowly killed us. We had won rights in theory—just not in practice. By the time the 2016 presidential election rolled around, women had reached a consensus: it was time to march.

Organize, March, Resist!

The Women's March was swiftly organized and, the day after Donald Trump's inauguration, record-breaking numbers gathered in cities and towns across the world to march in solidarity. Over the last several years, we had watched young men of color being shot by police, women being harassed at work and on the street, sexual assault occurring on a regular basis across

college campuses, trans and GLBQ folks still seeking basic human rights, and Indigenous women fighting to keep their land free from Big Oil. We all marched together. We found common ground through common denial of rights. We used our signs like shields to march into a battle we knew would not be ending anytime soon, but we made our message clear: we are back and we want our rights in theory *and* in practice this time.

Feats and Triumphs

Since that day in January, we have seen more women run for office. According the Center for American Women in Politics, 396 women have filed for US House seats and fifty women are predicted to run for US Senate seats.[5] If the number holds up, it will be record breaking. The absence of women in Congress has reached a critical point. Lawmakers are determining our rights without our voice, and little progress has been attained in addressing violence, sexual assault, poverty, and the continued issues of employment discrimination and harassment. Women lawmakers can bring the relief we have been seeking and know the necessity of change and the importance of being empowered to take care of ourselves and our families.

Another monumental achievement was the empowerment of thousands of women calling out predators with #MeToo. The #MeToo

movement was originally started in 2006 by Tarana Burke to help sexual assault survivors.[6] Used again by Alyssa Milano in 2017, the movement went viral, and men of power and fame were called out for sexual misconduct. As resignations were handed in and apologies issued, the country came to the grim realization that sexual misconduct was not only common, but also an accepted practice in every place from corporate boardrooms to the kitchens of mom and pop diners. The movement has given a voice to many survivors and encouraged even more women to report. The true change the #MeToo movement will make is yet to be determined, but already employers are on alert that misogynistic and criminal behavior will no longer be tolerated. Women are feeling more secure in shutting down unwanted sexual advances without the threat of losing their jobs or being otherwise penalized. A simple hashtag

with a complex meaning brought down some of the most powerful men in Hollywood and beyond. Never doubt the strength women will bring to a movement in order to achieve social change.

Lasting Effects

The Women's March encouraged unity among us all and demanded those in power acknowledge the discontent among us. The sheer number of marchers alone gave energy to have a second Women's March the following year. This time, marchers encouraged voting and getting people out to the polls. As the midterm elections loom, the attendees of the march are paving the way for women-centered positive change. Undeniably, the Women's March created a strong energy and will perhaps be remembered as one of the most important movements of the fourth wave.

The March has growing pains of course, like all the movements before it. Going forward, we will need to practice inclusivity and assure that all people have a voice, with focus on women of color and GLBTQ folks. We must be mindful that there is a perception among the younger activists that the Women's March is predominately middle-aged, middle-class, white women. While this may be statistically accurate, we cannot afford to let this become a reason to not participate. Marches must be open to everyone, and we must make certain we provide a welcoming and inclusive space. The movement must keep moving in order to be effective, and we all have a vested interest in seeing fundamental changes. We all need to stand together in a strong line of invincibility. Yes, there is room for improvement, but together we make lasting change. We must keep the big picture in mind, as the little things that divide us can ultimately destroy us.

NOTES

1. "The March," Women's March, n.d. Web. 28 January 2018.

2. Republican Senator Nancy Landon Kassebaum Baker from Kansas voted yea. Democratic Senator Barbara Ann Mikulski from Maryland voted nay.

3. Full list of democrats who voted in favor of Thomas: Richard Shelby, Alabama; Dennis DeConcini, Arizona; Sam Nunn, Georgia; Wyche Fowler, Georgia; Alan Dixon, Illinois; J. Bennett Johnston, Louisiana; John Breaux, Louisiana; J. James Exon, Nebraska; David Boren, Oklahoma.

4. *Planned Parenthood of Southeast Pennsylvania v Casey*, 505 US 833.

5. "Data Point: 2018, A Year of the Woman Like 1992?" Center for American Women in Politics, n.d. Web. 28 January 2018.

6. #MeToo, accessed January 28, 2018, https://https://metoomvmt.org/

●●●

Discussion Questions

1. The Women's March expressed a deep discontent among women and their respective countries. Politics were a clear catalyst for the march, but what other issues were represented?

2. A popular symbol of the first Women's March was the infamous pink pussy hat. While many women found the hat trivial, many others continued to wear it, and it was again popular at the second Women's March. Regardless of varying opinions, the hat has become a symbol of revolt and defiance. How can an accessory contribute to social change?

3. Much like the second- and third-wave movements, the fourth-wave movement also faces a lack of intersectionality. Why is this a persistent problem?

What You Can Do

- Make sure marches and protests are intersectional and every person attending feels welcome
- Respect one another's reasons for participating because other people's reasons might significantly differ from your own
- Do not diminish others' accessories, signs, slogans, etc. as meaningless; the movement belongs to us all, and inclusiveness sometimes calls for tolerance of things outside of your comfort zone

CHAPTER 15

Social Media As a Feminist Tool

By Connie Jeske Crane

It's January 2011, and the scene is a safety forum at Toronto's Osgoode Hall Law School. "I've been told I'm not supposed to say this," a Toronto police officer tells a group of female law students. But he says it anyway. Police constable Michael Sanguinetti's next bit of safety advice to the group was, "Women should avoid dressing like sluts in order not to be victimized."

The blame-the-victim riff, from a police representative, no less, touches off a firestorm that would have been hard to imagine before social media. Heather Jarvis, a co-founder of what became SlutWalk Toronto, heard about Sanguinetti's comment on Facebook.

"I was livid when I heard about it," she recalls, "and unfortunately not very surprised."

Together with Sonya Barnett, Jarvis conceived a protest walk to—yet again—raise the issue of blaming victims for rape. A Facebook page came first, then Twitter action. The movement attracted "a lot of people who have never engaged in activism and protests," recalls Jarvis. SlutWalk Toronto took place in May 2011 and drew about 1,000 participants. May 2012 saw a second annual event, and to-date, according to Jarvis, "over 200 cities around the world and counting have had SlutWalks, or SlutWalk-associated events— all different languages, cultures, contexts. It's astounding."

In 2012, Americans saw a similar "slut" comment and storm. After Georgetown University law student Sandra Fluke advocated for the inclusion of birth control in health insurance at religious institutions (like Georgetown), conservative radio host Rush Limbaugh railed at Fluke on air, calling her a "slut" and "whore." But a Twitter campaign (#FlushRushNow) mobilized quickly and led to a huge exodus of advertisers from Limbaugh's show.

In these social media triumphs, there is a strong feminist message. Slate.com sees a "recharging feminism," and the *New York Times* talks of Fluke and "feminist superstardom." Is it any wonder, then, that feminists (alongside gamers and shoppers) are embracing social media?

Women, as we know, are especially active online. According to statistics compiled by Cisco's Ayelet Baron, "women spend about eight percent more time online [than men]. In 2010, 76 percent of women visited a social networking site, compared to 70 percent of men. Specifically in North America, the social networking reach is 91 percent of women and 87.5 percent of males."

But here's a statistic that adds more context: Boston Consulting Group reports that women "control $12 trillion of the overall $18.4 trillion in global consumer spending." With projections like this, you can see why women are bombarded with pop-up ads for shoes, spa Groupons and the chance to join a gout study. Looked at another way, given the revenues at stake, you can also see why feminists banding together online could get an advertiser's attention.

Jarrah Hodge, editor of the Canadian feminist blog Gender Focus, sees social media as revolutionary. "I think social media has a lot of potential to connect feminists and to mobilize feminists and other progressive activists to resist

Connie Jeske Crane, "Social Media as a Feminist Tool," *Herizons*, vol. 26, no. 2, pp. 14-16. Copyright © 2012 by Herizons Magazine, Inc. Reprinted with permission. Provided by ProQuest LLC. All rights reserved.

Social Media

forms of electronic communication (such as websites for social networking and microblogging) through which users create online communities to share information, ideas, personal messages and other content (such as videos).

—Merriam-Webster

---

things in popular culture really quickly and effectively."

For feminism, social media is doing two things. First it's allowing broader access to feminist debates. Julia Horel, blog and community manager for the youth-driven *Shameless* magazine (shamelessmag.com), says, "I guess some of the big conversations in feminism have traditionally happened in the academy, and women's studies courses and that kind of thing. But having conversations, and questions, and arguments on all kinds of things on social media brings it to people who might not otherwise have an opportunity to be engaged."

Or, as Hodge says, "When I was in junior high school and we didn't really have social media, we were still reading teen magazines, but we had no way to connect with other people and challenge those ideas. Whereas we saw recently, with Julia Bluhm—a teen who challenged *Seventeen* magazine to use models that weren't Photoshopped—even though they haven't succeeded yet in that campaign, it's raised a lot of awareness." Social media's relative affordability, ubiquity and simplicity, adds Hodge, build inclusiveness. "You don't necessarily have to be a writer; you just have to be able to communicate honestly."

YOUNG FEMINISTS AND SOCIAL MEDIA

Secondly, Hodge says, social media can empower younger feminists. "They tend to have more of a voice online than in some mainstream feminist organizations" and are carving out more space for themselves online.

In her podcast series Tweeting Feminists, journalist Ronak Ghorbani interviewed well-known Canadian feminist Judy Rebick who observed, "Very few people my age really understand social media." And yet we see fantastic exceptions. Author Margaret Atwood, a passionate Twitter user, speaks proudly of getting Torontonians railing against library closures. Rebick herself told Ghorbani regarding social media: "I enjoy it. It's really fun, and I also use it politically—it's very useful politically."

Usually, in discussing social media activism, we hype this brave new world—Grrrl slays corporate dragon. But dig deeper and there's a more nuanced truth—social media with its dizzying upsides, but also a labyrinth-like underbelly. As Jarvis says, yes, SlutWalk co-founders added to a global conversation about violence against women. But they also received "a lot of harassment and threatening and bullying" and "horrible rape threats." So much, says Jarvis, that the group halted commenting on its YouTube site.

Then add sniping criticism from journalists. The *Globe and Mail*'s Margaret Wente wrote: "SlutWalks are what you get when graduate students in feminist studies run out of things to do." Feminists also dissed the newbie activists, especially around the use of the word slut. In *The Guardian*, feminists Gail Dines and Wendy J. Murphy wrote, "Trying to change [the term's] meaning is a waste of precious feminist resources." Jarvis feels the media often misrepresent SlutWalks. While participants dressed in all sorts of ways, she says, "Somehow the media kept putting out … images of two women in bras."

It's also stressful when, as an activist and blogger, you're unpaid but also have a day job. With social media activism, financial challenges are the unsung back story. SlutWalk Toronto is run by volunteers. While Jarvis's detractors tend to be well-paid (think tenured professors and established journalists), activists like her tend to do their advocacy work (blogging, media appearances, organizing) as volunteers. "The last year was one of the most overwhelming and challenging of my life," she says.

Deanna Zandt, a New York-based media technologist and author, is the first to acknowledge that a lack of pay is common for social media activists. "No one has an answer for this," she says, but "there are people who are studying it."

Right about here is where the power and challenges of social media intersect. Anyone who's been involved in social media for a while will be recognize the trajectory—an initial high where possibilities blow your mind, followed by a drift back down to earth.

So can social media be revolutionary? Or, as I sometimes fear, are we about to drown in a tsunami of cat videos, grinning vacation snaps and foaming vitriol? Exploring social media for this article, I'm gaining a renewed appreciation. The caveat? Success online, like offline, requires ingenuity, hard work and some lightsaber dueling against the dark side.

SOCIAL MEDIA CONSUMERISM

One of the biggest challenges is rampant, ad-riddled consumerism. On the one hand, you have weary activists (not to mention venerable institutions such as the *New York Times,* with its new paywall scheme) trying to make enough money online to survive. Alongside, we're witnessing rising corporate investment. Microblogging platform Pinterest, for example, recently made a $1-billion venture capital announcement.

For some, viability means advertising. The big danger here is losing authenticity via product placement. As one satirical bit from *The Onion* ("Women Now Empowered By Everything A Woman Does") reads: "Unlike traditional, phallocentric energy bars, whose chocolate, soy protein, nuts and granola ignored the special health and nutritional needs of women, their new, female-oriented counterparts like Luna are ideally balanced with a more suitable amount of chocolate, soy protein, nuts and granola…."

Of course, feminists are challenging the woman-as-consumer meme, notes Linn Baran, community outreach and promotions coordinator at the Motherhood Institute for Research and Community Involvement and a blogger at motheroutlaws. blogspot.ca. Baran says feminist blogging carnivals, radical mommy blogs and online petitions are all ways we can challenge the dominant narrative.

If you're skeptical about the power of blogging, talk to Sady Doyle. Today a prominent U.S. feminist writer and activist, Doyle writes about blogs politicizing her. "I suddenly saw more than just dating problems and wardrobe issues: I saw double standards, beauty standards, sexual policing and gender roles. And I began to understand, too, how small those concerns were, and how my

Jarrah Hodge of Gendre Focus believes social media connects and mobilizes feninists.

obsessive focus on them was intrinsically tied to my privilege."

Online, the trick is to keep your eyes wide open. Baran shares a favourite analogy from Jen Lawrence, whom *Toronto Life* magazine called one of "Toronto's pioneer mommy bloggers." In an essay for the book *Mothering and Blogging: The Radical Act of the MommyBlog*, Lawrence writes, "I think that blogging can be an incredibly powerful tool when it comes to building community, even if there are blog ads running down the sidebar.

"But I don't want blogging to become just another guerilla-marketing technique." She offers this analogy: "I don't want to be invited to a friend's home, only to discover I was really invited to a Tupperware party."

THE DOWNSIDE OF SOCIAL MEDIA

Of course, if you're being skewered online by nasty trolls, a Tupperware party could be tempting. Anyone who makes even mildly controversial statements online knows how much venom you can draw, and feminist statements remain lightening rods. The negativity, says Hodge, "can be really demoralizing, especially if you're someone who's new to social media."

Doyle, who launched a Twitter campaign called #MooreandMe after hearing filmmaker Michael Moore call sexual assault charges against WikiLeaks founder Julian Assange "a bunch of hooey," received rape threats for her action. Eventually her campaign wrung an apology from Moore. As she explained in her blog: "I'm being harassed, I'm being threatened, I'm scared for my physical safety to the point that I'm looking up dudes and seeing exactly what stalking consists of in case I have to press charges."

Jarrah Hodge at Gender Focus says bloggers can't rely on hosts to help if contributors receive threats. "Oftentimes, the companies that run the [larger] sites aren't very responsive," she says. Hodge aims to create a safer space for feminist dialogue on her blog by including a comments policy. "I cite reasons why I might remove your post. And I will never let hate speech or really disrespectful personal attacks stand un-countered."

For *Shameless*'s Julia Horel, it's all about "deciding what's worth your energy and what's not." Adds Jarvis, "It's sometimes blocking people from pages, removing comments," while accepting that feminist comments will see personal attacks. "You need support around and you need to realize your skin is going to get thicker."

INFORMATION OVERLOAD

Haters, advertisers, your 200 Facebook friends and the 50 blogs you're following—it's a lot to manage. While we see social media's value, there's a growing realization that it can be overwhelming and even addictive. Individuals and organizations are experimenting with boundaries: daily Facebook limits, Internet fasts and device-free weekends. We're just beginning to study what social media have done to us.

Information overload is a huge issue, agrees Joey Jakob, a Ph.D. candidate in communication and culture at Ryerson and York universities. "Social media allow us to have a kind of access we haven't been able to have," says Jakob, who

Media technologist Deanna Zandt says the freely available nature of social media can make organizing easier.

addressed a 2012 conference in Waterloo, Ontario, alongside such luminaries as Margaret Atwood and Jane Urquhart. "Do we even have the time and energy to think about [social responsibility] when we're just continuously overstimulated by continuous knowledge filtering in through social media?" asked Jakob.

"What we don't talk about enough is the actual amount of responsibility" our social media use involves, says Jakob. Consuming social media, Jakob thinks, requires us "to contextualize everything. It can be very tiring, I will admit it, to put everything in context, but I think if nothing else, that's our responsibility."

THE FUTURE

But how do we do this? How do we filter out junk and venom and develop a mindful, positive social media habit? As her recent book title, *Share This! How You Will Change the World with Social Networking*, suggests, Deanna Zandt is optimistic.

We will, says Zandt, learn to better handle the flood of information, and even the haters. "Some women are sort of turning it on their head and creating Tumblr blogs of the hate mail that they receive. … We don't have to be silenced."

Looking ahead, Zandt envisions social media activists continually informing and influencing

traditional power hierarchies. In her book, she writes that "the freely available nature of the tools reduces some of the complexity of organizing. We no longer have to rely on the old ways of top-down, or even organization-based, grassroots organizing." She concludes with clear-eyed confidence: "Technology isn't a magic bullet for solving the world's problems, but it's certainly a spark to the fastest fuse to explode our notions of power that the world has seen in a thousand years."

■ ■ ■

Discussion Questions

1. How does women's global consumer spending contribute to feminist social media?

2. Why is the use of a hashtag so effective?

3. What are some examples of backlash against feminist social media?

4. Do you think social media will continue to be a catalyst for social change?

What You Can Do

- Follow feminists on social media, and be aware of the current issues
- Be wary of interacting with those who post negative comments
- Report threats and inappropriate language
- Be active in posting your own material

CHAPTER 16

The Sweet Taste of Lemonade
BEYONCÉ SERVES UP BLACK FEMINIST HISTORY

By Cheryl Thompson

Beyoncé Giselle Knowles-Carter never ceases to amaze audiences. For nearly 20 years, she has consistently recreated herself, her music and her brand.

It is easy to forget that she began her career in 1998 at age of 16 as part of the girl group Destiny's Child. Since then, she's become one of the most recognized R&B/pop singers in the world—and one of the most critiqued. With each album, listeners delve into her creative subconscious, and her latest (sixth) solo project, *Lemonade*, is no exception. In fact, since the release of "Formation" in February and the title song in April, no artist, male or female, has garnered more buzz this year than "Bey."

Dropped the day before her performance during the halftime show at the Super Bowl, "Formation" is a not-so-subtle nod to the aesthetics of the New Black Panther movement—with its Afro hair, faux-bullet bandoliers and berets. The video features the singer sprawled atop a New Orleans police car, circa hurricane Katrina in 2005; a black youth dancing before a line of white police officers in riot gear; abandoned Louisiana homes; flashes of civil rights resistance; the Black church in Charleston, South Carolina in which churchgoers were killed; and a fierce all-woman dance troupe. It includes powerful lyrics like, "I like my baby heir with baby hair and afros/I like my Negro nose with Jackson Five nostrils."

This is a far cry from her previous girl-power anthems, such as "Who Run the World (Girls)" and "Flawless" (released in 2011 and 2013, respectively), which featured a sampling of Nigerian writer Chimamanda Ngozi Adichies TEDx talk, "We Should All Be Feminists." "Formation," make no mistake, is not about the universal "we" but the Black "us."

Following the Super Bowl, a *Saturday Night Live* skit, titled "The Day Beyoncé Turned Black," parodied a group of Beyoncé's fictional white fans responding to the new-found Black political consciousness of her music. The skit featured several confused white fans coming to grips with the fact that, after seeing "Formation," they realized for the first time that Beyoncé is a Black woman.

The skit was more than just parody. Beyoncé, like many mainstream R&B artists before her, has often had to balance being palatable to white audiences and Black audiences alike. This is not an easy task. The inability of Lauryn Hill, for example, to live up to mass appeal, came in spite of the fact that many regard *The Miseducation of Lauryn Hill* (1998) as one of the most important albums of all time. Hills music is scarcely talked about today.

It is very difficult for Black female artists to *be* Black (i.e. politically and socially attuned to the lives of Black women) and *be* feminist (i.e. place the struggles of gender and sexism above everything else) at the same time. *Lemonade* has made it clear indeed that Beyoncé struggles with this duality.

"Lemonade," the second track off the album, was first released as a 20-second teaser and then as a one-hour premiere on HBO. In the video for "Lemonade," the artist appears in cornrows (an African-descendant hairstyle consisting of tightly braided rows), angrily bemusing her ill treatment by men. It also sees her wearing a lemonade-inspired dress, wielding a baseball bat and smashing car windows. The video includes multiple scenes of Beyoncé's fierce all-girl company and can only be described as tumultuous.

What "Formation" and "Lemonade" reveal is that Beyoncé is letting out her inner Black feminist. By including appearances from the mothers of Trayvon Martin, Michael Brown and Freddie Gray, all children and young men lost to gun violence (most notably at the hands of police), Beyoncé is attuned to her times. And yet, mainstream reporting of the visual album was ablaze with chatter over "Lemonade's" suggestive infidelity lyrics.

The lyric, "He only want me when I'm not there/He better call Becky with the good hair" made critics wonder whether the relationship between Beyoncé and Jay Z was in trouble. Apparently, "Becky with the good hair" is a reference to fashion designer Rachel Roy. Beyoncé's sister, Solange Knowles, was seen on video footage fighting with Jay Z in a New York hotel elevator in 2015 after she accused him of being too close to Roy. In response to the video, Roy said she didn't care about "good hair," and, sadly, this tiff overshadowed much of the Black feminist overtones of "Lemonade."

Beyoncé's previous albums were about feminism, singular. However, *Lemonade* is specifically about Black feminism. For example, in an article for *Time* magazine, writer Omise'eke Natasha Tinsley called "Lemonade" "Black woman magic," noting that it is art—not autobiography. Tinsley also positioned Beyoncé as continuing in the tradition of Black women's music, wherein "trifling men have long been metonyms for a patriarchy that never affords Black women the love and life they deserve."

In the video for the song "Lemonade," Beyoncé poses on a New Orleans police car, a nod to hurricane Katrina's devastating impact on the city's Black residents.

Patricia Hill Collins, a professor of sociology at the University of Maryland, is often touted as one of the first theorizers of Black feminism. In her influential text, *Black Feminist Thought* (1990), Collins argued that black feminist thought must aim to clarify a standpoint of and for Black women. She also noted that is it vital to transcend group specific politics and move toward an understanding of how Black womanhood is uniquely positioned across two systems of oppression—race and gender. If we are to think intersectionally about Black women's issues, we need to open up the possibility of seeing and, more importantly, understanding how socio-cultural politics affect Black women's lives. To be Black and a woman means that structures of racial oppression and gender privilege are not separate issues but are integral to one's sense of self.

With *Lemonade*, Beyoncé uses her artistry to acknowledge this duality. As Jacqui Germain astutely noted on feministing.com, "Beyoncé using the specific cultural marker of 'Becky,' [a social trope for white womanhood] in *Lemonade* is less a question of who's excluding whom and why, and more so just us watching Beyoncé be the … multi-layered Black woman." Thus, when we focus on Beyoncé as an individual, we ignore the importance of Black women's lived experiences, especially in music.

"Formation" (above) and "Lemonade" reveal Beyoncé letting out her inner Black feminist.

Last year, the University of Victoria and the University of Waterloo both developed courses on Beyoncé. The University of Victoria School of Music course, titled Beyoncé, aims to explore how the superstar is positioned as a cultural product. The course Gender and Performance is an excursion into the singers albums, her feminism and critical race themes by the drama department at the University of Waterloo.

"I had to take up the work of this performer who is astute, an astute businesswoman, who is articulating a kind of feminism that is fascinating and very much of the 21st century," University of Waterloo drama professor Naila Keleta-Mae told CBC News. "She uses visuals and music to tell young people around the world what it means to be a woman, wife, mother and feminist, Keleta-Mae added in a subsequent blog on Huffington Post.

What is essential in any study of Beyoncé is an understanding of the historical continuum of Black women's performance. Beyoncé cannot be understood in isolation from the Black women artists who have come before her. As Angela Davis asserted in her book, *Black Legacies and Black Feminism* (1995), on blues singers Bessie Smith, Ma Rainey and Billie Holiday, such history must be acknowledged in critiques of contemporary Black women artists. The book dispels popular assumptions that the historical origins of second- wave feminism are white, arguing instead that, through their music (not their lives), Black women blues artists forged a template for understanding Black feminisms.

While Beyoncé has not struggled in the way that many blues artists in the 1920s and 1930s did, *Lemonade* reflects an increased awareness of a race/gender consciousness that speaks to the aforementioned challenges. To isolate her from this history is to misunderstand why she is both loved and incessantly critiqued in ways that her white contemporaries are not. "Formation," with its proud-to-be-black-don't-get-it-twisted aesthetic, even incited some authorities, including Toronto city councilor Jim Karygiannis, to claim that because of her "anti-police" message, Beyoncé posed a potential threat to police and the Canadian state.

I have not always been Beyoncé's biggest fan. I have questioned her politics, lyrics and public statements she's made about feminism. To me, *Lemonade* confirms that Beyoncé should not be framed as a feminist in isolation from other Black women artists who have come before her. She is, in the words of Angela Davis, part of the legacy of Black feminisms in music. Therefore, her art, not in her public statements, is where we need to locate her feminist politics.

Beyoncé's music, might be mere artistic expression to some, but her message is personal and political, the very definition of feminism.

■ ■ ■

Discussion Questions

1. How does *Lemonade* contribute to the understanding of black feminism?

2. Why is music such a powerful feminist tool for social change?

3. Music has always been popular is social movements, but women have struggled to gain as much recognition for it as men. How has the fourth wave increased female artist popularity?

4. How do music videos increase or enhance a feminist message within a song?

What You Can Do

- Support feminist artists on a local and national level
- Attend events and concerts
- Familiarize yourself with music and what makes it feminist
- Write your own music and songs

CHAPTER 17

The Future of Queer/Trans Activism

Julia Serano

The majority of my experiences as a trans activist and spoken word artist have taken place in what is increasingly becoming known as the "queer/trans" community. It is a subgroup within the greater LGBTIQ community that is composed mostly of folks in their twenties and thirties who are more likely to refer to themselves as "dykes," "queer," and/or "trans" than "lesbian" or "gay." While diverse in a number of ways, this subpopulation tends to predominantly inhabit urban and academic settings, and is skewed toward those who are white and/or from middle-class backgrounds. In many ways, the queer/trans community is best described as a sort of marriage of the transgender movement's call to "shatter the gender binary" and the lesbian community's pro-sex, pro-kink backlash to 1980s-era Andrea Dworkinism. Its politics are generally antiassimilationist, particularly with regard to gender and sexual expression. This apparent limitlessness and lack of boundaries lead many to believe that "queer/trans" represents the vanguard of today's gender and sexual revolution. However, over the last four years in which I've been a part of this community, I've become increasingly troubled by a trend that, while not applicable to all queer/trans folks, seems to be becoming a dominant belief in this community, one that threatens to restrict its gender and sexual diversity. I call this trend *subversivism*.

Subversivism is the practice of extolling certain gender and sexual expressions and identities simply because they are unconventional or nonconforming. In the parlance of subversivism, these atypical genders and sexualities are "good" because they "transgress" or "subvert" oppressive binary gender norms.[1] The justification for the practice of subversivism has evolved out of a particular reading (although some would call it a misreading) of the work of various influential queer theorists over the last decade and a half. To briefly summarize this popularized account: All forms of sexism arise from the binary gender system. Since this binary gender system is everywhere—in our thoughts, language, traditions, behaviors, etc.—the only way we can overturn it is to actively undermine the system from within. Thus, in order to challenge sexism, people must "perform" their genders in ways that bend, break, and blur all of the imaginary distinctions that exist between male and female, heterosexual and homosexual, and so on, presumably leading to a systemwide binary meltdown. According to the principles of subversivism, drag is inherently "subversive," as it reveals that our society's binary notions of maleness and femaleness are not natural, but rather are actively "constructed" and "performed" by all of us. Another way that one can be "transgressively gendered" is by identifying as genderqueer or genderfluid—i.e., refusing to identify fully as either woman or man.

The notion that certain gender identities and expressions are inherently "subversive" or "transgressive" can be seen throughout the queer/trans community, where drag and gender-bending are routinely celebrated, where binary-confounding identities such as "boy-identified-dyke" and "pansexual trannyfag" have become rather commonplace. On the surface, subversivism gives the appearance of accommodating a seemingly infinite array of genders and sexualities, but this is not quite the case. Subversivism does have very specific boundaries; it has an "other." By glorifying identities and expressions that appear to subvert or blur gender binaries, subversivism automatically creates a reciprocal category of people whose gender and sexual identities and expressions are by default inherently conservative, even "hegemonic," because they are seen as reinforcing or naturalizing the binary gender system. Not surprisingly, this often-unspoken category of bad, conservative genders is predominantly made up of feminine women and masculine men who are attracted to the "opposite" sex.

One routinely sees this "dark side" of subversivism rear its head in the queer/trans community, where it is not uncommon to hear individuals critique or call into question other queers or trans folks because their gender presentation, behaviors, or sexual preferences are not deemed "subversive" enough. Indeed, if one fails to sufficiently distinguish oneself from heterosexual feminine women and masculine men, one runs the risk of being accused of "reinforcing the gender binary," an indictment that is tantamount to being called a sexist. One of the most common targets of such critiques are transsexuals, and particularly those who are heterosexual and gender-normative post-transition. Indeed, because such transsexuals (in the eyes of others) transition from a seemingly "transgressive" queer identity to a "conservative" straight one, subversivists may even claim that they have transitioned in order to purposefully "assimilate" themselves into straight culture. While these days, such accusations are often couched in the rhetoric of current queer theory, they rely on many of the same mistaken assumptions that plagued the work of cissexist feminists like Janice Raymond and sociologists like Thomas Kando decades ago.[2]

The practice of subversivism also negatively impacts trans people on the MTF spectrum. After all, in our culture, the meanings of "bold," "rebellious," and "dangerous"—adjectives that often come to mind when considering subversiveness—are practically built into our understanding of masculinity. In contrast, femininity conjures up antonyms like "timid," "conventional," and "safe," which seem entirely incompatible with subversion. Therefore, despite the fact that the mainstream public tends to be more concerned and disturbed by MTF spectrum trans people than their FTM spectrum counterparts, subversivism creates the impression that trans masculinities are inherently "subversive" and "transgressive," while their trans feminine counterparts are "lame" and "conservative" in comparison. Subversivism's privileging of trans masculinities over trans femininities helps to explain why cissexual queer women and FTM spectrum folks tend to dominate the queer/trans community: Their exceptional gender expressions and identities are routinely empowered and encouraged in such settings. In contrast, there is generally a dearth of MTF spectrum folks who regularly inhabit queer/trans spaces.[3]

To me, the most surreal part of this whole transgressing-versus-reinforcing-gender-norms dialogue in the queer/trans community (and in many gender studies classrooms and books) is the unacknowledged hypocrisy of it all. It is sadly ironic that people who claim to be gender-fucking in the name of "shattering the gender binary," and who criticize people whose identities fail to adequately challenge our societal notions of femaleness and maleness, cannot see that they have just created a new gender binary, one in which subversive genders are "good" and conservative genders are "bad." In a sense, this new gender binary isn't even all that new. It is merely the original oppositional sexist binary flipped upside down. So now, gender-nonconforming folks are on top and gender-normative people are on the bottom—how revolutionary! Now, I understand the temptation for a marginalized group to turn the hierarchy that has oppressed them upside down, as it can feel very empowering to finally be atop the pecking order, but it's absurd to claim that such approaches in any way undermine that binary. If anything, they only serve to reinforce it further.

Subversivism's binary flip is very reminiscent of another binary flip that was forwarded by cultural feminists in the mid-1970s. While subversivism reverses oppositional sexism, cultural feminism sought to reverse traditional sexism by claiming that women were naturally creative and cooperative and therefore superior to men, who were seen as inherently destructive and oppressive. While it is always difficult to draw comparisons between different social/political movements for fear of oversimplifying them, there are other striking parallels between subversivism and cultural feminism that are worth bearing out. As historian Alice Echols describes in her book *Daring to Be Bad: Radical Feminism in America, 1967–1975*, cultural feminism evolved from its more outwardly focused predecessor, radical feminism.[4] While radical feminism—which asserted that neither sex was inherently superior to the other—actively engaged the mainstream public (and men in particular) to challenge and change their sexist ways, cultural feminism was a more insular movement, focusing on creating women-run organizations and women-only spaces rather than organizing public demonstrations. And unlike radical feminism, which attempted to accommodate a variety of different female perspectives (in fact, issues over "difference" in class and sexuality consumed much of the movement's energy), cultural feminists forwarded the idea of "sameness" and "oneness"—that all women were part of a universal sisterhood, united by their female biology.

This concept of female "oneness" was perhaps most responsible for cultural feminism's exclusionist, even separatist, tendencies. After all, if one believes in a female "oneness" that is distinct from, and superior to, maleness, then anyone who brings that distinction into question automatically becomes threatening. Indeed, that's exactly what happened throughout much of the 1970s and 1980s. Those women who disagreed with cultural feminist dogma—or who engaged in certain gender expressions and sexual practices that were associated with men—were derided as promoting masculine values and being

"antifeminist," and were accordingly excluded from the movement. Further, as Echols points out, while cultural feminists "used the language of sisterhood, they often assumed a patronizing stance toward those 'unliberated' women who were still living in 'The Man's' world."[5] This exclusionary shift from a movement that sought to benefit *all* women (i.e., radical feminism) to one that only sought to benefit a select group of women was made possible by cultural feminism's binary flip and its sense of "oneness."

The queer and transgender movements came into their own in the early 1990s in response to this sort of exclusionary "oneness" that was promoted by cultural feminists and many mainstream gay rights activists. The words "transgender" and "queer" came into vogue during this time as umbrella terms: "Queer" attempted to accommodate lesbians and gays as well as the growing bisexual and transgender movements; and "transgender" was used to promote a coalition of distinct groups (including crossdressers, transsexuals, butch women, femme men, drag performers, intersex people, etc.) that previously believed they had little in common with one another. These alliances were not based on a presumed shared biology or set of beliefs, but on the fact that these different groups faced similar forms of discrimination. In fact, the notion that transgender people "transgress binary gender norms" came about to create a cause for its varied constituents to unite behind, not as a litmus test or a criteria for them to meet. At that time, the idea of "shattering the gender binary" was outward-focused; if we could push our culture to move beyond the idea that female and male are rigid, mutually exclusive "opposite sexes," that would make the lives of all transgender constituent subgroups far easier.

Just as cultural feminism's binary flip fostered that movement's inward focus on women-only culture and spaces, I believe that the recent rise of subversivism may be an early sign that the more outward-looking, changing-the-world-focused transgender and queer movements of the 1990s are shifting into a more insular and exclusionary queer/trans community, one that favors only a select group of queers and trans folks, rather than all people who fall under those umbrella terms. Indeed, unlike our predecessors in the groups Queer Nation (who held public "kiss-ins" in suburban malls) and Transsexual Menace (who staged protests in small Midwestern towns where trans people were murdered), many in the queer/trans community these days often seem more content celebrating our fabulous queer selves or enjoying the safety of our own organizations and events.[6] While there is nothing inherently wrong with creating our own queer/trans spaces and culture, what troubles me is that we are clearly sacrificing diversity in the process. For example, in queer/trans spaces, one rarely sees MTF crossdressers (despite the fact that they make up a large portion of the transgender population) and there are very few trans women. Some might suggest that these groups are choosing not to attend of their own accord, but that only leads to the next question: *Why* are they choosing not to come? Often when trans women ask me when I'm performing next, and I tell them that it's a queer/trans event, they will tell me that they'd rather not go because they do not feel comfortable or safe in those spaces, that they have been dismissed or belittled at such events before. Even trans women who are dyke- or bisexual-identified often don't feel welcome or relevant in queer/trans spaces. And whenever a trans woman or ally points out aspects about the queer/ trans community that contribute to these feelings of irrelevancy and disrespect— such as the way our community coddles those who support trans-woman-exclusionist events or who make trans-misogynistic comments— we are described as being "divisive." This use of the word "divisive" is particularly telling, as it implies that "queer/trans" represents a uniform movement or community—a "oneness"—rather than an alliance where all voices are respected.

Perhaps the only thing more ironic than the fact that the trans-gender movement's "shatter the gender binary" slogan is now being used to enforce a new subversive/conservative gender binary is the fact that the queer/trans community's growing sense of "oneness" evolved out of a well-meaning attempt to prevent exclusivity. From the outset, many early transgender activists feared that one particular transgender subgroup might come to dominate the transgender community, that they would begin to police the movement's borders and enforce their own sense of "oneness." Because the exclusivity of cultural feminism and the mainstream "gay rights" movement seemed to center on disputes over identity— who counts as a "woman" or who is legitimately "gay"—many activists advocated the idea that the transgender coalition should be borderless, one where there was no set criteria for an individual to join. Many also worked to play down or blur the distinctiveness of individual transgender subgroups in order to prevent any kind of hierarchy from developing. The transgender movement, in effect, became an anti-identity movement.

In retrospect, I would say that the assumption that distinct identities would automatically lead to exclusivity was entirely misplaced. After all, an identity is merely a label, a descriptive noun to express one particular facet of a person's experiences. And if we look beyond gender and sexual identity politics, we can find many examples of flexible and fluid identities. For example, if I were to identify myself as a "cat person," nobody would be outraged or confused if I said I also loved dogs. Further, when I tell people that I'm a "musician," no one makes unwarranted assumptions about what instruments I play or what styles of music I prefer. Nonpoliticized identities like "musician" and "cat person" allow us to see that the recurring problems in gender and sexual identity politics arise not from identity per se, but rather from opposite-think (e.g., that a cat person cannot be a dog person, and vice versa) and from a sense of "oneness" (e.g., the assumption that all musicians are or should be punk rock guitarists.)

I believe that if the transgender movement had simply continued to view itself as an alliance of disparate groups working toward a shared goal (like making the world safer for gender-variant folks), it may have avoided such exclusivity while respecting the distinct differences and specific concerns of its various constituents. Instead, by promoting the idea that we must move beyond the supposedly outdated concept of "identity," the transgender movement has created its own sense of "oneness." Rather than viewing ourselves as a fragile political coalition of distinct subgroups, some activists instead encourage us to see ourselves as one big homogeneous group of individuals who blur gender boundaries. Rather than learning to respect the very different perspectives and experiences that each transgender subgroup brings to the table, the transgender community has instead become a sort of gender free-for-all, where identities are regularly co-opted by others within the community. These days, many transsexuals assume that they have the right to appropriate the language of, or speak on behalf of, intersex people; similarly, many cissexual genderqueers feel they have the right to do the same for transsexuals. This needlessly erases each group's unique issues, obstacles, and perspectives.

This sort of "gender anarchy"—where individuals are free to adopt or appropriate any identity as they please—might seem very limitless and freeing on the surface, but in practice it resembles gender-libertarianism, where those who are most marginalized become even more vulnerable to the whims of those who are more established. In this case, it leaves those of us who are cross-gender-identified susceptible to negation at the hands of the greater cissexual queer community. Indeed, it has become increasingly common for people who are primarily queer because of their sexual orientation to claim a space for themselves within the transgender movement.[7] This is particularly true in the queer women's community, which has become increasingly involved in transgender politics and discourses due to the recent sharp increase in the number of (1) previously lesbian-identified people transitioning to male, (2) dykes who now take on genderqueer or other FTM spectrum identities, and (3) non-trans queer women who seek a voice in the transgender community because they are partnered to FTM spectrum individuals.

Because of our history, the fact that cissexual queers now dominate transgender and queer/trans communities and discourses is highly problematic for those of us who are transsexual. During the 1970s, transsexuals and other cross-gender-identified queers were banished from the "gay rights" movement as it began to focus solely on sexual orientation. This was a calculated maneuver: By jettisoning cross-gender queers (who were typically seen as the "most deviant" by a reluctant mainstream public), sexuality-queers could make the case that they were just like "normal people" except for their sexual orientation. And from the perspective of a lesbian or gay person, this strategy was highly effective. Sexuality-queers, while still marginalized to a certain degree, have made tremendous legal gains with regard to domestic partnership, including reversing "sodomy laws" and gaining protection against discrimination. They now have their own social and political organizations, cable channels, university departments, and even their own Olympics. There are out lesbian and gay politicians and celebrities, and popular TV shows that revolve around lesbian and gay characters. Gay-themed jokes in the media are now more likely to make fun of someone for being homophobic than for being homosexual. Perhaps most significant of all, it has become generally accepted among most Americans—even among those who are stern opponents of "gay rights"—that there is natural variation in human sexual orientation. (Or, as the popular saying goes: "Some people are just born that way.")

As a direct result of the exclusion of cross-gender-identified trans people from the "gay rights" movement, public awareness and acceptance of our identities and issues are about twenty years behind those of lesbians and gays, because the transgender movement didn't gain momentum until the 1990s. Because of this exclusion, our cross-gender identities and perspectives are not acknowledged to nearly the same extent as lesbian and gay identities and perspectives. For example, when I come out to people as a transsexual, I am often barraged with highly personal questions about my motives, my physical body, and my male past. In contrast, I have never once been interrogated by someone upon coming out to them as a lesbian; that aspect of my person is generally accepted at face value. In other words, I am allowed to exist without question as a lesbian in ways that I am not allowed as a transsexual. In a climate where same-sex attraction has become a given while cross-gender identification has most certainly not, the merging of "sexuality-queers" and "gender-queers" (as seen in the queer/trans community) essentially subsumes transsexuals within the more well-established cissexual queer community. The more inclusive the word "trans-gender" becomes, the more thoroughly the voices of transsexuals and other cross-gender/cross-living individuals are drowned out by those who do not share our perspectives and experiences.

This "cissexualization" of transgenderism has taken a devastating toll on the ability of transsexuals to articulate our own perspectives and visions for gender activism. Rather than being listened to and appreciated on our own terms, we are instead forced to adhere to lesbian/gay rhetoric and values in order to have a voice within our own community. One can see this in the way that lesbian/gay-specific definitions of "passing" (as a synonym for "hiding") are inappropriately applied to our decisions to physically transition and live in our identified sex, or in the way that our descriptions of subconscious sex, gender dissonance, and physical transitioning are patronizingly dismissed by cissexual queers who favor social constructionist views of gender. It is evident in the way that queer theorists, ignorant of their own cissexual privilege, nonconsensually ungender us (or blur the distinctions between us and other queers) in order to artificialize gender; claim that "all gender is drag" without recognizing how dismissive that is to the transsexual

experience; and ignorantly apply the "gay rights" tactic of calling for the all-out demedicalization of transgenderism without considering the effects this would have on transsexuals' ability to access and afford hormones and sex reassignment procedures. Finally, as Viviane Namaste has pointed out in her books, the "cissexualization" of the transgender movement ensures that discourses about transsexuals inevitably revolve around the cissexual queer obsession over "identity" (who counts as a woman or man, who is legitimately queer), rather than examining the very real institutional obstacles and biases we face for being transsexual.[8]

I worry that the dominance of cissexual voices in the queer/ trans community, and the exclusionary practice of subversivism, are together fostering a sense of queer/trans "oneness" that excludes trans women such as myself. My fears stem not so much from my own concern about being excluded, or for the many other subgroups not mentioned here who also feel increasingly left out of this community. Rather, I fear that this inward, homogenizing trend represents a lost opportunity to learn from one another and to change the minds of the public at large. If we hope to correct this insular, exclusionary trend, then we must begin to (once again) think in terms of alliances rather than monolithic communities. Alliance-based activism begins with the recognition that we are all individuals, each with a limited history and experiencing a largely unique set of privileges, expectations, assumptions, and restrictions. Thus, none of us have "superior knowledge" when it comes to sexuality and gender. By calling ourselves an alliance, we explicitly acknowledge that we are working toward a common goal (how about "making the world safe and just for people of all genders and sexualities"?), while simultaneously recognizing and respecting our many differences. There can be no legitimate accusations of "divisiveness" in an alliance, as differences of opinion would be expected from the start. Thinking in terms of alliances can encourage us to move beyond the single goal of creating safe queer/trans spaces, to recognize that, in reality, there is no such thing as a "safe space." After all, the very notion of safety is often predicated on a presumed and exclusionary sense of "sameness" and "oneness." And unlike subversivism, which fosters a grim and belittling view of the heterosexual, gender-normative majority, alliance-based gender activism recognizes that the only way we will change society is by engaging the mainstream public and working with, rather than against, our straight allies.

If we hope to build alliances that are respectful of all queer and transgender perspectives, then we must stop talking about *the* gender binary system, as if there is only one. As a trans woman, I deal with lots of gender binaries: male/female, heterosexual/homosexual, cissexual/transsexual, cisgender/transgender, and so on. As someone who is marginalized in queer/trans spaces for not being "subversive" or "transgressive" enough, I find that calls to "shatter the (male/female) gender binary" sound hollow. And when cissexual queers try to frame all forms of gender/sexual discrimination in terms of "heterosexist gender norms," they deny the fact that, as a transsexual woman, I experience way more cissexist and trans-misogynistic animosity and condescension from members of my own lesbian community than I ever have from my straight friends and acquaintances. The truth is that whenever we enter a different space, or speak with a different person, we are forced to deal with a somewhat different set of binaries and assumptions. Indeed, my experience living in the San Francisco Bay Area—where most straight people I know are very comfortable with queerness, yet many queer people I know harbor subversivist attitudes toward straightness—makes it clear that there needs to be a more general strategy to challenge *all* forms of sexism, not just the typical or obvious ones.

Rather than focusing on "shattering the gender binary," I believe we should turn our attention instead to challenging all forms of *gender entitlement*, the privileging of one's own perceptions, interpretations, and evaluations of other people's genders over the way those people understand themselves. After all, whenever we assign values to other people's genders and sexualities—whether we call them subversive or conservative, cool or uncool, normal or abnormal, natural or unnatural—we are automatically creating or reaffirming some kind of hierarchy. In other words, when we critique any gender as being "good" or "bad," we are by definition being sexist. After all, isn't what drives many of us into feminism and queer activism in the first place our frustration that other people often place rather arbitrary meanings and values onto our sexed bodies, gender expressions, and sexualities? Is there really any difference between the schoolyard bullies who teased us for being too feminine or masculine when we were little, the arrogant employer who assumes that we aren't cut out for the job because we're female, the gay men who claim that we are holding back the gay rights movement because we are not straight-acting enough, and the people—whether lesbian-feminists of the 1970s and 1980s, or subversivists in the 2000s—who decry us for not being androgynous enough to be "true gender radicals"?

Some might argue that it's simply human nature for us to assign different values to different genders and sexualities. For example, if we tend to prefer the company of men over women, or if we find androgynous people more attractive than feminine or masculine ones, isn't that assigning them a different worth? Not necessarily. There is a big difference between rightly recognizing these preferences in terms of our personal predilections ("I find androgynous people attractive") and entitled claims that imply that there are no other legitimate opinions ("Masculine and feminine people are not sexy, period"). Similarly, there's a big difference between calling yourself a woman or a genderqueer because you feel that word best captures your gendered experience and using that identity to make claims or presumptions about other people's genders (e.g., assuming that "men" or "gender-conforming people" are your "opposites").

Some might also argue that there is such a thing as "bad" gender—for instance, a woman who feels coerced into living up to stereotypically feminine ideals. As someone who was closeted for many years, I can understand why someone might be tempted to describe genders that are enforced by others (e.g., stereotypical femininity or masculinity) as being "bad." The problem is that there is no way for us to know whether any given person's gender identity or expression is sincere or coerced. While we experience our own genders and sexualities firsthand, and thus are capable of separating our own intrinsic inclinations from the extrinsic expectations that others place on us, we are unable to do so on behalf of other people. We can only ever make assumptions and educated guesses about the authenticity of someone else's sexuality or gender—and that's always dangerous.

The thing that always impresses me about human beings is our diversity. Even when we are brought up in similar environments, we still somehow gravitate toward very different careers, hobbies, politics, manners of speaking and acting, aesthetic preferences, and so forth. Maybe this diversity is due to genetic variation. Or maybe, being naturally curious and adaptive creatures, we invariably tend to scatter all over the place, exploiting every niche we can possibly find. Either way, it's fairly obvious that we also end up all over the map when it comes to gender and sexuality. That being the case, if we take the subversivist route and focus our energies on deriding stereotypically feminine and masculine genders, we will inevitably disparage some (perhaps many) people for whom those genders simply feel right and natural. Furthermore, by critiquing those gender expressions in an entitled way, we actively create new gender expectations that others may feel obliged to meet (which is exactly what's now starting to happen in the queer/trans community). That is why I suggest that we turn our energies and attention away from the way that individuals "do" or "perform" their own genders and instead focus on the expectations and assumptions that those individuals project onto everybody else. By focusing on gender entitlement rather than gender performance, we may finally take the next step toward a world where all people can choose their genders and sexualities at will, rather than feeling coerced by others.

Notes

1. I do not have any problems with describing a gender as "transgressive" per se—I recognize how the notion that transgender people "transgress gender norms" has tremendously aided activists in articulating the discrimination that many of us face due to oppositional sexism. Neither do I have any issues with any specific gender identity or expression in and of itself. Things become problematic, however, when we move beyond simply claiming that "transgressive" genders are just as legitimate as any other gender, and into the realm of arguing that "transgressive" genders are better than "non-transgressive" genders. In other words, it is the value judgements often placed on "transgressive" gender identities and expressions (rather than those specific identities and expressions) that I critique with this piece. I should also mention that, throughout this book, I have placed the word "transgressive" in quotes. My reason for doing so is similar to the argument I have made regarding the word "pass." By talking about whether trans people "pass" or "transgress gender norms," we place undue focus on what a trans person "does" while ignoring the gendering and judgments of others. I would argue that a trans person doesn't "transgress" gender norms per se, but rather a gender-entitled public judges them as being either "transgressive" or "nontransgressive."

2. Hand-wringing by cissexuals over whether transsexuals either "reinforce" or "challenge" gender norms has dominated academic discourses on transsexuality for over thirty years now. Examples include Butler, Bodies That Matter, 121–140; Greer, The Whole Woman, 71; Jeffreys, Beauty and Misogyny, 65–66; Kando, "Males, Females, and Transsexuals," Kessler and McKenna, Gender: An Ethnomethodological Approach, 112–141; Judith Lorber, Paradoxes of Gender (New Haven: Yale University Press, 1994), 18–22; Nanda, Gender Diversity, 94–98; Lewins, Transsexualism in Society, 153–160; and Raymond, The Transsexual Empire. The issue is so pervasive that sociologist Henry Rubin has proposed "a ban on the question

of whether transsexualism and transsexuals are unequivocally subversive or hegemonic," because he believes that this "sort of scholarship fetishizes transsexuals." (Rubin, Self-Made Men, 163–164) For transsexual critiques of this myopic and cissexist practice, see Carol Riddell, "Divided Sisterhood: A Critical Review of Janice Raymond's The Transsexual Empire," in The Transgender Studies Reader, Susan Stryker and Stephen Whittle, eds. (New York: Routledge, 2006), 144–158; Namaste, Invisible Lives, 9–70; Namaste, Sex Change, Social Change, 6–11; Prosser, Second Skins, 1–60; and Valerio, "'Now That You're a White Man.'"

3. Serano, "On the Outside Looking In"; Tea, "Transmissions from Camp Trans."

4. Echols, Daring to Be Bad.

5. Ibid., 281.

6. Queer Nation and Transsexual Menace were activist organizations that regularly staged public demonstrations during the early 1990s to protest injustices and to increase queer and trans visibility, respectively.

7. Currah, Juang, and Minter, Transgender Rights, 154; Harris and Crocker, Femme, 219–220; Namaste, Invisible Lives, 60–65; Namaste, Sex Change, Social Change, 51–57, 89–90; Valerio, "'Now That You're a White Man.'"

8. Namaste, Sex Change, Social Change, 17–26, 60–81.

■ ■ ■

Discussion Questions

1. What does the author believe is necessary to challenge subversivism sexism?

2. The author states to correct the exclusionary trend, we must begin to think in alliances. What do alliances represent, and how do they help unify?

3. How does the author describe the unique prejudices transgender folk experience?

What You Can Do

- Be aware of language, treatment, and actions involving transgender communities, and contribute to educating others
- Become involved in activism and raising awareness
- Be an ally all the time, not just when there is an event or activity you find interesting
- Remember to be respectful and considerate of everyone

CHAPTER 18

The Personal Is Still Political

MOVING FORWARD

By Joanna Wall

The Personal Is Still Political

Social change requires walking down a long road of determination and perseverance. The past waves have contributed greatly to social change, but there is still much work to do. Sexual violence has continued to plague girls and women. Intimate partner violence is still a very real issue for many women. Equal pay has yet to come to fruition. Reproductive justice is a continuing battle with the unrelenting notion that women can't make decisions about their own bodies. And yet, we persist. We create new organizations and revamp the older ones. We work tirelessly in the political arena, so our personal lives remain personal. We share activist strategies and lend our voices to each other's movements, so we can continue to grow and support each other. Like the women before us and the women that will come after us, we do not give up hope and continue to fight for lasting social change.

The success the fourth wave has experienced so far can largely be credited to the fact that women have maintained their presence and demanded to be acknowledged. Momentum from the first Women's March encouraged us to take a closer look at what is going on in our country. Hope became reignited, and smaller, more personal movements began to appear. Some had been there, lingering in the fourth wave timeframe, and some are brand new. Social media really is a catalyst of organizing; once a small and successful movement gains public attention, others can adapt it and apply it to their own communities. Without the smaller grassroots movements, we would struggle to support the bigger ones and, by default, lose energy. There are too many movements to list here, but I would like to highlight some I have found to be exceptionally effective.

TAKE ROOT: RED STATE PERSPECTIVES ON REPRODUCTIVE JUSTICE

The Take Root conference started after students from the University of Oklahoma (OU) and Oklahoma State University (OSU) attended the Civil Liberties and Public Policy Conference at Hampshire University. The students returned to Oklahoma and wanted to do something similar, but focus on the unique issues women face in red states.[7] Organizing the conference quickly, the students presented the first Take Root conference in 2011 at OSU with the help of Dr. Carol Mason, then the director of the Women's and Gender Studies Department at OSU, and Dr. Jill Irvine, then Chair of the Women's and Gender Studies Program at the OU. There were over 100 attendees sharing ideas and collaborating on the future of reproductive justice.

The Take Root conference, now held at OU, is in its eighth year and hosts over 500 conference attendees each February. There are speakers from across the country teaching on issues that range from religious freedom to GLBTQ rights to sex education.[8] Take root essentially brings people facing similar restrictive laws and policies together and encourages them to become advocates. This incredible space, conceived of by a group of like-minded students, now facilitates the sharing of ideas to foster social change throughout the entire country.

LADY PARTS JUSTICE

Lady Parts Justice (LPJ) started in 2012 as a reproductive rights "rapid messaging hub."[9] Using humor as a medium, the founders share reproductive information to help facilitate change and education. [10] What makes LPJ so successful is a mixture of comedy and charisma that makes even the most jaded advocate smile.

Liz Winstead, one of the founders, has created an organization where comics can use their craft to address the seriousness of reproductive rights restrictions. LPJ is welcoming to all genders and non-binary people, and through the use of live shows, apps, podcasts, and videos, LPJ spreads it message to give people the power to fight back against restrictive politics. LPJ is fortunate enough to have some powerful supporters attached to it, including Sarah Silverman, Amy Brenneman, Dr. Willie Parker, and Chelsea Kane. With recognitions such as The Golden Probe, LPJ demonstrates humor while also calling out politicians who consistently vote against women's rights. Another highlighting of LPJ is the celebration of women comedians. Women comedians have struggled for recognition and equal treatment, so the popularity of LPJ has brought awareness to this issue as well highlighting talented women.

LPJ set out to do live shows in all fifty states. By accomplishing this, they raised awareness on reproductive justice, encouraged voting and political activity, and offered tools on how to be an advocate. LPJ may have big names behind it, but is still very much a grassroots organization which focuses on people who need support the most. LPJ members do amazingly simple things to help the reproductive justice movement. They may serve as escorts to abortion clinic clients or make homemade cards and cookies to give to abortion clinic staff to let them know they are appreciated. They say thank you to those in the trenches and celebrate the dedication the staff and practitioners have given to the movement. LPJ has effectively shown the country the absolute ridiculousness of anti-choice legislation while exposing the politicians behind the bills.

INCITE!

Incite! is made up of women of color, trans people of color, and non-conforming people of color. The organization started in 2000 when a group of women of color activists had a conference to address violence faced by women of color.[11] The founders recognized women of color were often excluded by organizations addressing violence against women and felt the need was too great to ignore any longer, so began Incite! The conference attendance ultimately reached 2000 participants with another 2000 people turned away due to space. The founders realized they had a movement on their hands and formally created the organization.

Today, Incite! has many grassroots chapters and affiliates across the country. Incite! encourages critical dialogue through writing, media, and other art forms and continues to hold follow-up conferences and community mobilizing events. The work they do intersects with the underlying racism that hinders women, trans people, and gender non-conforming people of color. Grassroots organizing is a main tool for the organization, bringing direct action to communities and immediate response to those who need it. Incite! serves as an important reminder of the absence of resources to the women of color and the powerful organizing and advocacy women of color bring to communities.

REBELLIOUS MAGAZINE FOR WOMEN

Rebellious Magazine is a magazine with a feminist perspective on Chicago culture. The magazine supports women-owned and operated businesses by publishing stories on them and facilitating business partnerships.[12] Karen Hawkins founded the digital magazine to promote women and feminist activities happening in and around Chicago.

Chicago, though considered progressive and politically liberal, still has work to do in promoting women, women owned businesses, and women organizations. *Rebellious Magazine* fills that void by sending weekly newsletters to keep subscribers up-to-date on feminist activities in Chicago. The effect of this has been to highlight women and their achievements by sharing their accomplishments via digital media. Perhaps you don't live in Chicago or anywhere close by, but you may read about a local actor, comedian, or artist, which in turn leads you to follow her work. Other interesting information in the magazine includes updates on women-only work spaces, women-only exhibits and shows, and news particularly relevant to women. Restaurant reviews are of women-owned restaurants only; travel tips and reviews highlight women-oriented activities and places to stay; news stories discuss women's health, politics, and activism. All the while, the magazine maintains inclusion by highlighting the voices of women of color and GLBTQ folks.

Rebellious Magazine is an excellent example of a local grassroots effort that reaches women nationally. This is something that can be replicated and fostered in many communities to reach thousands of women. This type of recognition and promotion can be invaluable in organizing and advocacy work. *Rebellious Magazine* is a perfect model for the use of digital media to promote feminist social change.

THE FUTURE OF FEMINISM

Every year, feminists around the world hear the whispers of a "post-feminist society" or hear in the hallways of their workplace, "feminism is no longer needed—we've reached equality." Clearly, we have not reached equality, and the need for feminist activism is as great as it has always been. The fourth wave has new ways to organize and promote and can reach millions of women with the click of a button. Organizations, like the ones mentioned above, continue to recruit and educate girls and women to challenge our patriarchal society. Grassroots organizations provide a community of sorts to collect ideas and organize. The social change that comes from this type of organizing is lasting and effective. Yes, we have a lot of work left to do, but rest assured women are up to the task and will fight for the equality we have been promised for so long. The fourth wave, like the waves before it, will have its struggles and setbacks. This will not hinder the desire for change nor will it hinder the dedication of women to the idea of equality. Whichever wave we grew up in, we must now lend our collective support to the fourth wave and empower these girls and women to continue the progress. We all have a voice (and a vested interest) in the movement, even if sometimes we have to search a bit to find it. The face of feminism should represent us all, and we need to embrace that idea to assist in the success of the fourth wave. Go march, hashtag, or tweet into the future, and keep the dream of equality alive. Our collective powerful voices will bring the change we need.

NOTES

1. "Our History." Take Root, n.d. Web. 4 February 2018.

2. "Program." Take Root, n.d. Web. 4 February 2018.

3. "About." Lady Parts Justice, n.d. Web. 4 February 2018.

4. Id

5. "History." Incite! n.d. Web. 4 February 2018.

6. "About." *Rebellious Magazine for Women*, n.d. Web. 4 February 2018.

• • •

Discussion Questions

1. What are some effective ways to ensure intersectionality in the fourth wave?

2. What do you see as the most significant issue for women today?

3. What should members of the fourth wave do differently than the third wave? The second wave?

4. The fourth wave is encouraging more women to run for political offices. What kind of difference can this make for women?

What You Can Do

- Consider running for political office
- Follow legislation that effects women
- Be present at events and rallies
- Know the statistics on issues effecting women, including domestic violence, sexual assault, poverty, etc.
- Volunteer, organize, create movements